Dostoevski the Adapter

UNIVERSITY OF NORTH CAROLINA
STUDIES IN COMPARATIVE LITERATURE

Editorial Committee

1 and 2: out of print.

3. R. C. Simonini, Jr. Italian Scholarship in Renaissance England. 1952. Pp. 125. Cloth $3.50.

4. Frank G. Ryder: George Ticknor's The Sorrows of Young Werter. Edited with Introduction and Critical Analysis. 1952. Pp. XXXII and 108. Cloth $3.50.

5. Helmut A. Hatzfeld: A Critical Bibliography of the New Stylistics Applied to the Romance Literatures, 1900-1952. 1953. Pp. XXII and 302. Cloth $6.-

6. Yearbook of Comparative and General Literature, I. 1952. Pp. VIII and 148. Paper $3.50.

7. Yearbook of Comparative and General Literature, II. 1953. Pp. X and 164. Paper $3.50.

8. Nan C. Carpenter: Rabelais and Music. 1954. Pp. XIII and 149. Cloth $4.25; Paper $3.50.

9. Yearbook of Comparative and General Literature, III. 1954. Pp. 196. Paper $3.50.

10. Charles E. Passage: Dostoevski the Adapter. A Study in Dostoevski's Use of the Tales of Hoffmann. 1954. Pp. X and 205. Cloth $4.50; Paper $3.50.

11. Werner P. Friederich and David H. Malone: Outline of Comparative Literature from Dante Alighieri to Eugene O'Neill. 1954. Pp. XII and 451. Halfbound $6.-

European Sales through Librairie E. Droz
8 Rue Verdaine, Geneva, Switzerland

UNIVERSITY OF NORTH CAROLINA PRESS

Dostoevski the Adapter

A Study in Dostoevski's

Use of

The Tales of Hoffmann

By

CHARLES E. PASSAGE

CHAPEL HILL   1954

Printed in U.S.A. by
The Orange Printshop
Chapel Hill, North Carolina

Dedicated

to the Memory of

SAMUEL HAZZARD CROSS

Professor in German and Slavic

at

Harvard University

whose Death on October 14, 1946

Withdrew an Inspiring and Revered

Teacher

TABLE OF CONTENTS

PREFACE

If the present work did no more than detail certain influences of the Tales of Hoffmann on the literary productions of Dostoevski, it could have been presented in much shorter form. It is hoped that it will serve other purposes as well. First among these is a badly needed critique of Dostoevski's writings of the pre-exile period, which have usually been accorded only cursory treatment in the hurry to get on with the major novels. They deserve a closer attention. No less important is the second purpose, to analyse the procedures of a great artist in the initial stages of his career. The investigation reveals that Dostoevski's works in the years 1845 to 1849 were neither effortless nor capricious, nor so "realistic" as has been thought, nor so radically new, nor so uniquely Russian, nor so independent as general opinion has held. In stating these things, no iota of detraction from Dostoevski's greatness is intended. The stature of his genius is rather enhanced by a better understanding of its operations.

It is to be hoped likewise that the present study may add some small measure of neglected due to Hoffmann, whose Romanticism is too noble and too enduringly human to suffer permanent eclipse in the anti-Romantic twentieth century. Dostoevski's use of his Tales attests the recognition of genius by genius.

Relative to the study itself, it may be said that it began in reverse order to the position the chapters now hold. It was the relationship of *Die Elixiere des Teufels* to *The Life of a Great Sinner* and *The Brothers Karamazov* that first prompted investigation of Dostoevski's early works, where "some influence of Hoffmann" has long been acknowledged in *The Double* and *The Landlady*. Except for the connections between the latter story and Hoffmann's *Der Sandmann* and *Der Magnetiseur*, and for the relationship between the plan of *A Novel in Nine Letters* and the plan of Hoffmann's *Haimatochare*, which was suggested to me in private conversation with Professor Cizevski of Harvard University, all instances of the Hoffmann-Dostoevski kinship are the result of my own observation.   Secondary sources have been of relatively little assistance.   Reading and rereading of the two authors in question account for the substance of this study.   Such prolonged reading in both writers was in itself a major experience among books.

Charles E. Passage

Dansville, New York
December 31, 1953

I
INTRODUCTION

To European and American readers Dostoevski has always seemed the most Russian of the Russians and by that token completely alien to the literary traditions of the West. Even in his native land he has come to pass for a unique genius who strode directly forth from youthful obscurity to the center of the literary stage and commanded almost instant attention by the power of his ideas, needing only the brief but timely introduction of the critic Belinski to present him to the public. Sometimes even this introduction seemed of negligible importance, and as for the thing which scholars call literary influence, it has been deemed almost an impertinence to seek it amid the self-evident originality of his characters and scenes.

Critics of all nations have, on the whole, accepted this tradition of *sui generis* as a fact and have proceeded to devote their attention to a multitude of facets of the man's personality and production: to his melodramatic life, to his political and social philosophy, to his religious message, to his "epilepsy," to his "schizophrenia," and many more. In reading through the long list of studies and biographies one might easily arrive at the conclusion that this author was born with his message ready in his head and of earthly equipment needed only pen and paper to set it down. Genius he was, and his originality from the very beginning was astonishing. But philosophy and psychology were subordinate to literature in his career. First and foremost he was a writer, a man whose business it was to tell a story. And story-telling is a craft that must be learned from somewhere. How did he begin?

A modicum of literary apprenticeship is usually conceded. Dostoevski, it is said, began where Gogol left off. His very first story, *Poor Folk* (1846), took for its central character a poor government clerk such as Gogol had portrayed in *The Diary of a Madman* and *The Overcoat* and developed him with an insight and a complexity far transcending Gogol. This was Gogol raised to a higher power.

Unfortunately, the fable of tradition has it, the brilliant realism, the newness and trueness of this first work was then compromised, despite repeated warnings from the wise Belinski, by Dostoevski's perverse return to a bookish enthusiasm of the

1830's when he came to compose his next important story, *The Double* (1846). All good advice to the contrary notwithstanding, he insisted on controverting his own realism by romantic fantasies in the manner of the famous Tales of Hoffmann. In the early 1830's the Russian reading public had known a veritable Hoffmann craze. Not only were the Tales admired, but their author was seriously reckoned a philosophical thinker. Major writers fell under his spell and imitated his work. Pushkin himself, normally cool to the Germanic Muse, produced the splendid *Queen of Spades* in Hoffmann's manner, and Belinski as prince of critics had led the chorus of praise for the German author's greatness. But in 1846-47 all this was past and done and it was folly on the part of a young author to revert to the worn-out mode of fifteen years ago. Thus the excellence of *The Double* was compromised and its author duly censured. Yet, the fable of tradition continues, Dostoevski persisted in his folly and in his next story, *The Landlady* (1847), allowed his genius to stray to the extremes of Romantic nonsense. Then the sharp rebuffs of critics and public alike brought him to his senses. Chastened by the experience he never again ventured in that false direction.

Besides Gogol and Hoffmann, some touch of Balzac is usually mentinoned in the earliest works, but, by and large, the impression is left that Dostoevski began his career immediately as a kind of super-Gogol and proceeded directly to an unalloyed originality. Now and again in subsequent works an alien strain is noted:—Russian readers could scarcely miss the resemblances to Pushkin's *Eugene Onegin* in the plot of *Uncle's Dream* (1859) ; the Tartuffe-like Foma Fomich in *A Friend of the Family* (1859) suggests that the author was not wholly unacquainted with Molière; in *The Insulted and Injured* (1861) the little girl Nellie with her English grandfather named Smith is clearly drawn after the little Nell of Dickens's *Old Curiosity Shop*; and something of Dickens's Mr. Micawber may be observed in the Marmeladov of *Crime and Punishment* (1866). But these are minor matters, and after 1866 even such casual influences cease and there is left only pure Dostoevski, spokesman of a uniquely Russian message in a uniquely Russian mode.

Doubtless this impression is the one Dostoevski would have liked. As the nationalistic urge in his nature deepened progressively into fanaticism he would have preferred to obliterate any non-Russian features in his past writings, and the last thing he would have admitted would have been a significant debt of inspiration to a foreign author, especially a German.

Such, then, is the tradition. It is quite wrong.

It is quite true that *The Double* compounded Gogolian realism with Hoffmannian fantasy, but if the story does not wholly succeed it is because, first, its author was experimenting for the first time with this extraordinary combination of elements, and, second, because the vast plan of the work outstripped the author's technique as well as the space alloted to its exposition. It is also true that Hoffmannian fantasy plays a large part in *The Landlady* and that *The Landlady* is one of Dostoevski's less successful tales. The fault, however, lies not with Hoffmann but with Dostoevski's technique, and in some degree with Dostoevski's taste. Furthermore, Dostoevski's Hoffmann episode does not end abruptly here as the tradition claims.

Between 1845 and his transportation to Siberian exile in December of 1849, Dostoevski composed twelve, or if you will, thirteen short stories and a sizable fragment of a novel. Of this number, not two but nine works derive from Hoffmann! And the four or five stories of non-Hoffmannian inspiration, excepting perhaps *Poor Folk* alone, are decidedly the weaker productions.

Careful study of these early stories will reveal that their young author was erperimenting in various idioms, Gogol's, Balzac's, Hoffmann's, now alone, now in combination. The most successful formula proved to be a combination: Gogol plus Hoffmann,—plus, of course, Dostoevski himself, for his transforming powers even at the beginning stage amounted to an extraordinary alchemy. With a regularity that can only have been deliberate, the character, the situation, or the motif from Hoffmann's tales is stripped of its Romantic qualities, then introduced into a setting of Gogolian realism where the highly imaginative force of the original is allowed to operate. The borrowings are varied and they are made from the most diverse of Hoffmann's tales. They are usually specific as opposed to the Gogolian element, which may be described as the realistic portrayal of a certain milieu, that of poor urban gentry, the insignificant clerks of the government offices, occasionally that of the city's truly destitute. In the last analysis it is the Hoffmann element that predominates and makes the story memorable.

Nor does Dostoevski's Hoffmannism end with the exile of 1849. The two short novels composed while still in Siberia, *Uncle's Dream* and *A Friend of the Family*, seem to have been written with the intention of making pleasant and entertaining rather than serious literature. The ex-convict, his precise status as yet undefined, even in the matter of residence permission, was steering clear of controversy and provocation. But after return to Petersburg in December 1859 he sought once again to put into effect his Hoffmann-Gogol formula, though now the formula is rendered more complex by the addition of still other elements. Essays were also made in wholly new directions in the immediate post-exile years, with *The House of the Dead* (1861-62), for example, which stands apart from all of Dostoevski's writing by virtue of its detachment and factual *rapportage*, or again with *Notes from Underground* (1864), which leads far afield from the previous works. In *Crime and Punishment* (1866) the Hoffmann element has been so thoroughly absorbed into the texture of the composition that its presence, while often felt, is difficult to demonstrate. With that novel begins the line of uniquely Dostoevskian productions.

Yet not even here, at 1866, may it be said that the Hoffmannian strain ceases. It reappears, for instance, in part of *The Eternal Husband* (1870). Possibly,—though the point is debatable,—it may enter the curious vision of beauty that so oddly recurs in *The Possessed* (1871-72), in *A Raw Youth* (1875), and in *The Dream of a Ridiculous Man* (1877). Far more important is the concept of the Great Sinner which emerges around 1870 as the theme for a master-novel in five volumes. Beginning as a kind of saint's protégé, but with imperfections unknown even to himself, the Sinner was to succumb to temptation, fall, live through a calendar of crimes, and ultimately achieve a true sainthood out of a chaos of evil. This is precisely the career of the monk Medardus, hero of Hoffmann's single finished novel, *Die Elixiere des Teufels*, a work which Dostoevski may be shown to have known in detail. The master-novel, *The Life of a Great Sinner*, was, of course, never written, but under the pressure of time and financial need, parts of its plan and materials were drawn into at least three of the last great novels, most particularly into *The Brothers Karamazov*. There, as Alyosha Karamazov, Hoffmann's monk and false saint Medardus receives his ultimate transformation.

Dostoevski's Hoffmannism was truly no slight episode. Rather it was a deep and far-pervading force. That this should be so strikes one at first as peculiar. Actually, there was nothing peculiar about it except the date. Hoffmann was a famous Romanticist. What is more, his name had been intimately associated with the development of Romanticism in Russia, and when that movement came to a close, it was natural to assume that his works belonged to a past era. The year 1841 marked the end of Russian Romanticism with a finality and abruptness common enough in survey outlines of literary history but truly rare in fact. The last works of Gogol, particularly *Dead Souls*, had opened perspectives of a new and exciting kind and the literary circles were agog with talk of the realistic ideal in writing. To Belinski, who had once led the chorus of Hoffmannizing Bacchanals but who had put all that sort of thing behind him in 1845, it must have seemed perverse indeed that his young protégé should wish to corrupt the fresh doctrine of realism with the old abandoned Romantic fantasy. What he did not realize was that this young protégé in his approach to Hoffmann was giving a wholly new interpretation to the old tradition.

In their native Germany the Tales had had an immediate and enormous success when they appeared, at first slowly between 1809 and 1813, then with astounding rapidity from 1813 to the last posthumously published item in 1823. (Hoffmann died in 1822.) Their immense European vogue did not begin, however, until the French translations spread them abroad in 1829 and the early '30's. Then they became the rage of the whole western world.

Oddly enough, the Russians made the discovery of the stories earlier than any other nation beyond the frontiers of the German language. In 1822, the year of Hoffmann's death, there appeared a translation of *Das Fräulein von Scudery*,[1] followed in 1823 by *Doge und Dogaresse* and *Spielerglück*.[2] The next year but one, 1825, brought not only two additional translations, *Eine Spukgeschichte* and *Die Marquise de la Pivardière*,[3] but also the first original Russian story "in Hoffmann's manner," the rather pale moralizing fairy-tale, *The Poppy-seed-cake Woman of the Lafërtov Quarter* by the nobleman dilettante who signed himself "Pogorel'ski."[4] One of the posthumous tales, *Datura fastuosa*[5] (1822), was translated in 1826. In 1827 the gifted young poet Venevitinov temporarily deserted his lyric muse to render *Der Magnetiseur*[6] into Russian, while in 1828 there appeared, again from the pen of "Pogorel'ski," a group of stories set in a frame-tale, a miniature *Serapionsbrüder,* entitled significantly enough *The Double, or My Evenings in Little Russia.*[7] Thus even before the advent of the major French translations and the general European vogue, Hoffmann's name was familiar to the Russian public. Thereafter came translations, imitations, adaptations, and articles of critical discussion in a steadily increasing flood. By 1830-31 magazines were going so far as to publish rival versions. From this impetus followed the remarkable productions of the Russian Hoffmannists,—such stories as Prince Odoevski's pleasing *The Improvisor,*[8] the journalist Polevi's earnest but over-solemn *Felicity of Madness* and *The Painter,*[9] all dating from 1833; Gogol's *The Portrait*[10] and Pushkin's *The Queen of Spades,* both of 1834; and again from Gogol *The Nevski Prospekt* and *The Diary of a Madman* in 1835.[11] With the publication in September of 1836 of Gogol's story *The Nose,*[12] a parody of Hoffmann, it may be asserted with the clarity of retrospect that the intellectual élite were beginning to turn away from Hoffmann. Among the wider public the popularity of the Tales is attested by further translations in the popular magazines through the remaining 1830's, but after 1841 there is evidence of rapid decline. Prince Odoevski's *Russian Nights*[13] (1844) came at extreme ebb tide. Moreover, its most Romantic story components had already appeared in individual printings, so that the collection was a kind of aftermath.

Pushkin's *The Queen of Spades,* finest of all the Russian tales "in Hoffmann's manner," is really a kind of anomaly, for Pushkin and the larger faction of the Russian Romantic school preferred by far the works of the English and French writers to those of the new German group. The smaller "German" faction,[14] however, saw in Hoffmann the very epitome of Romanticism, and in his stories they found formulations of philosophical and political ideas that would have made Hoffmann stare. For them, his thought content outweighed his merely literary value. When they read in *Der goldene Topf* or in *Meister Floh* or in *Prinzessin Brambilla* about those realms of Beauty to which the ardent heroes attained, they understood thereby glimpses of social Utopias, and when they wrote of the equivalent in their own stories they used terms strangely reminiscent of religious aspiration toward the Kingdom of God. Moreover, their heroes, unlike Hoffmann's, did not attain to those blessed lands. A common denominator of pessimism usually caused them to despair amid the conflict of real and ideal worlds and to end in madness,—not the ironic "madness" of Hoffmann, which meant a glad escape from Philistine stupidity down the corridors of the heart to the true, inner life,—but real, clinical, anguished madness. A not wholly objective school of critics has seized on this striking feature as a symbol for the psychic anguish of a whole nation utterly frustrated by the oppressive regime of Nicholas I. Be this as it may, many excellent minds in Russia for a whole generation derived much of their inspiration on the basis of a very broad misconception of the man and his works. Missing his essential joy and optimism, they distorted his dualism of Artist versus Philistine to mean a dualism, an irreconcilable dualism, of the contemporary world versus a Utopian condition, and spoke of it very like Christian prophets mourning amid This Vale of Tears for the sweet peace of Heaven. The sensitive who perceived the cleavage were destined to perish.

It is ironic that the decade which worshipped Hoffmann should have thus misread him, while a juster evaluation was achieved by the generation of the 1840's which no longer followed him. Dostoevski is the surprising exception. Belinski's anger at his apparent defection is understandable, for he still conceived of Hoffmann in the old sense. What he could not grasp was that his youthful protégé conceived of Hoffmann in a wholly new way, as a great literary artist, creator of characters that live and scenes that move, a master of vivid story.

This is not to say that the new evaluation was clear and precise in Dostoevski's mind in 1845. Had he been asked for a just appraisal at that stage, he would probably have been unable to give it. That was to come later. For the moment he knew only that Hoffmann's Tales teemed with life and color and excitement,—and that he had every intention of capturing and outdoing their excellence.

In the spring of 1845 Dostoevski was in his twenty-fourth year. Few joys other than those afforded by books had been his. From his birth in October of 1821 he had lived in the dreary cramped Moscow apartment of his parents together with his ever-increasing number of brothers and sisters. After 1830 he came to know something of the countryside of Tula Province where his father, now a widower, had purchased a small estate,

but for the most part that somber, indeed sinister, man preferred to live alone there to indulge in drunken debauches and
sprees of cruelty to his peasants. The latter, after enduring
much, finally could endure no more and one day in the summer
of 1839 they banded together and murdered their brutal master.
Word of the event produced in the eighteen-year-old son a violent effect, the exact nature of which has been the subject of
much discussion. He himself described it as an epileptic
seizure, and similar seizures were to characterize his whole life.

The news reached him at Petersburg where he had been a
student for over a year in the tuition-free Military Engineering
Academy. On the very first day at the school in 1838 he had
met a fellow student named D. V. Grigorovich, from whose
memoirs[15] we learn considerable about the future author. A
year younger than Dostoevski and somewhat malleable no doubt,
he easily fell under the control of his friend's strong and possessive will. "My relations with Dostoevski," he writes,[16] were
those of not merely attachment, but absolute subjection." This
domination extended apparently to more than one aspect of his
life. For one thing, it meant a revelation of the world of
books:—

> "Hitherto I had, like the rest of my colleagues, read nothing
> but textbooks and abstracts of lectures; not only because other
> books were forbidden in the College, but from lack of interest in
> literature.
> The first Russian books with which I made acquaintance I got
> from Dostoevski; they were a translation of Hoffmann's *Kater
> Murr* and *The Confessions of an English Opium-Eater* by
> Maturin (sic); the latter was especially prized by Dostoevski.
> His literary influence was not confined to me alone; three of my
> colleagues came equally under his spell—Beketov, Vitkovski, and
> Berechetski; in this way a little circle was formed, which gathered
> around Dostoevski in every leisure hour."

It had been a great disappointment to young Dostoevski that
his brother Michael was not able to be with him at the Petersburg Engineering Academy. The two brothers were much attached to one another, but Michael had failed to meet the physical
requirements of the school and had to be content with entering
later the other engineering academy at Reval. Letters passed
back and forth between them regularly, and these often dealt
with books. Fëdor read voraciously and seemed to delight in
detailing his achievements in reading to Michael. For a youth
of seventeen the list is more than creditable. He seems to have

devoured the whole French literature, both classic and contemporary, a great deal of English and German literature, some Greek and Roman authors, and apparently every native Russian literary production. He read all these pell-mell, expressing often as much gusto for lurid and trashy fiction as for the sedatest of the classics. On August 9, 1838 he challenges Michael concerning their respective reading lists:[17]

> "You plume yourself on the number of books you have read. . . . But please don't imagine that I envy you that. At Peterhof I read at least as many as you have. The whole of Hoffmann in Russian and German (that is, *Kater Murr*, which hasn't been translated), and nearly all Balzac."

The letter continues with a eulogy of Balzac and with more and more items calculated to overwhelm Michael with awe. A postscript adds:

> "I have a new plan: to go mad. That's the way: for people to lose their heads, and then be cured and brought back to reason! If you've read all Hoffmann, you'll surely remember Alban. (The reference is to the sinister mesmerist in Hoffmann's *Der Magnetiseur*.) How do you like him? It is terrible to watch a man who has the Incomprehensible within his grasp, does not know what to do with it, and sits playing with a toy called God!"

During the first two years at the Engineering Academy, Dostoevski's most intimate friend was not Grigorovich or any of the other school-mates who looked upon him as an oracle, but rather a man nine or ten years his senior, possibly a friend of his father's. He was a treasury official named Shidlovski who wrote poetry of lofty import but little merit and who later ruined himself with drink. Dostoevski always maintained that this man exerted a powerful influence on him and that it was by his direction that he came to read authors like Shakespeare and Schiller, Balzac and Hoffmann. To Michael he wrote on January 1, 1840:[18]

> "When last I met Shidlovski I took a walk with him in Ekaterinhof. What an amazing talk we had that evening! We were recalling the past winter, when we talked much of Homer, Shakespeare, Schiller, and Hoffmann—particularly Hoffmann."

Two impressions emerge from these remarks: a genuine enthusiasm for literature in general and for Hoffmann in particular, and a precocious mind. Little wonder that his graduation in 1843 and subsequent work as a designer in the War Ministry found him profoundly dissatisfied with his lot. Not only did he detest the work, but worse still, a transfer to some provincial post was impending. Recklessly he abandoned his post, determined to make his way somehow in the literary world.

With Michael he projected a translation of Schiller's collected works, but while his brother went dutifully about *Die Räuber* and *Don Carlos*, he himself was busy with a translation of Balzac's *Eugénie Grandet*, which he fancied would be more saleable. Secretly he was also working at a story of his own,—*Poor Folk*. The first draft was complete by November 1844, but the letters to Michael in the spring of 1845 speak of repeated revisions and of all the hopes and fears of an author for his first work. That spring, when the revisions were finally completed, he took his manuscript one day to his friend Grigorovich, who now also entertained literary aspirations and who could be counted on as a sympathetic and intelligent hearer. The story is well known, how Grigorovich "tore the manuscript from him by force, and took it to Nekrasov forthwith,"[19] how Nekrasov listened with wonder and wept at the final scene, and how Nekrasov took the manuscript in turn to Belinski with the cry that a new Gogol had appeared. Belinski, after listening, agreed that this was a new Gogol.

From non-entity to fame in one leap! The recognized chief critic of the day was telling him that he was the greatest living Russian author! It was incredible but true. Dostoevski was drunk with success. He swaggered and boasted by day, and by night found a frantic exhilaration in the dubious quarters of the city. With the approach of winter, even before the publication of *Poor Folk*, he began a new story which should outdistance the first one by far,—*The Double*,—though he had no doubt that the public would confirm Belinski's judgment of the first.

On January 15, 1846 *Poor Folk* did appear in Nekrasov's *Petersburg Miscellaney* and the public did indeed confirm Belinski's judgment of it. From the perspective of more than a century after the fact it is difficult to understand the furor created by this little epistolary novel. Its fifty-odd letters are exchanged by a pair of lovers, the aging Mr. Devushkin (Mr. Maidenley) and the young Miss Dobroselov (Miss Goodtown), although these persons live on opposite sides of the same courtyard. Mutual fear of gossip is the alleged excuse for writing, but it would seem that the author's shyness was the real reason for it. For into this unimpressive figure of a hero, awkward, yearning, desperately poor, lonely, proud, Dostoevski poured a good deal of autobiography and confession. Devushkin's story is brief but poignant: he loves, but his wretched poverty and unattractive person cause him to lose the girl; he is left alone and disconsolate. By literary affiliation he is patently another wretchedly poor and obscure government clerk like Poprishchin, the hero of Gogol's *Diary of a Madman*, though he is in no wise mad, and like Akaki Akakievich in Gogol's *The Overcoat*. Like the latter, he has an inadequate overcoat and he pays a visit in distress to a Very High Personage. His letter of July 8th is an ironic critique of Gogol's story which his beloved has lent him to read. In page after page of the story may be found reflexes of Akaki Akakievich, but if anyone wishes to examine the process of transformation into a character of purely Dostoevskian kind, let him read the letter of August 1st, with its searching analysis of poverty and pride.

Devushkin's experience is the essence of the work. His beloved Varvara is a personage created wholly from other books, and it is significant that her letters are frequently shorter than Devushkin's and that he frequently writes twice to her once. Her lengthy autobiographical account in her fourth letter does not offset the disparity, for it dwells unconvincingly on an idyllic rural childhood, a love affair with a gentle tutor in her family who died young, and the like. Paradoxically, however, the only "story" elements in the work belong to her. It is she who fled from hateful relatives to come to the city and try to earn an honest living; it is she who is harassed by the advances of a wealthy and sinister suitor; it is she who finally makes the decision to yield to him in her distress of poverty and marry him, thus leaving Devushkin to his loneliness. Some connection may exist between these events and the plot of Pushkin's *The Station Master*, a book which the lovers read and discuss in their letters, but the parallel cannot be pressed very far. The events are too slight and of too general a nature to warrant a search for a prototype.

The essentials of the story as a whole are drawn from personal experience,—such as the twilight walks about the city in the letter of September 5th, the description of poor lodgers in rented quarters, and the analysis of poverty,—and from the two tales of Gogol. Devushkin's final letter rises in lyric crescendo of despair paralleling the last pages of *The Diary of a Madman*.

By formula, the work may be called simply a combination of Gogol and Dostoevski. Of Hoffmann there is not a trace.

Meanwhile, during the long interval between Belinski's first approbation of *Poor Folk* and its publication on January 15, 1846, Dostoevski had worked strenuously in the composition of *The Double*, which was printed in the prominent journal *National Notes* within two weeks after its predecessor. Amid the praise for the first story there had been some voices of disapproval, some of them fairly vehement, and Dostoevski was eager to overwhelm these carping critics with the sheer power of his second production. His letter to Michael of February 1, 1846 reflects his excitement:[20]

> " 'Golyadkin',—(that is *The Double*),—is ten times better than *Poor Folk*. Our lot say there has been nothing like it in Russia since *Dead Souls*, and that is a truly brilliant achievement; they even say more. What don't they look for from me! 'Golyadkin' really has come off well. You will be sure to like him enormously. . . ."

These high hopes were destined to be quickly dashed. There is consternation in the letter of April 1, to Michael:[21]

> "My fame has reached its highest point. In the course of two months I have, by my own reckoning, been mentioned five-and-thirty times in different papers. In certain articles I have been praised beyond measure, in others with more reserve, and in others, again, frightfully abused. But it does pain and trouble me that my own friends, Belinski and the others, are dissatisfied with my 'Golyadkin.' The first impression was blind enthusiasm, great sensation, and endless argument. The second was the really critical one. They all—that is, my friends and the whole public— declare with one voice that my 'Golyadkin' is tedious and thin, and so drawn-out as to be almost unreadable. One of our lot is now going in for the perusal of one chapter a day, so that he may not tire himself, and in this way he smacks his lips with joy over it. Some of the public say emphatically that the book is quite impossible, that no one can really read it, that it's madness to write and print such stuff; others, again, declare that everything is from the life and that they recognize themselves in the book; now and again, it is true, I hear such hymns of praise that I should be ashamed to repeat them. As to myself, I was for some time utterly discouraged. . . ."

Reading between the lines, one concludes that the "hymns of praise" had been a good deal rarer than the disparagements, and, what is more important, that the attacks had shaken Dostoevski's confidence in his very self. The letter continues with an abject apology for himself and his work:

"I have one terrible vice: I am unpardonably ambitious and egotistic. The thought that I had disappointed all the hopes set on me, and spoilt what might have been a really significant piece of work, depressed me very heavily. The thought of 'Golyadkin' made me sick. I wrote a lot of it too quickly, and in moments of fatigue. The first half of it is better than the second. Alongside many brilliant passages are others so disgustingly bad that I can't read them myself. All this put me in a kind of hell for a time; I was actually ill with vexation."

This judgment of "Golyadkin" as an uneven work, as a fine idea imperfectly executed in haste and "in moments of fatigue" (dissipation?), was by and large a fair statement of the case. All his life Dostoevski was to maintain the same opinion, and at certain times in his post-exile career he toyed with the notion of rewriting the story to bring out its latent possibilities.[22] There are unhappy repetitions in the work. Some passages of fairly obvious content are spelled out in excessive detail, while others requiring much greater amplification are sketched in all too briefly. The result is that the reader finds himself going at one moment too slowly and at another moment far too fast. The clay was expertly prepared, but somehow the kiln was inexpertly fired, and the vessel which should have turned out a masterpiece emerged with imperfect contours and faulty glaze. The more's the pity, for the scope and concept of the tale are grand and imposing. It is easily the most significant work of his pre-exile years; in fact, it was not surpassed until *Crime and Punishment* twenty years later.

II
THE DOUBLE

Dostoevski's point of departure in the creation of *The Double* was clearly enough Poprischchin, hero of Gogol's *The Diary of a Madman*, a short story. Upon this fundamental figure, now rechristened Golyadkin (Poordevil), it was his intention to graft the whole lore of "Doppelgängerei" and his own analysis of that lore. The prime difficulty, which he could not resolve, was the disparity of the two things. The lore of "Doppelgängerei" implied whole volumes, not only stories and novels, but even philosophical tracts, for the theme itself, so far as it entered literature, was but an elaborated detail out of the complex of German Romantic thought. Yet he went ahead with the almost impossible task of forcing so much matter into the compass of a short novel, drawing from sources which were, to be sure, related in theme, but widely different in artistic form. The finished work as we have it may be defined as a combination of the basic character and theme from Gogol's *Diary of a Madman*, a brief bit of Gogol's *The Nose*, possibly another brief bit from "Pogorel'ski's" *The Double, or My Evenings in Little Russia*, an episode from Hoffmann's *Kater Murr* (a novel), important features from Hoffmann's *Die Abenteuer der Sylvesternacht* (a short story), and still more important features from Hoffmann's *Die Elixiere des Teufels*, a full-length and complex novel. The wonder is that the result was not a hopeless hodgepodge. It must be admitted that the work is not crystal clear, but it must also be admitted that the twenty-four-year-old author had in mind a conception of sheer genius,—which lay just beyond his technical powers at that stage of his life. In the completed work trivialities are juxtaposed with passages of astonishing force and grandeur, and in the last analysis it is the latter which prevail.

The thirteen chapters of *The Double* occupy a time-span of four days, of which the first and fourth far transcend the second and third in importance. (Compare the structure of *The Idiot*.) Essentially there is only one character, as in the crucial Gogol tales, *The Diary of a Madman* and *The Overcoat*, all other persons being seen only as they appear to the hero. The true scene of action is the hero's mind, the whole tragedy is an inner tragedy. We behold despair in the act of tearing the edifice of Reason down to ruin.

On the morning of the first of the four days Yakov Petrovich Golyadkin, a titular councillor, is discovered in the act of waking. It is striking that on the very first page of this "realistic" narrative such a point should be made of the hero's uncertainty as to whether he is awake or asleep. A state of waking dream was a favorite Romantic and Hoffmannian subject. Golyadkin does awaken, and into a quite habitual world, a real and sorry world of shabby clothes, shabby furniture, and shabby existence. The reader craving realism may at this point feel assured that he is not being misled into some Romantic fantasy.

Yet why do things look at Mr. Golyadkin, rather than he at them?

> "The dirty green, smoke-begrimed, dusty walls of his little room with the mahogany chest of drawers and chairs, the table painted red, the sofa covered with American leather . . ., and the clothes taken off over night and flung in a crumpled heap on the sofa, *looked at him familiarly.*"

On the following page of the story Mr. Golyadkin examines his bill-fold:

> ". . . . the roll of green, grey, blue, red, and particolored notes *looked at Golyadkin,* too, with approval."

Things in this room seem to be alive with a life of their own:

> ". . . . the samovar standing on the floor was beside itself, fuming and raging in solitude, threatening every minute to boil over, hissing and lisping in its mysterious language, to Mr. Golyadkin something like, 'Take me, good people, I'm boiling and perfectly ready.' "

In a truly realistic story things are not "looking" and "talking" like the animated objects that fill the houses of Archivarius Lindhorst or Prosper Alpanus. However, the realism-craving reader of 1846 might take comfort that the room was filled with objects that were perfectly normal, exactly identified and minutely described.

Mr. Golyadkin is attended by a rascally servant named Petrushka, blood brother to the rascal Selifan who attended Chichikov in *Dead Souls* and to the barber in *The Nose*, but even before summoning him Mr. Golyadkin darts out of bed to look into the little round looking-glass that stood on the chest of drawers:

> "What a thing it would be," he exclaims, "if I were not up to the mark today, if something were amiss, if some repulsive pimple had made its appearance. . . ."

The second section of Gogol's *The Nose,* that parody of Hoffmannian "Doppelgängerei," begins:

> "Kovalyov the collegiate assessor woke up early . . . stretched and asked for a little looking-glass that was standing on the table. He wanted to look at a pimple which had come out upon his nose the previous evening. . . ."

Upon looking into that little mirror Kovalyov was horrified to behold that "there was a completely flat space where his nose should have been." During the remainder of the story he has to contend not only with his marred countenance but with the nose itself which turns up in public dressed in the uniform of a civil councillor to play against him all the nasty tricks of an *antagonistic double.* Happily Mr. Golyadkin finds only reassurance in *his* mirror.

Now *The Nose,* while it reduced "Doppelgängerei" to an absurdity, drew part of its subject matter from Hoffmann's *Die Abenteuer der Sylvesternacht,* particularly from the last section of that tale which dealt with Erasmus Spikher's lost mirror-image, one of the many variants of the "double" theme. Dostoevski's story is related twice over to the *Sylvesternacht,* directly, and through the Gogolian derivative, and it is by no accident that Mr. Golyadkin's first action on this day is to run to look into his mirror. More than once he will encounter mirrors and mirror-like reflections, and with subtle indirection it is implied that his Double, the second Mr. Golyadkin, is his mirror-image.

After the state of waking dream, the objects with life of their own, and the dubiously Romantic motif of the mirror, the story continues in pure Gogolian vein as Mr. Golyadkin inspects the second-hand livery which Petrushka has acquired for this special day. Dressed now in his best clothes, he has the servant drive him into the center of the city. They pass some insolent young puppies of clerks who act much as similar young clerks used to act with Akaki Akakievich. Mr. Golyadkin is outraged at their insolence. His employer also passes, and Mr. Golyadkin is filled with the same anxious servility that used to mark the poor clerk Poprischchin. As the scene becomes more urban we are aware that this is to be, in Gogol's sense, a "Petersburg story." The subtitle, in fact, is "A Petersburg Poem."

The destination, surprisingly enough, of this trip is the office of Krestyan Ivanovich Rutenspitz, Doctor of Medicine and Surgery. "Rutenspitz" (whip-tip) is surely not intended as very friendly humor, and "Krestyan" may well be a bi-lingual pun: "Christian," a German name, and "krest'yanin," the Russian word for peasant. Quite possibly the doctor represents a fragment of autobiography and sarcasm, recalling a German doctor named Riesenkampf who had been a fellow-roomer with Dostoevski in the dark days just after graduation from the Engineering Academy in 1843.

Chapter II gives an account of Mr. Golyadkin's visit to the doctor. It is a very strange call. Utterly at a loss for words, he cannot for the life of him tell Rutenspitz why he has come. Obviously he is not a stranger to the doctor and the latter clearly considers him a nuisance. The prescription is to be as before: go out with friends, "not to be hostile to the bottle," avoid solitude. To all this Golyadkin keeps insisting that he is "quite all right," "just like other people." Launched into speech now, he talks faster and faster, overwhelming the bewildered doctor with office gossip, tales of enemies that surround him, of the plots they hatch to destroy him, but coming back to the assertion that he is "quite all right," "just like other people." What is more, he is a man of action, he can take care of himself. The doctor is all at sea; after all, Dostoevski implies, he is only a German. Suddenly Golyadkin fixes him with his eye, stares, then bursts into tears and sobs uncontrollably. For an instant reality is present to his conscious mind, he *knows* he is unbalanced, and he weeps for hopelessness and helplessness. The final speech of Poprishchin in the madhouse is moving, but this passage is ten times more terrifying and more moving. The strange interview ends. As he passes out the door Golyadkin loses his feeling of utter surrender. Arrogantly he says to himself: "That doctor is extremely silly. He may treat his patients all right, but still . . . he's as stupid as a post."—This scene with an actual doctor, even though the doctor does little, shows Dostoevski's awareness of the medical nature of schizophrenia and removes his hero from all dualism of a merely symbolic nature. This man is beset with a real mental illness, not a division of alliances between the Real and the Ideal or between the Good and the Bad. This chapter had no literary source, it was based on direct observation from life.

From the doctor's office Golyadkin goes on a fantastic shopping tour. (Chapter III.) He visits various stores, prices articles, changes money into smaller denominations, orders furniture enough to supply six rooms, but winds up his business with the actual purchase of only a pair of gloves and a bottle of perfume.   In his dream world he is preparing for marriage with his employer's daughter, Klara Olsufevna, again paralleling Poprishchin's infatuation with *his* employer's daughter.   Golyadkin next goes to a restaurant for lunch and there he examines himself anew in the restaurant mirror.

Now he is ready for the real errand of the day, a call at the home of his employer Olsufi Ivanovich.   It is Klara Olsufevna's birthday and a party is being given.   Mr. Golyadkin has no invitation but he believes it is his right to appear.   Petrushka drives him to the door, he enters, and is refused admittance by the servants.   In the presence of arriving guests he is told, in fact, that the master has given strict orders *not* to admit him. Precipitately he rushes back to the carriage and orders Petrushka to drive home.   In the next moment he reverses the command and they drive back to the house,—a superb symbol for a mental fixation,—but even as they do so, Golyadkin is stricken with terror and once again, without even stopping, the carriage swings out into the street and disappears.

Up to this point the story has presumably presented realistic facts and actions.   This realism is none the less ambiguous.   It would be more correct to say that the story has presented the eerie unreal world seen by a man in the shadow of madness. These events are Mr. Golyadkin's fantasy.   The fantasy is about to pass into delirium.

Several hours later Klara Olsufevna's birthday party is in full swing.   (Chapter IV.)   But Mr. Golyadkin is to be found huddled in the darkness and bitter cold—on the back stairs to his employer's apartment!   He has been there a long time.   And all that time he has been debating how he can slip in and join the party, for he is "all right," he is "quite well," he is "just like everyone else," he belongs here.   Finally he summons the courage and darts in, throwing aside his coat as he goes.   The whole company is appalled.   His prepared speeches die on his lips, he can say nothing.   The women retreat from him, the men sneer, his employer is shocked, Klara hides.   All this is seen through Golyadkin's eyes and the kaleidoscope turns of his mind make a brilliant passage of imaginative writing.   The impressions of the room mingle with impressions gained from

books he has read. He recalls the French minister Villesle, the
Turkish minister Martsimiris, the beautiful Margravine Luise,
the Jesuits, his own room, Petrushka. He thinks that if the
chandelier were suddenly to fall how he would rush to save Klara.
The butler approaches. Golyadkin tells him one of the candles
is about to fall out of the chandelier. The butler assures him
that the candle will not fall and says that someone outside wishes
to speak at once with Mr. Golyadkin. They argue. A tear glit-
ters on Golyadkin's eyelash. He will not go. He feels like an
"insect," yet he turns and walks straight toward Klara Olsufevna
and asks her to dance with him. The young lady shrieks, everyone rushes toward them, Golyadkin is torn away from her and
propelled laughing, talking, explaining, apologizing, out into the
vestibule. His hat and coat are thrust upon him. Then he
feels himself falling, then lying in the outer courtyard, while
the orchestra within strikes up a new piece. He stands per-
plexed, then

> "he started off and rushed away headlong, anywhere, into the
> air, into freedom, wherever chance might take him."

To some degree this scene is an intensified version of Dostoevski's own feelings about refined soirées and his place in them.
On one occasion he had been so mortified by an ill-timed argument with the young and somewhat patronizing Turgenev that
he rushed out of the house. When his coat was held for him he
was so excited that he could not get his arms into the sleeves.
In utter exasperation he seized the coat and ran out into the
night in precipitate flight.

But here may be seen an example of how autobiographical
experience is blended with literature to the transformation into
something quite new.

In more than one story of Hoffmann's the hero turns from an
"impossible situation" and flees as fast as his feet will carry him
from the scene. In the opening section of *Die Abenteuer der
Sylvesternacht* the narrator, identified only as the "travelling
enthusiast," attends a New Year's Eve party at the home of the
Justizrat. Among the guests is Julie, his former beloved,—she
will become Giulietta, the Venetian courtesan of Act II of Offenbach's opera,—who treats him so heartlessly that he becomes
desperate. Her repulsive husband, the frivolousness of the
dancing and card-playing guests increase his desperation until

he suddenly leaves the party and runs "out—out into the stormy night." The next section, *Die Gesellschaft im Keller,* begins:

> "To walk up and down Unter den Linden may at other times be pleasant, but not on St. Sylvester's Night (i.e. New Year's Eve) amid a good sound frost and snow-squalls. Bare-headed and coat-less as I was, I finally realized that as icy shivers pierced through my feverish heat. Away I went across the Opera Bridge, past the Palace—I turned a corner, ran across the Schleusenbrücke past the Mint.—I was on Jägerstrasse close by Thiermann's store. . . ."

Just so, at the beginning of the new chapter (V), Mr. Golyadkin

> "ran out on the Fontanka Quay, close to the Izmailovski Bridge,"

and later, after his adventure with the stranger, discovered that he

> "had run right across the Fontanka, had crossed the Anichkov Bridge, had passed part of the Nevski Prospekt, and was now standing at the turning into Liteini Street,"

whence he goes eventually down Italianski Street to his own house on Shestilavochni Street. Hoffmann was the poet of Berlin and Gogol and the young Dostoevski were the poets of Petersburg. How uncannily all three authors meet again here: the "travelling enthusiast," Akaki Akakievich, and Mr. Golyadkin, all know the streets of the capital on a night of wind and snow and bitter cold, when a fierce emotion drives them to their fates. When Akaki Akakievich stumbled out of the office of the Person of Consequence into the stormy night, he found that

> "In an instant it (the storm) had blown a quinsy into his throat, and when he got home he was not able to utter a word;"

while Dostoevski describes this flight of Golyadkin's as taking place on

> "an awful November night—wet, foggy, rainy, snowy, teeming with colds in the head, fevers, swollen faces, quinsies, inflammations of all kinds and descriptions. . . ."

The verbal echo is from Gogol, but the party, the flight, and the destination are paralleled in Hoffmann. The "travelling enthusiast" finally entered a beer-cellar where all the mirrors were draped over with cloth out of deference for the client Erasmus Spikher, who had surrendered his mirror-image to the temptress Giulietta and therefore could not bear to look into mirrors where he could not see himself. With him is Peter Schlemihl, the man who had sold his shadow. (Hoffmann here borrows him wholesale out of Chamisso's famous fairy-tale.[1])

In short, the "travelling enthusiast" encounters two men who have lost their doubles. Mr. Golyadkin is about to lose his, not just his shadow or his mirror-reflection, but the half of his psychologically sundered self.

The plan of the *Sylvesternacht*, which the story has now begun to parallel, is here interrupted but will be resumed later. At this particular juncture Dostoevski's mind may be seen to swerve suddenly to another scene from Hoffmann's works where the hero does not simply encounter other men with doubles,—and lost doubles at that,—but encounters for the first time his own double. It is the fine passage toward the end of Part I, Section 2 of the novel *Kater Murr*,[2] where Kreisler abruptly flees from a somewhat different kind of "impossible situation" and rushes out into the palace gardens of Sieghartshof. It is late afternoon.

"Kreisler paused in the middle of the bridge which led across a broad arm of the lake to the fisher-hut and looked down into the water, which reflected with magic shimmer the park, with its wonderful groups of trees, and the Geierstein which towered above them and which bore its white-shining ruins upon its brow like a crown. The tame swan that answered to the name of Blanche was paddling about the lake, its lovely neck proudly held aloft, rustling its flashing wings. 'Blanche, Blanche,' cried Kreisler aloud as he stretched out both his arms, 'sing thy loveliest song and do not think that thou wilt then die!' . . .

Dark clouds were moving up and throwing broad shadows across the mountains, across the forest, like black veils. Muffled thunder was rolling off to the south, louder rushed the night wind, rushed the brooks, and simultaneously individual tones of the weather-harp resounded like organ tones. Startled, the birds of the night arose and swept through the thicket shrieking.

Kreisler awoke from his dreaming and glimpsed his dark form in the water. It seemed to him as though Ettlinger, the mad painter, were looking up at him from the depths. 'Hoho,' he shouted down, 'hoho, are you there, beloved Double, old comrade?— . . . . If they have sent you down undeservedly to Orcus, I'll pass on all sorts of news to you!—Know, honored madhouse inmate, that the wound which you dealt that poor child, the beautiful Princess Hedwiga, still has not healed. . . . Do not attribute it to me, my good fellow, that she takes me for a ghost, specifically for your ghost.—But when I am at leisure to prove to her that I am no disgusting spook, but the Kapellmeister Kreisler, along comes Prince Ignatius cutting across my path, who is obviously laboring under a 'paranoia,' a 'fatuitas,' 'stoliditas,' which, according to Kluge is a very pleasant kind of actual folly.—Don't ape all my gestures, painter, when I am **talking seriously to you!**—Again? If I weren't afraid of a head cold, I would jump

down to you and beat you properly.—Devil take you, clownish
mimic!'
    Kreisler quickly ran away."

The identity of the mad painter Ettlinger is one of the points
left by the author for clarification in the third and last part of
the novel, but that part was never written. Some scholars have
deduced that he was the actual father of Kreisler and hence that
his madness foreshadows that of Kreisler, but these are unresolved questions. Kreisler standing on the bridge and looking
at his own image in the water below addresses the image as
"Double," yet speaks to him as though he were the mad Ettlinger
who had attacked and wounded the Princess Hedwiga.

    The first drops of a beginning rain drive Kreisler immediately
afterward to seek shelter in the fisher-hut where his friend, the
wise Meister Abraham, lives. As he approaches the cottage he
receives a shock:

    "Not far from the door, in the full glow of the light, Kreisler
    caught sight of his own image, his very self (sein eigenes Ich),
    walking along beside him. Seized by the profoundest horror,
    Kreisler plunged into the cottage and sank pale as death into the
    arm-chair."

To behold one's double signified, according to folk beliefs, one's
approaching death. Meister Abraham inquires what has happened to affect his friend so strongly:

    "With difficulty Kreisler got possession of himself, then spoke
    in a hollow voice: 'It cannot be otherwise, there are two of us—I
    mean I and my Double, who leaped out of the lake and pursued
    me here.—Have mercy, Master, take your dagger and strike the
    rascal down—he is mad, believe me, and can destroy us both. He
    conjured up the storm outside.—Spirits are abroad in the air and
    their chorale rends the human heart!—Master—Master, lure the
    swan here—it shall sing—my song is frozen, for the Double (der
    Ich) has laid his white cold hand upon my heart, he will have to
    take it away if the swan sings—and go down again into the lake."

Meister Abraham laughs and quickly explains away his friend's
terrors: the sounds are made by the wind in the weather-harp,—
a sort of giant Æolian harp made of tuned steel strings and
stretched between buildings in the open,—and the vision of the
Double walking beside him was an optical illusion created by
the lighted lamp and the concave mirror in the entryway. To
convince Kreisler, Abraham steps outside and immediately two
Abrahams may be seen in the twilight. For the moment, the
whole episode seems to be reduced to comic error caused by an

optical illusion. What Hoffmann might have made of it in the unwritten part of the novel no one can say, but it is surely meant to be more than a comic error. It symbolizes Kreisler's present fear of madness and his sense of impending catastrophe and undoubtedly prefigured some future situation in reality; in other words, potentiality pressing forward to become fact.

In the case of Mr. Golyadkin, madness and catastrophe are also potentialities pressing forward to become fact, not in the future but at the present moment. His frantic and random flight from Klara Olsufevna's party into the stormy darkness brought him, when "it was striking midnight from all the clock towers in Petersburg," to the Izmailovski Bridge.

> "At last Mr. Golyadkin halted in exhaustion, leaned on the railing in the attitude of a man whose nose had suddenly begun to bleed, and began looking intently at the black and troubled waters of the canal. There is no knowing what length of time he spent like this. All that is known is that at that instant Mr. Golyadkin reached such a pitch of despair, was so harassed, so tortured, so exhausted, and so weakened in what feeble faculties were left him that he forgot everything. . . ."

Suddenly terror strikes him. "Was it my fancy?" he asks himself. The import of the question is not disclosed to the reader immediately, but presently a stranger passes, at sight of whom Mr. Golyadkin's terror increases. Again the figure approaches, makes no answer to Mr. Golyadkin, and vanishes. Mr. Golyadkin begins to run. The figure appears anew running parallel to him. As they approach Mr. Golyadkin's house it outdistances him, goes up his stairway, through his doorway, is received by Petrushka without question, and when Mr. Golyadkin arrives in his room, there is the figure sitting on his own bed. The figure is identical to himself in every detail. It is his Double. Here the chapter and the first day of the story end, with all clarification postponed,—in good Hoffmannian fashion,—until another time.[3]

The two-fold connecting link between the two stories and with the *Sylvesternacht* was undoubtedly the mirror-image. Kreisler had identified his reflection in the water with the reflection in the concave mirror in Abraham's vestibule and believed that his Double had risen from the lake to follow him. In all likelihood Dostoevski conceived originally of a reflection of Mr. Golyadkin in the waters of the canal but this became impossible when he placed the time at midnight in the midst of storm. Yet it is on a bridge that the second Mr. Golyadkin first appears to him and then, as in Kreisler's case, reemerges later to follow him home.

For Mr. Golyadkin, however, no swan shall sing, that is the Heavenly Grace of music is not vouchsafed to him, nor shall any Meister Abraham comfort him. Dostoevski's hero, in contrast to Hoffmann's, is utterly alone. He differs from his prototype further in that it is understood, despite the *coming* of the Double, that the self has split under the strain of anguish, has broken in two, and that the Double is Mr. Golyadkin's illusion. It is a part of his personality which has escaped the control of his rational mind and now seems to have a separate existence. The author's "clinical" attitude was new in fiction in 1846, yet it is prefigured in several respects in the most elaborate of Hoffmann's "Double" stories, the novel *Die Elixiere des Teufels*, and from that work Dostoevski now proceeded to draw further materials for the amplification of his theme.

The second period of twenty-four hours in our story occupy Chapters VI and VII and are pitched in a much lower key than the preceding section.

When Mr. Golyadkin awakes the morning after his midnight encounter on the Izmailovski Bridge, he recalls the previous events but dismisses them as more intrigues on the part of his enemies at the office. After delaying over several pipes he goes to work as usual. Scarcely is he settled at his desk when a door opens and through it comes his Double, the second Mr. Golyadkin. The latter is a clerk too, and he will work at a desk just *opposite* the real Mr. Golyadkin, that is in the position of a mirror image. (Is the reader intended to imagine that a mirror hangs on the office wall?) Cold sweat stands out on Mr. Golyadkin. When the Double goes briefly into the inner office Mr. Golyadkin takes the opportunity of speaking with the chief clerk, Anton Antonovich. The latter acknowledges the presence of a new office member who bears a striking resemblance to Mr. Golyadkin—(Does Dostoevski mean to say that all clerks look alike as a class?)— and asks him whether they are related. To Mr. Golyadkin it seems preposterous "to talk of a family resemblance when he could see himself as in a looking-glass." The talkative Anton Antonovich rambles on about Doubles and remarks that an aunt on his mother's side saw her Double just before her death. At the end of the office day Mr. Golyadkin makes haste to leave his work, but there in the street inexplicably his Double is to be found walking beside him. Humbly, deferentially, in halting sentences such as the real Mr. Golyadkin would have used, the new clerk requests his friendship, and Mr. Golyadkin, touched by the request, asks him home to supper.

Chapter VII presents the supper scene. It is a comico-pathetic one of a very lonely and friendless man who has had to create a second self to bear him company. At this point the situation strikingly resembles the beginning of "Pogorel'ski's" *The Double or My Evening in Little Russia,* where the author's Double appears for just this reason to the lonely nobleman and bachelor on his remote Ukrainian estate. The "Evenings" are the account of the discussions they had and the stories they told each other.[4] But where these two Antoni's were much concerned with philosophy and literature, the two Golyadkins find much pleasure in chit-chat about the city. Theirs is a cozy feast of small talk. Before long they call each other "Yasha,"[5] make mutual confessions, and even plot a little counter-conspiracy to confound the intriguers at the office. From the concluding paragraphs it is clear that Mr. Golyadkin is drunk and for a moment it looks as though the whole story might prove an alcoholic hallucination. The second day stands as a comic interlude in the whole work.

On the morning of the third day Mr. Golyadkin awakes to find no trace at all of his guest. (Chapter VIII.) When Petrushka brings the tea his manner is so ambiguous and he speaks so strangely about "the other one" that Mr. Golyadkin is alarmed. After the brief *entente cordiale* the dualism is about to enter its antagonistic phase.

Arriving at the office, Mr. Golyadkin finds his worst fears confirmed. His Double, last night so friendly, so confiding, has preceded him and already is busy at the task of destroying his reputation with his superiors. He blithely takes credit for the work which Mr. Golyadkin performs subserviently; he taunts him for his slowness, his shyness, his bald spot, his middle-aged paunch-belly; he makes a fool of him before the other clerks; he exposes all his fears, all his wounded pride, for the whole world to see. In the face of such treatment Mr. Golyadkin meekly bows and even takes a certain satisfaction from his deliberate humility.

It is clear that the new Mr. Golyadkin is the latent aggressive phase of Mr. Golyadkin's character and that this phase is slipping from his control. The Double is clever, he is successful, he is both sly and gay, he is a man of action, in short, a devil of a fellow. He has another trait, which since Dostoevski's time has come to be thought of as a commonplace in schizophrenics: he is implacably hostile to the milder phase of the split personality. His sole aim is to destroy the antithetical self. A struggle to the death is the only possible course now.

It is in this deadly struggle of the antithetical selves that we find embodied much of the matter of Hoffmann's novel *Die Elixiere des Teufels,* not in the form of story elements now, though some of these will enter presently also, but rather as a distilled essence. *Die Elixiere des Teufels* relates the life of the runaway monk Medardus from the time of his apparent sainthood in his monastery, through his flight into the world and the mad course of passion and crime he pursued there, to his ultimate return to the monastery and his holy death. In this case, the Double of Medardus is not a hallucination but an actual person, Count Viktorin, half-brother to the monk. Not only do they look absolutely identical, but there is at times an interpenetration of their personalities and experiences that goes beyond a rational explanation. At each stage of Medardus's strangely guided journey through the world Viktorin appears, and each time the deadly enmity between the two comes close to destroying the sinning, yet never fatally lost Medardus.

When first they meet, Viktorin is discovered sitting on the edge of a mountain cliff overlooking the Devil's Chasm. The monk, seeing him there apparently in a position ready to fall, attempts to save him, but at the touch of his hand Viktorin does fall and Medardus is horrified to think that he has actually caused the young man's death. Presently a groom appears, greets Medardus as his master, and from his talk it becomes plain that Viktorin had been planning to adopt monk's garb, pose as the Confessor of Euphemie, the adulterous wife of a certain Baron von F., and carry on his nefarious love affair under the cloak of religion. Straightway Medardus allows the groom to guide him to the castle of Baron von F. and there lives out Viktorin's evil plans. The result is tragedy thrice compounded and eventually Medardus flees from the house with the guilt of two murders upon him. Just outside the gate, when the pursuit is hot behind him, Medardus once again meets Viktorin's groom whom "chance" has prompted to come to his master with horses, coach, and a complete wardrobe.

On the way to the "mercantile city" the coachman loses his way in the darkness and Medardus is forced to become the guest of a forester. In the forester's house lives a half-mad monk in whose habit is sewn the name-tag: Medardus. His biography as retold by the forester is the story of Medardus's own child-hood,—just as the life-story told by the second Mr. Golyadkin to the first in Chapter VII was actually the life story of the real Mr. Golyadkin. When Medardus, now dressed as a nobleman, is shown this fugitive monk, who is, of course, Viktorin, the latter passes into a kind of frenzy of hatred and screams:

> "Come up to the roof-top. There we shall wrestle with each other, and whoever throws the other down shall be king and drink blood!"

The spectacle fills Medardus with horror, and of himself, he says:

> "More than ever divided within myself, I became ambiguous to myself, and an inner horror came over my own being with a destructive power."

The "monk" Viktorin, who of late had been quite calm and lucid, now reverts to a bestially raving madness so that the forester decides he must be sent away lest he harm some member of the family in the forest-house.

Considering himself well rid of this creature "whose appear-ance reflected his own Self with features distorted and ghastly," Medardus continues his travels, coming eventually to a *Resi-denzstadt,* where he is presented at court. To the same court comes Aurelie, whom Medardus knew and loved at the home of her father, Baron von F. and whose brother, Hermogen, he had murdered. She denounces him as her brother's murderer, with the result that he is arrested and imprisoned. With lies born of desperation, he steadfastly maintains he is a Polish gentleman on his travels, but he is caught in the web of his own falsehoods until, suddenly, Viktorin is discovered in a madhouse of the same city and the crime is fastened upon him. Medardus is set free. In meditation of the state of affairs, he says:

> ". . . the conviction arose in me that it was not I who had been the ruthless criminal at the castle of Baron von F., who slew Euphemie, Hermogen, but rather that that deranged monk whom I had met at the forest-house had committed the deed. . . ."

Once his "innocence" is established, a wave of good fortune pours over the unrepentant sinner. Aurelie retracts her accusation and now admits that she loves Medardus. Their wedding day is set. It coincides precisely with the day appointed for the execution of Viktorin, and as the ceremonies begin, the hangman's cart passes the palace with the victim. Glimpsing Medardus at the window, the wretched Double cries:

> "Bridegroom, bridegroom! Come . . . come up to the roof . . . to the roof . . . there we shall wrestle with each other and whoever throws the other down shall be king and drink blood!"

The sight and the challenge of his other self sting Medardus into telling the truth. He laughs as he wildly declares his true identity, then turns, stabs Aurelie, leaps out of the window, cuts the prisoner's bonds with the same dagger, and vanishes through the crowd. That night in a dark forest Medardus drops to the ground from exhaustion. As he makes an effort to rise he is seized from behind by Viktorin, still in monk's garb. "You can't run," he laughs, "you can't run, you've got to carry me!" Then begins a fierce struggle which goes on and on in the darkness until consciousness is lost.

Three months later Medardus comes to himself:

> "A gentle warmth pervaded my inner being. Then I felt a movement and a prickling in all my veins. This feeling was transformed into thought, but *my Self was divided hundredfold*. Every member had its own movement, its own awareness of life, and the head commanded the members in vain. Like faithless vassals, they refused to assemble under its leadership. Now the thoughts of the separate parts began to circle like gleaming dots faster and faster, until they formed into a fiery circle. This became smaller as the speed increased, until at last it seemed a motionless ball of fire. . . .
> These are my limbs that are stirring, I am waking up."

He is in a monastery in Italy. He is lying in bed dressed in the habit of a monk. In the habit is sewn the name-tag: Medardus.

A long section of Italian adventures follows, until Medardus finally arrives at the monastery in Germany from which he had originally set out. His arrival is even more dramatic than if he had come simply from his own adventures, for a few days previously a beggar in rags had presented himself at the monastery gate, declaring himself to be Medardus the runaway. He was taken in but the prior doubted the alleged identity. Then illness came upon the man and, with death imminent, he summoned the

prior and confessed that he was not Medardus but Count Viktorin. His confession is one of the most striking passages in
the novel.

> "It seems to me that I must soon die, but first I must un-
> burden my heart. You have power over me, for however much
> you try to conceal it, I perceive that you are St. Anthony and
> that you know best what evils your elixirs cause. I had high
> plans in mind when I determined to represent myself as a clerical
> gentleman with a big beard and a brown cowl. *But when I actually
> looked into myself, the strangest thoughts seemed to arise from
> within me and embodied themselves in a corporeal form which
> was horrible and which was my own Self.* This second self had
> fearful power and hurled me down, as from out of the black
> stones of the deep chasm the princess, snow-white, rose out of the
> swirling, foaming waters. The Princess took me up into her arms
> and washed my wounds, so that presently I felt no pain. I had
> indeed become a monk, but the Self of my thoughts was stronger
> and drove me on so that I had to murder the Princess who had
> rescued me and whom I loved very much, and to murder her
> brother as well. They threw me into a dungeon, but you yourself
> know, holy Anthony, in what way you carried me off through the
> air after I had swilled your accursed drink. The green Forest-
> King entertained me badly, despite the fact that he recognized my
> princely rank. *The Self of my thoughts appeared at his home
> and did all sorts of hateful things to me, and since we had done
> everything together, wanted to remain in a joint relationship with
> me.* That was arranged, but soon after, as we were running
> away from there, because people wanted to *cut off our head*, we
> separated again. When the foolish Self, however, kept trying
> always and forever to feed upon my thoughts, I knocked it down,
> whipped it hard, and took its coat away."[6]

Shortly after this confession Viktorin apparently dies, but his
death, like his confession, was illusion. His body, brought to
the monastery courtyard preparatory to burial, mysteriously
vanishes. He returns for the great solemnities at which Aurelie
is to take the veil of a nun. While Medardus undergoes his last
and hardest temptation, watching, as a humble monk among
fellow-monks, his beloved becoming the bride of Christ, Viktorin suddenly appears in the throng of worshippers, rushes
into the sanctuary, and fatally stabs Aurelie, thus fulfilling the
act once before attempted by Medardus. As Aurelie, now the
nun Rosalia, dies, the murderer vanishes as suddenly as he had
appeared. Not long afterwards Medardus dies, a manifest
saint.

If the complex and melodramatic events of this novel seem remote from Mr. Golyadkin's situation, it must be remembered that Dostoevski was deliberately transposing this romantic subject matter into what he considered Gogolian comedy and that he was doing this within the confined limits of a short story about an obscure office employee. In Chapter XIII we shall see a more concrete borrowing from Hoffmann's novel, but just now we should keep in mind that the intensity of the Medardus-Viktorin conflict underlies the antagonism of the two Golyadkins. It should be noted further that Dostoevski has not given roughly equivalent will to both phases of the divided personality but that the "real" Mr. Golyadkin meekly suffers while his aggressive Double is wholly active. Typical of this is the conclusion of Chapter VIII where, having emerged together from the office on this difficult day, the insolent Double is seen suddenly departing gaily in a cab while Mr. Golyadkin is left standing forlorn and alone by a lamp post.

With Chapter IX the story reverts to the general outline of *Die Abenteuer der Sylvesternacht*. After the "travelling enthusiast's" unhappy evening at the soirée of the Justizrat and after his wild flight through the streets of Berlin, he arrived coatless and exhausted in a certain beer-cellar where he encountered Peter Schlemihl, the man without a shadow, and Erasmus Spikher, the man without a mirror-image, that is to say, two men whose Doubles were lost. Mr. Golyadkin now goes to a restaurant and there has a new encounter with his Double.

He is very hungry when he arrives. He orders a pie, sits down and eats it. Then he goes to pay the cashier. With astonishment he is told that he has consumed not one but eleven pies. He protests indignantly, but, not wishing to make a scene, he agrees to pay. All of a sudden he becomes aware of the reason for his plight:

> "In the doorway of the next room, almost directly behind the waiter and facing Mr. Golyadkin, in the doorway which, till that moment, our hero *had taken for a looking-glass*, a man was standing—not the original Mr. Golyadkin, the hero of our story, but the other Mr. Golyadkin, the new Mr. Golyadkin."

As we would now say, Mr. Golyadkin, with his meek phase predominant, had cautiously eaten according to his poverty, then with a shift of his aggressive phase into predominant position, he had eaten ten more pies, not so much from hunger as from the will to torment and to humiliate his other Self.

The remainder of the chapter departs again from the *Sylvesternacht* pattern to take Mr. Golyadkin home to write a letter of protest about his Double's conduct. Here Dostoevski does not play quite fair with the reader. In each of several details he is evasive when we would most like to know precisely what happens. Petrushka, for example, merely laughs slyly when his master gives him the letter to deliver. While waiting for his return with the answer, Mr. Golyadkin walks to the home of his employer but does not enter. He comes back home and falls asleep. When Petrushka does finally return, the fellow is thoroughly drunk and unable to answer any questions. He declares at one minute that he delivered the letter and in the next minute says there *was* no letter. Golyadkin indignantly dismisses him. Then his eye catches something on the table. It is a letter, the answer to his protest. It tells him that he is a fool. He immediately writes a reply in which he urgently requests an interview in which to explain himself. When he awakes next morning this letter has disappeared. The question rises as to whether there ever were any letters except as Mr. Golyadkin composed them, both originals and replies. Quite possibly he maintained both parts of the correspondence himself. Or, still more probably, there is simply no rational explanation. The episode surely represents Dostoevski's version of that part of *The Diary of a Madman* where Poprishchin acquires the very informative letters written by the two dogs, Madgie and Fido, to each other. At any rate, the episode shows once again that Dostoevski was indeed writing his story with *The Diary of a Madman* for a basis.

In the same way, Chapter X shows that most closely related in his mind to the Gogol basis was Hoffmann's *Sylvesternacht,* for now the strange dreams that beset Mr. Golyadkin as he sleeps from the third far into the fourth and last day of his story are the exact counterpart of Chapter 3 of the Hoffmann tale. After his encounter with Schlemihl and Spikher in the beer-cellar, the "travelling enthusiast" repaired to a room at the "Golden Eagle" for the night. There, as he slept until far into the morning, he was beset with strange dreams.

The dreams take the form of a phantasmagorical recapitulation of the New Year's Eve party at the home of the Justizrat. There, the "travelling enthusiast" reports,

". . . I was sitting on the ottoman next to Julie. But presently it seemed to me as though the whole company were a funny

Christmas display at Fuchs's store, or Weide's, or Schloch's, or some other, and the Justizrat a dainty sugar-plum figure with a note-paper jabot. . . ."

The siren Julie again offers him the goblet of steaming punch from which the blue flame rises. Erasmus Spikher in the form of a squirrel leaps upon his shoulder and warns him that Julie is a figure come to life out of the monitory paintings of Breughel, Callot, and Rembrandt. With his squirrel tail he beats the blue flame and cries: "Drink not! Drink not!"

"But now all the sugar-plum figures of the display came alive and moved their hands and feet comically. The sugar-plum Justizrat tripped up to me and in a faint little voice cried: 'Why all the fuss, my good fellow, why all the fuss? Stand on your own good feet, for I've been noticing for some time now how you are walking around in the air over the chairs and tables.'"

Again Julie tempts. This time it is Peter Schlemihl who cries to the "travelling enthusiast": "This is Mina who married Rascal." (Characters out of Chamisso's *Peter Schlemihl*.) In approaching to say this, Schlemihl has stepped on several of the sugar-plum figures, causing them to groan aloud.

"These now multiplied by the hundreds and by the thousands and tripped up around me and up my person in a motley and loathsome throng. They buzzed around me like a swarm of bees.

The sugar-plum Justizrat clambered as far as my collar, which he clutched tighter and tighter. 'Accursed Justizrat!' I cried, and started up awake."

It is a bright clear day and already eleven o'clock in the morning.

Mr. Golyadkin's dreams also review the past. He beholds his superior Andrei Filipovich in an attitude of condemnation. He sees himself a distinguished guest in a distinguished gathering, until, just as his success is most brilliant, the other Mr. Golyadkin comes to spoil it. He sees himself rushing out into the street to hail a cab,

"but with every step he took, with every thud of his foot on the granite of the pavement, there leaped up as though out of the earth a Mr. Golyadkin precisely the same, perfectly alike, and of a revolting depravity of heart. And all these precisely similar Golyadkins set to running after one another as soon as they appeared, and stretched in a long chain like a file of geese, hobbling after the real Mr. Golyadkin, so there was nowhere to escape from these duplicates—so that the real Mr. Golyadkin, who was in every way deserving of compassion, was breathless with terror; so that at last a terrible multitude of duplicates had sprung into being; so that the whole town was obstructed at last by duplicate Golyadkins, and the police officer, seeing such a breach of de-

corum, was obliged to seize all these duplicates by the collar and
to put them into the watch-house, which happened to be beside
him. . . . Numb and chill with horror, our hero woke up. . . .

It seemed as though it were rather late in the day. It was
unusually light in the room. The sunshine filtered through the
frozen panes and flooded the room with light. . . .

It actually was one o'clock."

The motif of the multiplying doubles will occur again at the
dénouement.[7]

We are now at early afternoon of the fourth and last day.
The rest of Chapter X is devoted to another office sequence, unfortunately not very well differentiated from the former one.
At the end of the day Mr. Golyadkin invites his Double and
rival to a coffee house for a serious consultation. Their colloquy
there (Chapter XI) is very interesting from the viewpoint of
modern psychology, and it has no connection whatever with
Hoffmann. The Double constantly makes off-color remarks
about the waitresses and also flirts shamelessly with them, while
the real Mr. Golyadkin lowers his eyes and confesses that he is
"absolutely pure." The sexual suggestions sink deep into consciousness. The two leave the coffee house, take a cab together
and drive to the home of Olsufi Ivanovich. There the Double
goes in, while the real Mr. Golyadkin flees away. He goes to a
tavern, and while there draws from his pocket a letter which
he had no idea existed. How it came into his pocket he cannot
imagine. (The motif of the Madgie-Fido letters from *The
Diary of a Madman* again.) It is an appeal from Klara Olsufevna to rescue her that night from her tyrannical parents
and a hated suitor. Mr. Golyadkin is intensely preoccupied by
this letter, so much so that he occasions a scandalous scene in
the tavern by attempting to leave without paying his bill. The
bill paid, he hurries home to plan the rescue of Klara. At home
he finds the official notice of his discharge from his position, and
Petrushka is packing his effects preparatory to leaving his
service.

Feverishly brooding over his plans for rescuing Klara, Mr.
Golyadkin takes a cab (Chapter XII) and tells the driver to take
him to the Izmailovski Bridge. No sooner started in that direction than he changes his mind and has the driver take him to
the home of "His Excellency," one of his higher superiors. It
is now early evening.

His Excellency has guests. But, no matter. Mr. Golyadkin goes right into the midst of the assembled guests. The light is so brilliant that he is dazzled.

> "At last our hero could distinguish clearly the star on the black coat of His Excellency, then by degrees advanced to seeing the black coat and at last gained the power of complete vision. . . ."

The mirror-reflection of every shiny surface now fascinates him. Readers of Hoffmann's *Sylvesternacht* will recall how Erasmus Spikher shrank from the sight of a highly polished snuff-box because it resembled a mirror. Mr. Golyadkin's gaze is held by the flashing star, then it is caught by the patent leather shoes on His Excellency's feet. His words are, of course, utterly unintelligible to His Excellency. The situation becomes more desperate by the minute, and now, "through a door which our hero had taken for a looking-glass" comes the impertinent Double to delight in his discomfiture. With his eyes on His Excellency's patent leather shoes and his mind pondering the nature of leather, polish, rays of light in artists' studios, Mr. Golyadkin is lost in a morass of gibberish. Suddenly he feels himself seized, propelled toward the door. "Just as it was at Olsufi Ivanovich's," he thinks. And so it is. His coat is tossed into the street after him. Then he finds himself in a cab. To the driver he cries to drive to the Izmailovski Bridge.

It is not clear just what Dostoevski intended by this fixation of Golyadkin's to return to the Izmailovski Bridge. Perhaps the unfortunate hero wished to return to the place where the Double went forth from him, in the hope of inducing the Double to return to him once more.

The foregoing chapter (XII), interesting as it is, is nevertheless regrettable in that it makes for repetition both of Chapter IV and the final Chapter XIII. No doubt Dostoevski wished to convey the impression of reality spinning about Mr. Golyadkin's consciousness in faster and faster tempo. Unfortunately, the reader sometmes feels as though he were spinning too.

The grand climax of *Die Elixiere des Teufels* occurs at the ceremonies where Medardus watches with renunciation while his beloved Aurelie is made a nun. In religion she takes the name Rosalia for the saint whose intercession for Medardus and for his sinning ancestors has been a recurrent theme of the book. The monastery church is full of people for the occasion, music rolls through the incense laden air, masses of flowers adorn the high altar. It is as though all the senses were receiving their consecration. As the bride of Christ, her vow spoken, waits to have her hair shorn, suddenly the wild Viktorin makes his way to her and stabs her to death by the altar. He escapes forever, but manifest miracle attends the death of the beautiful nun, while to Medardus comes the mysterious painter in his customary purple mantle to speak the final words of consolation. The painter is actually the monk's sinful ancestor five generations removed, whose sin is now expiated and whose miraculously prolonged life may now find rest. Heaven and Hell are present at this culminating scene of the novel, which has the form of a saint's legend, for this is the triumphant overthrow of the works of Evil by the Powers of Good.

The final chapter of *The Double* is not *like* this scene, but it is *analogous* to it. This whole finale, at which Mr. Golyadkin appears once again at the home of Olsufi Ivanovich, presents neither a realisitic room nor realistic guests. The previous visit in Chapter IV may be called realistic in so far as it correctly portrayed what a half demented man saw, but this time Dostoevski is not merely repeating himself. Mr. Golyadkin here appears before a kind of Last Judgment.

Not only the drawing-room but the entire house is described as being full to overflowing. There are "masses of people, a whole galaxy of ladies." They are there, row on row, like the heavenly hosts. Klara Olsufevna is there, dressed in white, with a white flower in her hair,—like an angel. Olsufi Ivanovich is enthroned in an arm-chair like a heavenly judge. Mr. Golyadkin's office superiors are there and they gather about the judge. A solemn hush falls. The Double stands in the throng at some remove from the soul awaiting judgment. White, dazzling light pervades the whole place. At a sign from the superiors, the perfidious Double takes Mr. Golyadkin's hand, then bends and kisses him "with his Judas kiss":

> "There was a ringing in Mr. Golyadkin's ears, and a darkness before his eyes; it seemed to him that an infinite multitude, an unending series of precisely similar Golyadkins were noisily bursting in at every door of the room;"

The door does indeed open and the Double, with vicious delight, identifies the newcomer as "Krestyan Ivanovich Rutenspitz, doctor of medicine and surgery, your old acquaintance." Judgment has been passed, and this stern policeman of heaven will take him away to outer darkness. He is led down the stairs:

> "Faint with horror, Mr. Golyadkin looked back. The whole of the brightly lighted staircase was crowded with people; inquisitive eyes were looking at him from all sides; Olsufi Ivanovich was sitting in his easy-chair on the top landing, and watching all that took place with deep interest. . . ."

It is the condemned soul's last lingering look backwards toward Paradise.

And now, a final touch from *Die Elixiere des Teufels*. When Medardus, elegantly dressed as a nobleman and travelling about the world, met his Double in monk's garb at the home of the forester, the effect was to send the wretched Viktorin back to his previous state of raving madness, so that the forester felt compelled to send him away for safety's sake. Medardus watched his departure:

> "When I came down, a rack-wagon bedded down with straw was standing in front of the door ready to leave. The monk was brought out. With face deathly pale and distorted, he allowed himself to be led along quite patiently. He answered no question, refused to take anything to eat, and scarcely seemed aware of the persons about him. They hoisted him into the wagon and tied him fast with cords, inasmuch as his condition seemed doubtful and they were not at all sure there would not be a sudden outburst of his inwardly repressed fury. As they secured his arms, his face became convulsively distorted and he emitted a low groan. His condition pierced my heart. He had become closely related to me, indeed it was only to his ruin that I owed my salvation. . . . Only as they started to drive away did his glance fall upon me, and he was suddenly seized with profound astonishment. Even when the wagon was disappearing into the distance (we had followed it as far as the wall) his head remained turned and his eyes directed toward me."[8]

So, now, as Mr. Golyadkin is conducted down the shining stairs from the white light to the waiting darkness, "the malignant Mr. Golyadkin junior in three bounds flew down the stairs and opened the carriage door himself," and once the doomed man is seated inside and the vehicle gets under way, several persons, including the Double, run alongside. But "Mr. Golyadkin's unworthy twin kept up longer than anyone," and he follows the carriage for some distance, gesticulating and throwing farewell kisses.

Mr. Golyadkin, half suffocated with fright, finally addresses Rutenspitz:

> "I believe . . . I'm all right, Krestyan Ivanovich. . . ."

But a great voice "stern and terrible as a judge's sentence" rings out:

> "You get free quarters, wood, with light, and service, the which you deserve not."

Two fiery eyes stare at him from the darkness.

He is on his way to the madhouse, a real madhouse, like the one to which Poprishchin was sent. But he is also in Hell, the outer darkness pierced by two eyes of a watchful demon.

> "Our hero shrieked and clutched his head in his hands. Alas! For a long while he had been haunted by a presentiment of this."

So ends the remarkable story.[9]

III
A NOVEL IN NINE LETTERS

Early February 1846 had witnessed the publication of *The Double* and the high enthusiasm of Belinski and the other critics for the story, but scarcely was the month out when the enthusiasm turned first cool, then sharply hostile. By April 1, the author was taking rueful inventory of the faults in his work, as was seen in the letter of that date, previously cited, to his brother Michael.[1] The same letter brightens up, however, as he speaks of two new stories currently under way which will surely recoup his fortunes, *The Whiskers that were Shaved Off* and *The Story of the Abolished Public Offices*. But neither the summer nor the autumn brought either of these two apparently Gogolian pieces to realization and before the end of the year both were abandoned. Nor were his fortunes recouped. A letter to Michael on November 26 testifies to the steadily mounting hostility of his former literary friends.[2]

The year ended rather dismally, with only one work to succeed *The Double* in print. In October, *National Notes* published the short story *Mr. Prokharchin*, another tale with a poor clerk as hero. The title character is a miser who becomes distraught with the suspicion that his fellow clerks are seeking to rob him of his hoard, falls ill, goes insane, and finally dies. Contemporary critics identified the literary sources as Pushkin's *The Covetous Knight* and Balzac's *Eugénie Grandet*, which Dostoevski had translated two years earlier, though the mold of the work as a whole is, of course, borrowed from the creator of Poprishchin and Akaki Akakievich. The publication of *Mr. Prokharchin* was a small success amid large disappointments.

An undated letter to Michael in the autumn of 1846 assures his brother that he has "heaps of original, vital, and lucid thoughts that all yearn to come to birth."[3] Perhaps there were too many, so that they crowded each other by turns out of the center of attention. With the new year he set to work on a full-length novel called *Netochka Nezvanova*, but financial need demanded something for quicker completion and sale, and the novel fragment was put aside. It was to be resumed two years later. Meanwhile, the best he could muster was a little comic story entitled *A Novel in Nine Letters*, actually composed in 1845 along with *Poor Folk*, but now submitted to *The Contemporary*, which published it in January 1847.

The nine letters which compose the "novel" are exchanged between two Petersburg business associates in approximately daily sequence from the 7th to the 17th of an unspecified November. To heighten the mystification which is the principal intention of this comedy of errors, their names are Pyotr Ivanich and Ivan Petrovich. Although they are partners and friends, every appointment to meet and discuss their difficulties is missed through all these November days, and the letters proceed in a crescendo of mutual irritation. Pyotr begins the trouble by hinting that he is not pleased by the visits made to himself and his wife by a certain young man named Yevgeni Nikolaich, whom Ivan has introduced to him some three weeks ago. Ivan retorts that Yevgeni is a perfectly respectable young man and, in turn, suggests that Pyotr has not dealt honestly in a recent business matter of common concern. Failure to get together to clarify matters intensifies the anger of both parties until they denounce each other furiously as blackguards in Letters 6 and 7 respectively. The last two letters are dedicated to reciprocal revenge.

Letter 8, from Ivan to Pyotr, encloses a love-note from Pyotr's wife to Yevgeni. It is dated November 2. Ivan announces that he and his wife Tatyana, who is pregnant, are leaving on a journey to Simbirsk but will leave Yevgeni as Pyotr's friend.

Letter 9, from Pyotr to Ivan, encloses a love-note from Ivan's wife to Yevgeni. It is dated August 4, the eve of her marriage to Ivan. Pyotr adds that Yevgeni will not be staying in Petersburg but happens to have a business trip to make,—to Simbirsk.

Such *badinage* about cuckoldry,—even to the hint that Yevgeni may be the father of Tatyana's unborn child,—is not at all in Hoffmann's manner of writing. Yet the little story has a Hoffmannian model in *Haimatochare,* one of the late Tales (January 1819) that were gathered into the posthumous collection entitled *Die Letzten Erzählungen.*[4] It can scarcely be said to add any more to Hoffmann's achievement than *A Novel in Nine Letters* adds to Dostoevski's.

Haimatochare is made up of fifteen letters which Hoffmann himself, in a foreword declares were furnished him by his friend Chamisso, author of *Peter Schlemihl,* who came into possession of them during his journey around the world, 1815-1818. The first letter, from J. Menzies to the Governor of New South Wales, Australia, requests permission to include an old friend and

fellow scientist, A. Broughton, among an expedition presently
to sail for O-Wahu (i.e. Oahu, Hawaii).   Letter 2, from the
Governor, grants this permission, while Letter 3 describes the
voyage aboard the ship *Discovery*, Captain Bligh commanding.
In Letter 4 Menzies describes ecstatically a find he has made in
a forest near Hanaruru (Honolulu) : drawn as if by magic, he
had come upon the "daintiest, prettiest, dearest 'Insulanerin' "
he has ever seen.   ('Insulanerin' presumably means "island
girl.")   He seized her, brought her home, named her "Haimatochare" (Greek for "Blood Beauty"), built her a lovely bower,
and spends all his hours near her.   Letter 5 states Broughton's
exasperated complaint to the Governor that Menzie's infatuation is negating the scientific value of the expedition.   At this
point begins the parallel with Dostoevski's story.

The following seven letters (No. 6-12) trace a quarrel of
mounting fury between the two scientists over the question of
rightful possession of Haimatochare and culminate in a challenge, and the acceptance of the challenge, to a duel with pistols.
Letter 13 contains Captain Bligh's sober report to the Governor
of the death of the two men, one found with a bullet through his
brain, the other with a bullet through his heart.   Near their
corpses lay a box marked "Haimatochare."   It contained a
small and curious insect, which the man Davis at first took for
a louse.   The insect had been discovered by Menzies—among the
dorsal feathers of a pigeon shot by Broughton.   The final two
letters are concerned with the disposal of the specimen at sea
amid mock-heroic ceremonies.

The subject matter of Dostoevski's story is apparently his
own invention, intended no doubt to rival Gogol's unique humor[5]
but falling considerably short of it.   But the form of the work,
the whole idea of an anecdote of preposterous misunderstand-
ings presented in a sequence of letters, came from a rather obscure item among the Tales of Hoffmann.

THE LANDLADY

Neither *Mr. Prokharchin* nor *A Novel in Nine Letters* re-captured Dostoevski's prestige or won him back his friends among the literary critics. The months of 1847 dragged along as drearily as the months of 1846 had done. With the projected novel *Netochka Nezvanova* now definitely put aside for some future time, he was working on a story, a little shorter than *The Double,* which he hoped would vindicate him as an author. It was published in October 1847 by *National Notes* with the title *The Landlady.*

It cannot be justly claimed that *The Landlady* is one of Dostoevski's most successful creations, yet, with all its faults, it is a story with a certain memorable intensity. Certainly, by style as well as by content, it stands apart from everything else he ever wrote. Parts of it are intended to create the impression of folk ballads, a twilight of uncertainty pervades the whole tale, there are attempts to portray moods of dim langor and sensuous beauty. Above all, mystification, a common element in Dostoevski's writings, is here carried to an extreme which sometimes irritates more than it intrigues.

The setting is Petersburg, but not the glittering Nevski Prospekt or even the government offices and the residences of office workers, rich and poor. Rather, the story unfolds in the outlying sectors where the very poor form almost a community apart. The nominal hero, Vasili Mikhailovich Ordynov, is, we are told, a scientist, though in the three years that he has been living as a recluse in his rented room full of books, the only work mentioned is the assembling of notes for a book on church history,—an odd subject for a scientist,—and toward the end of the story he destroys even these from sheer weariness and indifference. That he is a "scientist" at all must be credited to the literary mileiu of the 1840's, which no longer permitted heroes to be painters and live in studios amid "picturesque confusion." But, the author says, he has the *soul* of an artist. This is hardly flattering to artists, for Ordynov's soul, indeed his whole personality, consists almost wholly of indistinct and blurred sensation, a tender apparatus of feeling with no definite traits of character at all. He feels intensely and narrates his feelings, but he does nothing. Through most of the story he is

ill of an illness which is never defined. Its symptoms are a recurring weakness, fainting, susceptibility to dream phantasma-
gorias during states of half-sleep. Though these symptoms are
intensified when he is in the presence of "the landlady," he is,
even before his first encounter with her, singularly devoid of
will and drifting in a dream. He is never fully awake, nor does
he desire to wake.

A decade earlier, his literary counterpart would not only have
lived in a garret studio and painted "sublime" pictures, but
would also have longed for Italy and died, if necessary, for Art.
A decade later, this same basic type would wake and aspire to
apostleship of social reform or religious regeneration. For the
present, Ordynov and Dostoevski's other passive heroes, merely
dreaming, constitute an indeterminate middle, psychologically of
great significance both for the author and the age[1]

As the story opens, this shy youth has set out in quest of a
new rooming house, since his former landlady is about to leave
Petersburg. Through the twilight he is guided by a mysterious
power to enter a certain parochial church. A passage unique in
Dostoevski's works seeks to present the church and the Vesper
service then in progress as a kind of vision of mystic beauty.
Candles shine, ikons richly gleam, the twilight awesomely deepens
as the gorgeous rites proceed. The whole description is odd
enough with its author to arrest attention. One recalls that
set-piece of deliberately gorgeous description which Gogol added
as an after-thought to *Taras Bulba,* when the youthful hero
witnesses a Roman Catholic Vesper service in the beleaguered
Polish city. The resemblance is more than fortuitous. Moreover, both may derive from the lavish splendor of ecclesiastical
descriptions in *Die Elixiere des Teufels.*[2]

As the last sun-ray departs from the windows of the cupola
and night has descended, Ordynov's gaze is caught by a curious
couple who have just entered the church, a strikingly austere old
man and an amazingly beautiful young woman. They proceed
to the shrine of the Virgin, where the young woman kneels and
prays and weeps. Ordynov hears her sob echo through the
building. He watches them leave, fascinated by the smile that
contends with "some childlike fear and mysterious horror" in
the young woman's face.

On the following day Ordynov returns to the church for
Vespers but the real object of his curiosity does not appear.

His third visit is more rewarding. He watches the beautiful girl at her prostrations before the Virgin's shrine, his heart almost suffocated with ecstasy. He follows her and her escort to their house, to which he himself then goes the following morning to inquire whether they have a room to rent. Their surly Tatar porter will give him no information even for a bribe; the austere old man, who opens the door, is obviously ill-disposed to the intrusion, but in answer to Ordynov's inquiry the beautiful girl immediately says: "We have a lodging to let." An hour later Ordynov is installed in his new quarters, the proprietor of which has, in disgruntled fashion, identified himself only as "Ilya Murin, artisan."

From this point forward Ordynov is hardly more than an observer, and it is Murin and Katerina, the "landlady," who engage the principal interest in the story. The complexities of the narrative will require a summary.

Chapter II

Unable to elicit information about his hosts from either the Tatar porter or an old female servant and unable to settle his mind to his books, Ordynov takes a long walk in a drenching rain, returning chilled and half sick. He is overtaken with a fever. All sense of time is lost. All that he knows is that there are waking intervals during which he realizes that he is being tended by the beautiful landlady. In one of these intervals she reveals her name and says that her master has many books, just as Ordynov does, but that they are religious books from which he reads to her. In semi-conscious moments Ordynov senses passionate kisses upon his lips. Fantastic dreams also pass through his mind, recollections of an idyllic childhood and visions of journeys in outer space.

Waking at some indefinite time, he peers through a crack in the partition and observes Murin, apparently ill and lying on a bed from where he reads to Katerina who is listening raptly as she reclines on a couch alongside the bed. Ordynov gets up, wrenches open the bolt, and staggers into their room. Murin, in fury, snatches a gun from the wall and fires it at the intruder. When the smoke rises, the unharmed Ordynov sees the old man writhing on the floor in an epileptic fit.

Chapter III

The convalescent Ordynov goes for a stroll. A second talk with the Tatar porter yields only the extra information that Murin was once a merchant and owner of boats on the Volga and that through some misfortune involving the burning of a factory, he had gone mad.

Next Ordynov encounters an old friend, Yaroslav Ilich, who takes him to a restaurant for a chat. Confirmed gossip that he is, Yaroslav Ilich tells what he has heard of Murin. He too has been told that Murin was once an owner of Volga barges and of a factory which had burned. Some close and dear relation perished in the fire, the loss of whom cast Murin into a fit of melancholy in which he apparently tried to murder some young merchant. Since that event the old man has been doing penance. Furthermore he gives private audiences, presumably to tell fortunes, and takes fees for these extraordinary interviews.

More puzzled than enlightened, Ordynov goes home. He hears Katerina praying and sobbing in the adjoining room. As he falls asleep in the twilight he feels Katerina's kisses again upon his lips. He clasps her in his arms.

PART II
Chapter I

Lying in Ordynov' arms, alternately ecstatic and hysterically weeping, calling him brother and protesting that she is his sister, Katerina relates the story of her life. It is an incoherent tale of long ago in the region by the Volga. During an absence of her father's, "he"—Murin—came to her house, whether as her mother's lover or in pursuit of her, is not clear. Jumbled together in the narrative are scenes where her mother cursed her for an illicit love and threatened to expose her unknown parentage; where her father, pale and distraught, went down to his factory one stormy night and there perished by stumbling into a red-hot cauldron; where she fled in the night with Murin and lived as his mistress while he directed a gang of thieves. Then again she recalls a young merchant lover, Alyosha, who stayed with her during an absence of Murin's. They planned to flee together in a boat, but Murin suddenly appeared and said there was need to leave that part of the country at once. With Murin she went down to the river. Alyosha was in a boat. Murin asked him to ferry them across the river. The three were in the boat together. There was a storm. The two men quarrelled, each threatened to throw the other into the water.

Just at this climax Katerina is interrupted by Murin. From the doorway he sternly bids her come to him. She presses a last kiss on Ordynov's lips, then meekly follows the old man. There is a total silence from their room. Ordynov staggers and collapses on his bed.

Chapter II

Two days later Ordynov wakes to the sound of Katerina's singing. As he makes his way to her, she gaily welcomes him and commands Murin to do likewise. The old man apologizes for the shooting, calls the young people brother and sister, and calls for wine. A fantastic drinking scene begins. Flushed with wine, Katerina challenges Murin to tell her fortune and tell it honestly, to tell her in particular when her term of bondage to him will end. The old man grows pale, his eyes burn. He says something about the hearts of maidens and the power of youthful beauty, then his voice chokes, he becomes inarticulate, and a tear runs down his cheek. Ordynov tries to lead Katerina away. He stops to take a knife to kill the old man, but as he looks at him, Murin's eyes open and diabolical laughter fills the room. Ordynov drops the knife, which Murin, rising, kicks away. Katerina sinks at Murin's feet murmuring "Alyosha! Alyosha!", and with powerful arms the old man picks her up and crushes her to his bosom.

With horror Ordynov whispers: "She is mad!" and rushes out of the house.

Chapter III

When Ordynov goes to confer with Yaroslav Ilich next morning, he is startled to find Murin sitting with his old friend. For the sake of Yaroslav Ilich the old man is playing a patently false rôle of the not too well educated, but honest peasant, who has known Katerina since childhood. Even as a small girl her mind was affected, and certain terrible events which resulted in her parents' death have made her actually insane. He refers to her as his wife and says he never crosses her in her whims. He quite understands Ordynov's feelings and both he and his wife will pray for the unfortunate young gentleman.

Bewildered and furious, Ordynov leaves to think by himself in quiet. A crowd gathers around him as he sits lost in thought by a fence. Suddenly Murin stands before him, but gone are all the servile manners and pretensions to awkwardness of a few minutes before. The girl is mad, it is true, he declares. Sometimes she takes a great fancy to some young man, but surely no one will blame Murin for defending what is rightly his. Ordynov agrees to quit the house. Then Murin presents him with a cushion, a gift from Katerina, and says in a fatherly tone: "Now mind, don't hang about or harm will come of it."

For six months Ordynov lives with a conventional and dull German family named SHpis (Spies), tormented by the lingering doubt that Katerina might after all have been quite sane and in the power of an evil man. One day he encounters Yaroslav Ilich who tells him that Murin's house was recently found to be the headquarters of a smugglers' gang. The owner of the house was the chief.

"And Murin?" asks Ordynov.

Yaroslav Ilich at first does not recollect the name. Then he says he has heard that Murin and his wife had left three weeks ago to return to "their own parts."

On this ambiguous note the story ends.

What is Murin: a brigand, a fiend, a madman, a stern old peasant with a protective interest in an insane orphan girl, an aging and justifiably jealous husband, or an evil man with aspirations to power over human beings? With only the text as a basis of judgment it might be impossible to decide, so intricately has Dostoevski interwoven reality and irreality, but on the basis of Hoffmannian sources one may arrive at some shrewd deductions. Even so, the answer is complex.

First of all, he is, though in a sense which must be modified later, a sinister hypnotist by virtue of his relationship to Alban, the central figure of Hoffmann's early tale, *Der Magnetiseur*.[3] Here must be recalled the post-script, previously cited,[4] of Dostoevski's letter of August 9, 1838 to his brother Michael:

> "I have a new plan: to go mad. That's the way: for people to lose their heads, and then be cured and brought back to reason! If you've read all Hoffmann, you'll surely remember Alban. How do you like him? It is terrible to watch a man who has the Incomprehensible within his grasp, does not know what to do with it, and sits playing with a toy called God!"

It is no exaggeration to say that the late 18th century discovery of hynosis (magnetism, mesmerism) by the Swiss, Franz Anton Mesmer (1734-1815), made possible the whole vast system of thought common to the German Romanticists, thought which through a century of amplification and change ultimately emerges as modern psychology. Proceeding from the phenomenon of hypnosis, these German thinkers elaborated an imposing philosophy of the dual self, composed of the "sidereal" phase. and the "adamitic" phase. The former was the essential one. It was contained within the human individual, yet participated in the life of the universe as a whole; it was without relation to time; it was normally mute, except as it manifested itself in dreams, visions, premonitions, and the like, and it was inaccessible, except through a medium such as hypnotic evocation. Compared to it, the adamitic self was a mere external shell, which shallow rationalism persisted in mistaking for the real personality.[5] Among the many debated matters relevant to hypnosis, there was the question raised by Franz von Baader as to what would happen if the essential self somehow came under the domination of an evil man with mesmeric powers.

As a kind of answer to this question Hoffmann composed *Der Magnetiseur,* in which the evil Alban seeks to take possession of other selves in order to arrogate to himself the life forces within them and thereby make himself super-human. Unfortunately it is not one of Hoffmann's best stories, though its long "philosophical" preamble helped more, perhaps, than any other passage in his works to win him the reputation of a profound thinker,—at least in Russia.

Alban is described as in love with Maria, the daughter of a certain Baron, and in order to be near her, has insinuated himself into the Baron's family. By exercise of his mesmeric powers he has alienated Maria from her true lover, Hipolyt. But not entirely. Love is also a mighty force. Maria follows the dictates of love and goes to marry Hipolyt. At the very moment of pronouncing her vows at the altar, the evil power destroys what it could not completely possess. The bride collapses and dies on the floor of the church. Well aware of the source of this evil power, Hipolyt challenges Alban to a duel. Again the evil power is triumphant. Alban runs his opponent through, then disappears from the country. Overcome with grief, the Baron himself dies, but before his death he comes to believe that Alban may be no other than a certain sinister "Major" whom he had known years before in the Army and who once tried to murder him in his sleep by means of hypnotic suggestion.

Hoffmann was apparently aware of the shortcomings of his story as he had composed it in 1813, and six years later retold it essentially, though with new characters and with the new title of *Der unheimliche Gast*.[6] The result was unhappily inferior to the original, though the narration is more smoothly conducted. The evil mesmerist is now called Count S——i. He finds that he can command the affection of the girl Angelika only when she is in his presence. If he so much as leaves the room, her thoughts revert directly to her betrothed Moritz. Presently Moritz is summoned to his regiment, and with the young rival out of the way, Count S——i is able to persuade Angelika to marry him, though only after Moritz has been long at the wars and after the report has been brought of his death. The fateful wedding does not come to pass, however, for one day the old count dies, quite naturally and peacefully in the garden at the stroke of noon. At that very moment Angelika, who is inside the house, faints. When she revives, a joyous premonition tells her that Moritz is returning from the war, indeed that he is even now close by. She runs out of the door into the very arms of her rightful betrothed.

To this main plot is attached a substory concerning a neurotic girl named Margurite, a disciple of Count S——i. She had learned some part of her master's skill and had used it to prolong the absence of Moritz even after the war had ended and other soldiers had returned home. A letter from the Count, addressed to her and delivered after his death, shows him to have been aware of the evil of his actions and resigned in advance to defeat in the quest for Angelika's love. By such conscience-pangs and by his harmless death in a sunny garden, the Count becomes a sorry figure after the Satanic self-willed Alban.

Dostoevski apparently lumped the two stories together as one, and tentatively it may be stated that Murin as an evil man with hypnotic powers like Alban and Count S——i, while Katerina corresponds to the young girl-accomplice Margurite compounded with the beloved Maria-Angelika. Ordynov, then, is the unsuccessful lover, parallel to Hipolyt. These equivalencies are exact up to a certain point.

In view of Dostoevski's remark about Alban as

> ". . . a man who has the Incomprehensible within his grasp, does not know what to do with it, and sits playing wiah a toy called God,"

one might expect that his own Murin would be imbued with some grand ideas and plans, but we find instead a man of rather modest aspirations. It is true that to possess utterly and completely one human being is no slight achievement, and he does so possess Katerina. As Ordynov beholds them through the crack in the partition (Part I, Chapter II), the old man's domination seems as complete as the most unqualified egotist might desire:

> "On a bench beside the bed lay Katerina with her arms about the old man's chest and her head bent over his shoulder. She was looking at him with attentive, childishly wondering eyes, and seemed, breathless with expectation, to be listening with insatiable curiosity to what Murin was telling her. From time to time the speaker's voice rose higher, there was a shade of animation in his pale face; he frowned, his eyes began to flash, and Katerina seemed to turn pale with dread and expectation. Then something like a smile came into the old man's face and Katerina began laughing softly. Sometimes tears came into her eyes; then the old man tenderly stroked her on the head like a child, and she embraced him more tightly than ever with her bare arm that gleamed like snow, and nestled ever more lovingly to his bosom."

And the last view we get of the pair (Part II, Chapter II) shows her, as it were, adoring at Murin's feet, from where he sweeps her with fierce ardor into his arms. Yet between these two points in the story she has defaulted in her submission to her master by making love to Ordynov, and Murin himself suggests that on previous occasions she has fallen in love with other young men. His domination would seem to falter from time to time.

Moreover, if he has such extraordinary powers, why should he live in a wretched slum, endure poverty, and ply a trade of "consultations," on a par with shabby palmists and tea-leaf readers, for small fees? If he practices hypnotic therapy, as seems fairly certain, the work could have only a benevolent motive, which we do not expect from the equivalent of Alban, or a utilitarian bread-winning purpose, which seems equally out of character. Sometimes he terrifies his clients, but it is no mighty necromancy to impose upon the simple citizens of the metropolitan poor districts who come to him for consultations.

Now, in Prince Odoevski's *The Improvisor*,[7] a Hoffmann-derived story of 1833, clients also came to the mysterious house of Segeliel, and strange events transpired there, though the police, try as they would, could never discover anything amiss. Upon some of these clients Segeliel performed marvellous cures, while upon others, his enemies, disaster and ruin fell. But in this case the motivation is quite clear: Segeliel is in league with the Evil One, from whom he derives his healing and his destructive powers, and his fee for healing is an unnamed request, undoubtedly the sale of the client's soul to the Devil. Segeliel earns his luxury by recruiting ever more agents for Satan, but if such is Murin's course, he has the work without the reward. It may be fairly said that this is not Murin's course. He does share with Segeliel the practice of mysterious consultations with odd clients, but the motif is introduced as a tantalizing clue leading nowhere. Murin is not an evil image transposed from Romanticism to the "realistic" slums of Petersburg.

If we equate Murin with Alban and Count S——i, we are forced to declare that Dostoevski restricted his mesmerist's power to a few nameless clients and a girl over whom his domination wavers to a distressing degree. The evil in him is equally tempered. Even assuming he took her from her true lover, as Alban sought to take Maria and as Count S——i sought to take

Angelika, there is something admirable about his devotion, and there is no compelling sympathy of the reader with Ordynov to make it morally imperative that Murin surrender the girl to him. Yet Katerina stresses repeatedly that Murin is evil, even a kind of devil:

> "A wicked man corrupted me," she tells Ordynov. "It was *he* who ruined me! . . . I have sold my soul to him. He says that when he dies he will come and fetch my sinful soul! . . . I am his, I have sold by soul to him. He tortures me, he reads to me in his books. . . . He says I have committed the unpardonable sin . . ."

Her tale of her childhood and of her flight with Murin (Part II, Chapter I) certainly portray a stage when the Satanic aspects of the man were much more readily seen than at any point where the reader sees him.

There is another odd circumstance of Katerina's recollections of her childhood: they have a certain nightmarish quality in common with the dreams that Ordynov dreams of his own childhood as he lies ill with the fever. (Part I, Chapter II.) The connection between the two and many details in each cease to be puzzling if one reads Hoffmann's tale, *Der Sandmann*,[8] not the well known middle section about the hero's infatuation with the life-size doll (Act I of Offenbach's Opera), but rather the opening pages with their extraordinary portrayal of a small boy's terrors.

It is with a letter that Hoffmann begins *Der Sandmann*. The hero, Nathanael, is writing from his university town to his friend Lothar concerning a recent unnerving encounter with a sinister vender of barometers and other instruments, named Dr. Giuseppe Coppola, whom he considers to be possibly identical with the evil man Coppelius, the bane of his childhood.

When he was a small boy, bed-time was announced with the well known phrase: "The Sandman is coming." His mother had explained that the Sandman threw sand into the eyes of tired children to make them sleep, but his nurse had told him something far more frightening about the sleep-fairy. According to her, he was

> ". . . an evil man who comes to children when they don't want to go to bed and throws handfuls of sand into their eyes so that they burst blood-covered out of their heads. These he puts into a bag and carries for food to his children in the half-moon. The latter sit there in the nest and have hooked beaks like owls, with which they peck out naughty children's eyes."

The impressionable child was obsessed with this ghastly theme. Nathanael recalls in his letter how he had always loved frightening stories about witches, cobolds, elves, and the like,

> ". . . but always at their head stood the Sandman, whom I sketched everywhere in chalk, in charcoal, on tables, cupboards, and walls, in the strangest, most revolting forms."

By a natural transition, he had identified the Sandman with the hateful visitor, Coppelius, who frequently came to his parents' house at nightfall. Sometimes he was put to bed before Coppelius came, sometimes it was necessary to sit with him at the supper table. How the children loathed him! His repulsive face with its mocking leer filled them with horror, but worst of all was his malicious pleasure in reaching out his "huge, knotted, hairy hands" to touch a cake or a fruit as it lay on their plates, well knowing that they would not be able to eat it after his touch. Waking and sleeping, the boy was haunted by the figure of Coppelius-Sandman.

Similarly, Ordynov dreaming during his fever, recalls first an idyllic childhood, then the whispering stories materializing into shapes of horror told by "some old woman, mournfully nodding her white, grizzled head before the dying fire," and most of all an evil man. Into the idyll of his childhood

> ". . . a being began suddenly to appear who overwhelmed him with a child-like terror, first bringing into his life the slow poison of sorrow and tears; he dimly felt that an unknown old man held all his future years in thrall, and, trembling, he could not turn his eyes away from him. The wicked old man followed him about everywhere. He peeped out and treacherously nodded to the boy from under every bush in the copse, laughed and mocked at him, took the shape of every doll, grimacing and laughing in his hands, like a spiteful gnome: he set every one of the child's inhuman schoolfellows against him, or, sitting with the little ones on the school bench, peeped out grimacing from every letter of his grammar. Then when he was asleep the evil old man sat by his pillow . . . he drove away the bright spirits whose gold and sapphire wings rustled above his cot, carried off his poor mother from him forever, and began whispering to him every night long wonderful fairy tales, unintelligible to his childish imagination, but thrilling and tormenting him with terror and unchildlike passion. But the wicked old man did not heed his sobs and entreaties, and would go on talking to him till he sank into numbness, into unconsciousness."

(The note of precocious sexuality is wholly lacking in Nathanael's recollections.)

At no point is it made explicit that the evil old man of Ordynov's dream is the same Murin in whose house he now lies dreaming his dream, but the connection will be made in a most interesting way by Katerina, whose childhood story takes up the Coppelius motif where Ordynov leaves off and carries it forward through further parallels.

At a certain point, Nathanael recalls, Coppelius ceased his visits. A year perhaps elapsed. Then, one evening as the family sat at supper, the familiar tread, heavy as iron, was heard on the stairway. His mother turned pale and said: "That is Coppelius." Gloomily his father agreed, but vowed that this would be "the last time." The family were sent off to bed and his father went to meet the visitor alone.

On the occasion of a former visit, the boy had stolen unobserved into his father's room to watch what Coppelius might do. From behind a curtain he had seen both men don black smocks, open a cupboard which revealed a hidden forge where a blue flame burned, and proceed to work at the fire with strange instruments. Ghastly eyeless faces had appeared in the room, at sight of which Coppelius had called for "Eyes, eyes!" The horror of the spectacle had caused him to cry out and betray his presence, whereupon Coppelius had seized him, held him on the hearth, and begun to choose red-hot coals to put in his eyes. Only his father's frantic appeals had saved him. Then, as Coppelius had started to remove the boy's hands and feet, a merciful oblivion had befallen him, from which he awoke finally to his mother's tender caresses. Thus uncommon terror overtook him the evening of this new visit. He went to bed, however, and slept. At midnight a violent explosion shook the house. Screams were heard. Dense smoke poured from his father's room. The father was found, hideously burned and dead beside the hearth.

In Part II, Chapter I of *The Landlady*, Ordynov is roused from his sleep by the weeping and the caresses of Katerina. He comforts her, then questions her about her life. The question agitates her violently. She laments that she is accursed, that she is her mother's murderess, that she is in thrall to Murin. Incoherently she begins a flood of reminiscences about her childhood in a distant place by a river, presumably the Volga. One night, she says, her father was called away by the news that his barge had been wrecked on the river.

> "Mother and I were sitting alone. I was asleep. She was sad about something and weeping bitterly . . . and I knew about

what! . . . Suddenly at midnight we heard a knock at the gate; I jumped up, the blood rushed to my heart; mother cried out . . . I did not look at her, I was afraid. I took a lantern and went myself to open the gate . . . It was *he*! I felt frightened, because I was always frightened when he came, and it was so with me from childhood ever since I remembered anything! . . .

He was all wet and shivering; the storm had driven him fifteen miles, but whence he came neither mother nor I ever knew; we had not seen him for nine weeks. . . . He threw down his cap, pulled off his gloves—did not pray to the ikon, nor bow to the hostess—he sat down by the fire . . ."

Five nights later catastrophe overtook her family.

"Towards evening . . . father came in, surly and menacing, as he had been stricken with illness on the way. I saw his arm was bound up, I guessed that his enemy had waylaid him on the road, his enemy had worn him out and brought sickness upon him. I knew, too, who was his enemy, I knew it all. He did not say a word to mother, he did not ask about me. He called together all the workmen, made them leave the factory, and guard the house from the evil eye."

That same evening she allowed herself (apparently) to be seduced by Murin. They were planning to run away together when all at once the cry was heard that the factory was on fire. Soon thereafter she saw workmen carrying her father's corpse and overheard them say:

"He stumbled, he fell down the stairs into a red-hot cauldron; so the devil must have pushed him down."

An interval elapsed. Suddenly she felt herself seized by the shoulders. It was Murin.

"he was singed all over and his kaftan, hot to the touch, was smoking."

(Again, as with Ordynov, there is the note of precocious sexuality which is not to be found in *Der Sandmann*.)[9]

For all the incoherence of Katerina's narrative, Ordynov understands her very well because, the author says,

"her life had become his life, her grief his grief, and because her foe stood visible before him. . . . The wicked old man of his dream (Ordynov believed this) was living before him."

The implication is that Katerina's life has not *become* Ordynov's life, but rather that her life *had been* his life. From a literary-historical point of view they have, it is obvious, shared the experience of Nathanael's childhood between them, but there is a further and much more interesting aspect to this interpenetration of existences. A common motif of German Romantic thought was the extra-rational participation of the "sidereal self" in

experiences of which the "adamitic self" or rational consciousness could not know. Hoffmann's *Meister Floh* is a tale where
the whole narrative is a progressive revelation of a former life
together, both to the characters themselves and to the reader.
The fact that Dostoevski in *The Landlady* does not exploit the
theme may indicate that he knew the idea well from reading
Hoffmann and took it for granted. Or again it may be a coincidence resulting from his deliberate mystifications. Evidence
is lacking to prove the former, but if he did make use of the
complex motif from *Meister Floh*, it would be one of the very
rare instances where he shows a concern with the great *Märchen*
for which Hoffmann is justly famous.

For the remaining portion of Katerina's narrative Dostoevski
drew, as Gesemann suggests,[10] on Gogol's early Ukrainian tale,
A Terrible Vengeance.[11] The evil necromancer who dominates
that story is a monster of crime. He is a traitor, compounding
now with the Catholic Poles, now with the Moslem Turks; he
has sold his soul to Satan for earthly pleasures; he pursues his
daughter, also named Katerina, with an incestuous passion. In
a scene intended as a climax of horror, the young woman's husband, Danilo, spies on his villainous father-in-law as the latter
invokes the soul of the sleeping Katerina to leave its physical
body and appear before him. The reluctant and sorrowing soul
knows what the rational mind does not know, namely that this
evil father murdered her mother years before. The young husband apprehends the old sorcerer and throws him in prison,
whence he is to be taken, tied to the tail of a wild horse, and
dragged to death across the steppes. Through Katerina's simplicity the old man escapes, but ultimately he meets a horrendous death,—"a terrible vengeance,"—at the hands of supernatural forces.

From this source Dostoevski drew, in all likelihood, the romantic literary theme of incest. The scene in the boat on the
river may possibly be connected with a section of Gogol's tale,
where Danilo and *his* Katerina make a memorable crossing of
the Dnepr while the dusk is troubled by the rising of the evil
dead from their graves on the bank. More striking is the imitation of the high-flown diction of Gogol's early period. In
fact, Dostoevski goes even further in this unique passage of his
writing to introduce phrases from the old ballad cycles of
Russia. Lovers refer to each other as "bright falcons"; set

epithets occur, such as "fair maid," "maiden queen," white hand" (for a man) ; there is talk of "goblets," "caskets," "board" (table), "vessel" (boat) ; and the lapse of time is indicated by the phrase "Two dawns have passed." Ballad-like also is Katerina's flight with Murin on horseback, her head nestled in his bosom as they rode, and the farewell to her horse at the river's edge. Even the old poems of Russia are drawn into the complex matter of this story.

Some time back the question was posed: Just who and what is Murin? Our discussion up to this point has established several details of his literary ancestry:—he is a sinister hypnotist by virtue of his derivation from Alban in Hoffmann's *Der Magnetiseur*; he holds mysterious "consultations" reminiscent of Segeliel in Odoevski's *The Improvisor*; he enters the lives of Katerina and of Ordynov as an evil figure directly traceable to Coppelius in Hoffmann's *Der Sandmann*; and there is an unresolved question as to his incestuous love for Katerina which is connected with the monstrous villain of Gogol's *A Terrible Vengeance*. All of these literarily related figures are strikingly evil.

All of these "explanations" of Murin fail to account for the character as a whole. If he belonged exactly in a category with any one of the four named characters it would be odd indeed that he should attend Vespers frequently, that he should read religious books, and that he should commit in the course of the story proper no evil act except to fire a gun at the rashly intruding Ordynov, for which unpremeditated violence he shortly apologizes.

The Russian scholar Rodzevich recognized years ago the connection between *The Landlady* and Hoffmann's two stories, *Der Magnetiseur* and *Der Sandmann*;[12] Gesemann perceived the relatively minor connection with Gogol's *A Terrible Vengeance*. All of these relationships are valid. But in the last analysis they illuminate only isolated parts of the work, leaving the central character of Murin and the story as a whole quite as puzzling as before.

The truth of the matter is that Dostoevski was again compounding story elements as in the case of *The Double*, though in not quite the same way. It seems most likely that he began that story with the intention of blending the theme of Gogol's

Diary of a Madman with the general plan of Hoffmann's *Die Abenteuer der Sylvesternacht* and that the latter work attracted like a magnet other scenes and other notions of "Doppelgängerei" from Dostoevski's wide reading in Hoffmann and elsewhere. What resulted was a basically Gogolian pattern overlaid with these diverse motifs from various sources. In the case of *The Landlady* we are confronted with a procedure of story "incapsulation."

Without further ado, let it be understood that Katerina is mad. To her deranged mind Murin *seems* to be an evil creature, half supernatural, like Coppelius. In her jumbled narrative she speaks of him in such terms, but then proceeds to speak of him in terms of an incestuous father like the one in Gogol's *A Terrible Vengeance,* which he also *seems* to her to be, just as the real journey she must have made from the Volga region to Petersburg *seems* to her to have been made ballad-fashion on horseback with her head nestled in her lover's bosom. As for Murin's mesmeric powers, they too are an illusion,—Ordynov's illusion,—for to him Murin *seems* to be a sinister hypnotist like Alban. For one set of "seemings,"—Katerina's,—Dostoevski used Hoffmann's *Der Sandmann*; for another set of "seemings,"—Ordynov's,—he used Hoffmann's *Der Magnetiseur.* But for the story as a whole, within which these "seemings" are "incapsulated," he used still another work of Hoffmann's, *Der Artushof.*

It is from the great counting-house in Danzig, the Artushof (Arthur's Hall) that the story takes its name. Here in the late afternoon the daily crowds dwindle, half-light fills the building, and the old mural paintings seem about to come alive and restore the mediaeval splendor of the place. Here, on such a late afternoon sits a young clerk named Traugott, lost in a daydream and idly sketching a pencil copy of one of the murals when he should be drafting a business letter for Herr Elias Roos, his superior and prospective father-in-law. His fancy is wholly engaged by the painting, a mediaeval cavalcade in which a handsome youth is shown holding the bridle of a black horse mounted by a gloomy faced man in rich apparel. A word of praise for his pencil copy startles him, and he looks up to behold the very same persons at his side. Before he can recover from his astonishment they vanish in the crowds. Mr. Roos is irate to find a drawing where he had counted on finding a business letter prepared for despatch, but an associate calms his anger, makes other arrangements for the letter, and then compliments young Traugott on the excellence of his art.

The young man is troubled. He would like to become an artist, but all circumstances conspire to make of him a business man and the husband of the pretty and wealthy Christine Roos. Doubting his artistic vocation, he resigns himself to a conventional existence. One day the mysterious old man and the handsome youth reappear in the Artushof and Traugott is able to intervene before the old man commits himself to a clearly inadvisable business transaction. At first the old man is resentful of the intrusion, but when the youth reminds him that this is the young artist of the previous occasion, he relents and introduces himself as Godofredus Berklinger and the youth as his son. He claims further to have painted the mural in question, which Traugott knows to be at least two centuries old. No explanation of the time discrepancy is advanced. The son invites Traugott to come to see his father's other paintings. Berklinger suppresses an impulse of annoyance and, with a sharp scrutinizing glance at Traugott, makes the invitation specifically for the next morning.

Upon arrival at the appointed time, Traugott finds the son dressed in old German costume and the father eager to display a recently completed picture entitled "Paradise Regained." The visitor is bewildered to hear his host discuss in detail the canvas before them, for the canvas is completely blank. The old man becomes ever more excited as he talks, until, at the peak of excitement, he collapses. Sadly the son explains that such frequently befalls his father, who was once a great artist, and displays several earlier pictures to prove the statement. The pictures are indeed excellent. The son further adds that his father is dominated by "an unhappy thought" which involves both their lives in misery.

Among other paintings, there is one depicting a beautiful girl in old German costume and with features closely resembling those of Berklinger's son. The latter identifies the girl as his unhappy sister Felizitas, then, with tears in his eyes, hurries the visitor away. Deeply moved by the portrait, Traugott turns to Berklinger, who has now revived, and asks him to accept him as a pupil in painting. The old man accepts the proposal with joy.

Day after day Traugott studies under his new master, neglecting his business duties and postponing his marriage to Christine Roos. Berklinger is delighted with his pupil and always welcomes him enthusiastically, yet does everything in his power to keep him apart from his son. A private conversation between the young people will set him directly in a rage. Thus a winter passes.

One spring day Traugott arrives late, at twilight, and is astonished to hear the sounds of a lute coming from one of the rooms of Berklinger's house. He opens a door and beholds the girl Felizitas in the very costume of her portrait. She is, of course, Berklinger's "son." Traugott falls on his knees before her, "the beloved of his soul," but at that very moment feels himself seized by the collar and dragged out of the room.

> " 'Infamous wretch!—Rascal unparalleled!' screamed old Berklinger, pushing him away, 'so that was your love for Art—You want to murder me!' And with that he thrust him out the door. A knife flashed in his hand. Traugott fled down the steps. Dazed, indeed half mad with delight and terror, Traugott ran to his own house."

After hours of sleeplessness, he rises and hastens to Berklinger's house, only to find that the painter and his "son" have left for parts unknown.

Here the action-parallels with *The Landlady* break off, though it may well have been the ambiguous sequel that gave Dostoevski the idea for his own tale of mystifications.

Traugott eventually learns that half of Danzig was aware that the old painter was insane and that his putative son was actually his daughter Felizitas in man's clothing. The prophecy of "an ignominious death" if his daughter were ever to marry explained his extreme hostility to all suitors. The pair are now living in "Sorrento." Assuming that "Sorrento" can only be in Italy, Traugott abandons business and Christine to flee to the land of Love and Art. On the way, however, his excitement cools and he does not go to Sorrento but tarries in Rome to study painting. There he encounters another father and daughter couple, strangely like Berklinger and Felizitas, yet not the same. The daughter, Dorina, with whom Traugott falls in love, has "the features of Felizitas but is not she";—"it was the same picture painted by Raphael and Rubens." At this juncture business matters summon the young painter home to Danzig, and there he learns that the "Sorrento" of Berklinger is an estate of that name located not far distant. In the interim Berklinger has died: he burst a blood vessel one day upon discovering a young man in the very act of proposing to his daughter. After a decent interval Felizitas married,—not the suitor in question, but a jurist from near-by Marienwerder.

At first Traugott laughs bitterly, but then declares that Felizitas will always be his ideal, that she is "the creative art that lives within him." He starts back for Italy and Dorina.

Here, then, is the core-story of *The Landlady*: an impressionable young man goes to the poor home of a mysterious couple, an old man and a young girl, and for a time becomes intimately involved in their lives. Insanely jealous of any and all suitors for his daughter's hand, the old man attempts to kill the intruder,—Berklinger by drawing a knife on Traugott, Murin by firing a gun at Ordynov,—and when the attempt fails, he takes his daughter with him and vanishes without a trace.

Now *Der Artushof* is an art-tale, one of several in this category among Hoffmann's works, and its primary concern is with the problem of conventional life versus an artist's dedication. For an artist to marry his "ideal" is to lose the ideal and to descend to commonplace existence. Traugott escapes the patently Philistine Miss Roos as well as Felizitas, who herself opts for a conventional married life with the jurist from Marienwerder. Whether he will escape Dorina is left an open question. What could so have caught the fancy of Dostoevski in such a story? Probably it was the tantalizing mystery that pervades the work, for Dostoevski dearly loved mystery. The transformation of the story-material was, however, another problem.

If one takes the figure of Godofredus Berklinger and cancels out all his art-characteristics, one will arrive very near to an accurate description of Dostoevski's Murin. Both are commoners, poor and obscure, known to people about them as "queer fellows"; both accept fees for small services; both have endured some unspecified misfortune, either through their own fault or as innocent victims, and as a result are marked with a lucid madness, the supreme obsession of which is to prevent the approach of any suitors to their jealously guarded daughters; both live amid circumstances of suspicion, yet within the range of the stories proper neither commits any known evil deed, with the exception of their attempted violence to the respective heroes. Above all, both are good.

Herewith is answered our original question: What is Murin? He is a pathetic old man with a lucid madness, solely concerned with keeping his daughter with him. Whatever may have been involved in his past, he is genuinely pious, sincerely reads his religious books, and attends Vespers with true reverence. That he speaks Tatar is of no significance; that he may be an Old Believer is equally without significance; that his house was a meeting place for thieves is a coincidence. He *is* subject to epileptic seizures, but his sinister mesmeric actions are the illusions of his lodger, as his devil-rôle is the illusion of Katerina.

Dostoevski's next step, typical of his incessant will *plus ultra,* was to make his equivalent of Felizitas Berklinger insane *also.* Neither girl had a particularly active rôle to play. It consisted largely of enduring the bizarre caprices of an insane but loving father. But by making Katerina's illusion of Murin a main concern, Dostoevski was able to raise her to the position of title-character in his story.

It was to Traugott that the greatest violence was done in recasting him as Ordynov, for to remove Art from Traugott was to remove almost everything there was in him. Nothing was left but a great sensitivity and dreaminess, and this is precisely the definition of Ordynov, who is a fair candidate for the most hyper-sensitive youth in Russian fiction. This "scientist" has "the soul of an artist" because Traugott *was* an artist. The character-vacuum thus created was compensated by making his illusion of Murin a primary feature of the narrative. His ultimate fate, however, is different from that of his predecessor.

Traugott suffers a bitter disillusionment upon learning of the marriage of Felizitas, but he shrugs the disappointment off and returns to Italy, to Art, and to Dorina, in keeping with the essentially optimistic attitude of Hoffmann. In Russia, Hoffmann-derived heroes consistently perish in madness and despair. Ordynov is no exception. For a time after quitting Murin's house he was merely dispirited and dull. Only the church bells, reminding him of his first meeting with Katerina, could rouse him from his torpor. Then, amid tears and anguish, he would relive his experience, which now begins to take on a religious significance for him. His new landlady,

> "a devout old Russian woman, used to describe with relish how her meek lodger prayed and how he would lie for hours together as though unconscious on the church pavement. . . ."

In other words, he now prostrates himself and prays as Katerina used to do. And like Katerina, he is, in all probability, mad.

Even minor details, hitherto unnoticed in *The Landlady*, take on new meaning by collation with *Der Artushof*. Early in the story, for example, Ordynov, in search of new lodgings, takes and pays in advance for a room in the home of a German family, but disregards the fact to follow Murin and Katerina and find other quarters in their house. After leaving them he returns to the quarters rented in the home of the German SHpis (Spies) and his pretty daughter Tinchen. Obliquely Dostoevski thus alludes to a set of "Doubles" for Murin and Katerina, but leaves the theme undeveloped. The presence of SHpis and his daughter Tinchen is the residue of the "other" Berklinger and the "other" Felizitas, Dorina, who was "the same subject painted by a different artist."

Again, the gossip-loving Yaroslav Ilich has an analogue in *Der Artushof* in the person of the unnamed broker from whom Traugott derives his "factual" information concerning the lives and whereabouts of Berklinger and Felizitas. Once the heroes are launched on their fantastic adventures, it is only from these informants that the reader obtains "reliable" facts.

Or again, take the opening scene of *Der Artushof*, the late afternoon dusk amid which the figures of old Berklinger and his "son" emerge, as it were, into the imposing mediaeval building from one of the ancient paintings on the wall. This passage Dostoevski has metamorphosed into a church interior,—in terms of Gogol's *Taras Bulba* Vesper scene, or from *Die Elixiere des Teufels*, or whatever,—and amid the awesome twilight there brought forth the mysterious old man with the beautiful Katerina on his arm.

Finally, *Der Artushof* may itself be defined as the story of a succession of illusions. Like *The Landlady*, its basic realities consist of a few unglamorous facts. Everything depends, not on what Traugott saw, but on what he thought he saw. Dostoevski merely multiplied the illusions, presenting not one mad person as seen by two sane ones, but a madman as seen by a second person who is also mad and by a third person, Ordynov, who is going mad. Thus three deranged minds are placed like mirrors at odd angles to the simple realities they reflect, and, as it were, turning and swaying, their surfaces blemished and misted, they catch the partial and imperfect images of each other until the whole story takes on the quality of a kaleideo-scope. The artistic fault was two-fold: an excess of irony, leaving the reader more irritated than pleased, and an excess of gloom and horror. What Dostoevski probably intended was a horror-story in the Hoffmannesque manner, psychologically deepened, yet undercut with ironic (Gogolian?) humor, and more akin in spirit to *Der Sandmann* and *Der Magnetiseur* than to *Der Artushof*. Too often he achieved an effect of mere absurdity incongruously commingled with grisly nightmare.

Yet for all its shortcomings, *The Landlady* has about it the persistence of a haunting dream. The figures of Murin and Katerina dog the memory. The work does not deserve the neglect with which it has usually met.

V

THE SHORT STORIES OF 1848

Whatever the virtues or faults of *The Landlady* may be, it is difficult to see how Dostoevski could have imagined for one moment that any story of its type, however brilliant, might please Belinski and the circle of realist minded critics. Yet he had eagerly looked forward to its publication in October 1847 as a logical means of regaining his lost favor. He was quickly undeceived. Grigorovich in his memoirs describes the reaction:[1]

> "About this time Belinski said in a letter to Annenkov: 'Dostoevski's *The Landlady* is terrible stuff! He has attempted a combination of Marlinski and Hoffmann, with a dash of Gogol. He has written other novels besides but every new work of his is a calamity. In the provinces they can't stand him at all, and in Petersburg even *Poor Folk* is abused; I tremble at the thought that I shall have to read this novel once more. We've been well taken in by our 'gifted' Dostoevski!'
> So Belinski wrote, the most honest man in the world, and he meant every word of it most honestly and thoroughly. Belinski never flinched from declaring his opinion of Dostoevski, and all his circle echoed him."

No less distressing was his record of publication. It was now approaching two years since he had brought out *Poor Folk* and *The Double* within a fortnight of each other. Since then only *Mr. Prokharchin* and *A Novel in Nine Letters* had been printed, and their anniversaries were upon him. Something had to be done. The novel fragment of *Netochka Nezvanova* tempted him to continuation, but that would take too long. The public must not be allowed to forget him, and, besides, he needed money. He solved the problem by turning out a series of short stories of uneven length and uneven quality, but all of much more modest proportions than *The Double* or *The Landlady*. They are all minor works of a great author.

1. POLZUNKOV

Panaev and Nekrasov, friends of Belinski, had by now no strong enthusiasm for Dostoevski, but at the beginning of 1848 they printed the first of these short stories in the *Almanach* or special issue of *The Contemporary*. Entitled *Polzunkov* (Crawler) from its principal character, it is hardly more than an expanded anecdote about an April Fool's joke that woefully miscarried.

Engaged to his employer's daughter but offended at something her father had done, Polzunkov submits his resignation and simultaneously announces that he wishes to renounce all claims to the young lady's hand. Then he cries "April Fool," laughs off the whole affair, and is presumably pardoned by all parties concerned. His employer bides his time, allowing Polzunkov to work very hard and long at the office, and meanwhile, under pretext of urgent need, gets back the dowry money which had been advanced to his employee. In due time Polzunkov receives an official letter dismissing him from service. His employer has allowed the April Fool letter to be submitted in earnest.

The memorable thing about the story is not the anecdote proper but the fact that Polzunkov himself has struggled for some time to get the attention of a group of guests at an evening party in order to tell them this story of self-humiliation. He prefers to be heard and mocked at rather than not be heard at all. He is the first of Dostoevski's self-tormenting buffoons, the line of whom will end in that remarkable figure, the father of the Karamazovs.

There is no perceptible Hoffmannian trait in the story.

2. ANOTHER MAN'S WIFE AND THE HUSBAND UNDER THE BED

In January of 1848 *National Notes*, which was to publish all the rest of Dostoevski's output of this year, carried the brief humorous tale called *Another Man's Wife*. Intended as hilarious farce somewhat in the vein of *A Novel in Nine Letters*, the work is made up chiefly of a confused and confusing dialogue between a jealous husband and a jealous lover, both of whom are lurking in a dark Petersburg street to spy on their respective lady-loves. The lady-loves prove to be one and the same person, the wife of the former. As they approach the door together, the lady emerges with a third man, clearly her present lover. With staggering self-assurance she manages to bamboozle all three. Sending the third man for a carriage, she tells the other lover that this was her husband. When he indignantly points to the actual husband standing only a few feet away, she runs to the husband and tells him that she has just been rescued from an accident by the very man with whom he has been keeping the jealous vigil. The third man returns with the carriage. Nothing daunted, the lady pretends that she has not seen him in weeks, introduces him to her husband, and calmly gets into the vehicle, ordering her husband to join her. Even as she bids good evening to the two lovers on the kerb, she manages to convey an assignation to one and an arch hint of a rendezvous to the other. The dazed husband drives away with his wife, leaving the philandering gentlemen, no less dazed, behind.

Like a new installment of a comic strip, Dostoevski followed up this episode with a new adventure of the cuckolded husband in December. Entitled *The Jealous Husband,* it takes the husband to the opera where he sees his wife in a box with a strange man. His curiosity is thwarted by the fact that the box in question is immediately above him so that he cannot observe it, but when a love-note drops on his bald head from above he immediately concludes that it involves a secret tryst of his wife's. He goes to the appointed place, stalks in despite the protests of servants, only to find himself confronting a perfectly strange lady. At the approach of her husband he rushes to hide under the bed. There he discovers another gentleman who had hidden at *his* approach. The lady's dog betrays them both. He seizes the dog and strangles it, and in the resulting furor the first lover escapes, leaving our hero to tell the unlikely truth to the husband. Returning home, he finds that his own wife has been waiting for him these many hours. As he draws forth his handkerchief to mop his perspiring brow, he pulls out the corpse of the little lap-dog which he had stuffed into his pocket in his bewilderment.

If the first story was only mildly funny, it was at least innocuous, whereas the sequel is in sheer bad taste. Gay farce was not Dostoevski's strong point. Yet he combined the two pieces under the title of *Another Man's Wife and The Husband under the Bed* for his collected works in 1860 and retained them in the new augmented collection of 1865. It is under this title that the double story is now known.

Again there is no perceptible trait of Hoffmann in the story.

3. A FAINT HEART

In quite a different vein is the tale *A Faint Heart,* which was published in February of 1848. It is perhaps the most pleasing and intrinsically interesting of the series. It is also, of all Dostoevski's works, the nearest equivalent to a short story of Gogol, in length, in the simplicity of its linear structure, and in its sympathetic poor clerk hero.

For all of that, this particular poor clerk, Vasya Shumkov,—

he is never referred to as Vasili,—is marked with a certain seraphic quality that is uniquely Dostoevskian. He is a hard-working fellow, happy in the blessings which fortune has conferred upon him: he has a considerate employer, a stable job, a loyal friend in his room-mate Arkadi, a lovely fiancée, and prospective parents-in-law who like him cordially. With all this and his gentle, cheerful disposition, it would seem that nothing could possibly go wrong. Yet there is something very wrong. He confesses his difficulty to Arkadi on New Year's Eve after a delightful visit the two have made to the family of his fiancée. He has been assigned a considerable quantity of work at the office, but he has neglected it in the midst of his excitement over his engagement and is now filled with remorse at his failure in his duty. The New Year's holiday is devoted to ardent work at his task, but, try as he will, conflicting emotions and self-reproach keep him from making any real headway. Arkadi becomes worried as Vasya continues work hour after hour without rest, and determines to keep awake himself in order to force Vasya to go to bed before too long a time. His good intentions fail him, he drifts off to sleep, and wakes in the middle of the night shocked to see Vasya still writing. Then Arkadi notices with horror

> "that Vasya was moving a dry pen over the paper, was turning perfectly blank pages, and hurrying, hurrying to fill up the paper as though he were doing his work in a most thorough and efficient way. . . .
>
> 'Vasya, Vasya, speak to me,' he cried, clutching him by the shoulder. But Vasya did not speak; he went on as before, scribbling with a dry pen over the paper.
>
> 'At last I have made the pen go faster,' he said, without looking up at Arkadi."

Arkadi hurries out in search of a doctor. Meanwhile Vasya quits his task in despair and goes to the office where he presents himself to be arrested and sent away as a conscript soldier. His employer is amazed, all the more since the work assigned was not urgent at all. He watches, deeply grieved, as Vasya is led away, not to become a soldier but to be committed to the madhouse.

Forty of the forty-eight pages of the story proceed in an atmosphere of the coolest, most unambiguous realism, then suddenly the turn to madness arrestingly symbolized by the blank sheets of paper, the most memorable element in the whole work. Quite properly, the symbol may be traced to *Ritter Gluck,* the very earliest of Hoffmann's Tales (1809).[2]

This is the story in which the unnamed narrator makes the acquaintance of an odd, middle aged musician who finds an uncommon exasperation in the afternoon band playing in the Tiergarten. Since the narrator is also much concerned with music, the conversation is prolonged on that subject. Some months later the two meet again accidentally outside a theatre where Gluck's *Armida* is in progress. The eccentric musician seizes the narrator by the arm and urges him to come home with him. There he assures him he shall hear *Armida.* They go to an old house in a side street, pick their way up a dark stair, and arrive at a room richly furnished in an antiquated style. A piano occupies the middle of the floor, while on a shelf in a corner are lined up the volumes of Gluck's complete works. The volume marked *Armida* is taken down and placed on the music rack and the strange musician asks the narrator to follow the score carefully and to turn the pages at the proper time.

But the pages are completely blank, except for the staves which are lined in. There is not a single note of music on them and they are yellow with age. The musician then proceeds to play *Armida,* Gluck's *Armida,* but with new and striking modifications of the original score. By watching the movements of his eyes, the narrator turns the blank pages at intervals. When the playing ceases, the narrator, struck with wonder, cries out: "Who are you?"

The musician looks at him solemnly, then without a word withdraws to an inner room. Presently he returns, dressed in 18th century court costume, a dress-sword at his side. He advances majestically and with a strange smile says:

"I am the Chevalier Gluck."

Opinions differ as to the interpretation of the story, as they differ about the date and circumstances of its composition, but it is probably based on a personal experience of Hoffmann's in Berlin in 1807-1808 and almost certainly is intended to depict a lucid madman then alive and with extraordinary musical gifts, who suffers from the delusion that he is "the Chevalier Gluck." That he is the ghost of the real Gluck, who died in 1787, is the unlikely claim of the editor Ellinger.[3]

Whatever the conflict of opinions, Dostoevski, we may be

sure, understood the "Chevalier Gluck" to be a madman. Given his close acquaintance with *Der Artushof,* as may be seen from the use he made of it in writing his own story *The Landlady,* he may well have been aware of the parallel motif there, when the mad painter Berklinger demonstrates at length his masterwork "Paradise Regained" upon a perfectly blank canvas. In any event, it must be granted that Dostoevski has adapted the borrowed motif with great skill and put it to highly effective use. Nor should it fail to be observed that the transformation has exchanged a pessimistic tone for the original optimistic one. Hoffmann's mad musician found untold solace in the music he created, while his delusion of being Gluck, far from harming him, was actually a source of happiness and pride. For Dostoevski's poor clerk, on the other hand, those blank sheets of paper contain his commitment to the hell of the madhouse.

4. AN HONEST THIEF

Within two months, Dostoevski followed up *A Faint Heart* with a new story called *An Honest Thief,* published in April of 1848 under the original title of *A Chapter from the Tales of a Worldly-wise Man.*

The central character is a friendless old drunkard named Emelyan Ilich, who lives upon the hospitality of a retired soldier. The latter can hardly eke out a living as a tailor, but sheer compassion for Emelyan Ilich prevents him from driving the old fellow away. One day the host discovers that a pair of riding breeches is missing. Quite naturally it occurs to him that Emelyan Ilich may have sold them for drink. Accusation elicits only protests of innocence from the old man, and prolonged suspicion after his denial humiliates him to the point where he declares that he will leave his benefactor forever. The tailor lets him go, confident that nightfall will see his return. But three days pass and no news comes of him. On the third night the poor creature comes back, ill with fever and apparently without food since his departure. The illness is fatal, and as he lies dying, he confesses that he did indeed sell the riding breeches in order to buy drink. He hopes that after his death his old cloak may fetch enough cash to reimburse his benefactor.

As the story stands, there is no clear indication of a source in Hoffmann, yet certain facts exist to suggest that there may be a connection after all. Emelyan Ilich's obsession with gratitude relates him to Vasya Shumkov in *A Faint Heart*; the two stories were written close together in time; in *A Faint Heart* Dostoevski borrowed only an isolated motif from Ritter Gluck. Now let us suppose that *Ritter Gluck* was in his mind at this period and that he passed Hoffmann's title character through that same process of transformation by which the personages of *Der Artushof* were made into those of *The Landlady.* Removing all connection with art so that only a residue of externals remains, Hoffmann's musician is left as a forlorn old man who wanders friendless about the great city; place him then in the "realistic" poor quarters of Petersburg and give him death instead of salvation through music, and we have something very close to Emelyan Ilich. Both works are two-men stories, with one main character and one narrator who tells the events after the fact.— This frankly undemonstrable thesis has against it chiefly the fact that the "honest thief" is a drunkard, not a madman. But Dostoevski had written three stories with madness as the principal theme, most recently *A Faint Heart,* and possibly he was anxious to try something new. At all events, he was never again to employ the theme of madness in the sense in which it occurs in *The Double, The Landlady,* and *A Faint Heart.*

5. A CHRISTMAS TREE AND A WEDDING

Shortest of all the tales of 1848 is the fifth, *A Christmas Tree and a Wedding,*[4] which appeared in *National Notes* in September.

Through the eyes of an unidentified narrator the author presents the scene of a Christmas party in a wealthy home. The lively children have stripped the Christmas tree and are playing with their new toys, all except one little eleven-year-old girl, who is "quiet, dreamy, pale, with big, prominent, dreamy eyes, exquisite as a little Cupid." One of the guests comments on the 300,000 ruble dowry of this little girl, and the narrator observes the undue interest which this remark evokes in Yulian Mastakovich, a pompous middle aged man to whom the hosts pay considerable deference.

From behind an ivy-arbor in a quiet parlor the narrator further observes how Yulian Mastokovich comes to watch the little girl as she is playing with the poor governess's little boy, and overhears him muttering arithmetic. He is computing the interest on 300,000 rubles for five years. Then he approaches the girl, dismisses the little boy irritably, and is about to kiss the girl when he is interrupted by the arrival of other guests.

Five years later the narrator passes a certain church where a wedding party is just coming out the door. The groom is Yulian Mastakovich and the bride is the same little girl, now a pale and melancholy figure. An on-looker remarks that her dowry is 500,000 rubles,—just what Yulian Mastakovich had calculated.

Ostensibly this very brief tale is concerned with the cynical pursuit of money, but it has, especially in view of later works of Dostoevski, the suggestion of sexual depravity in the lust of the middle aged man for an eleven-year-old girl. If it does pre-figure the child-rape motif hinted at in *Crime and Punishment* and specifically treated in *The Possessed,* one would not expect to find Hoffmann analogues. Nevertheless there seem to be in this little story certain echoes from widely different tales of Hoffmann.

First a minor analogue which may be fortuitous.—*Meister Floh* opens with a Christmas party for children, from which the hero, Peregrinus Tyss, goes to distribute gifts to the poor children of the bookbinder Lämmerhirt. In the seventh and last chapter he comes again to Lämmerhirt's house and there en-counters the bookbinder's lovely daughter Röschen, who will become his wife. Röschen, however, had not been present at the time of his first visit since she was living then, in time of war, with a cousin of the family in another place.—A family Christmas scene, with children discovering toys beneath a lighted Christmas tree, also marks the opening of *Nussknacker und Mausekönig.*

In *Signor Formica,* however,—a work which Dostoevski singles out for praise in *Three Tales of Edgar Poe* (1861),[5]— Hoffmann does treat the subject of inappropriate marriage be-tween an old man and a young girl, though as a theme for comedy. Comic likewise is the handling of the same theme in *Die Brautwahl,*[6] where the preposterous old Privy Secretary Tusmann is in love with Albertine Vosswinkel, the daughter of an old schoolmate. In Chapter III we learn that

> "Tusmann watched Albertine grow up, and on her twelfth birthday, after handing her a bouquet of fragrant flowers which the most famous florist in Berlin had himself tastefully arranged, he had kissed her hand for the first time with a dignity and a gal-lantry that no one would have thought him capable of. From

that moment the thought arose in the mind of the Commission
Councillor (the girl's father) that his schoolmate might well marry
Albertine."

The idea grew until it became a settled decision, and a formal
betrothal took place on the girl's eighteenth birthday, the point
at which the story begins. The plot, of course, is devoted to the
removal of the fatuous and infatuated old suitor and to the
trials and ultimate triumph of the young hero's quest for the
young heroine.

Closer to the mood of Dostoevski's story is an episode in the
fourth chapter of *Datura fastuosa*,[7] where the fourteen-year-old
Gretchen is approached by the devilish Fermino Valies. In this
rather atypical work of Hoffmann more than one touch of extraordinary psychology is to be found. Characters of great purity
are juxtaposed with characters of depravity and lust, and there
is an intense, yet curiously passive, resistance to the force of
the latter, parallel to the vegetable strength in the plants among
which the good characters spend their lives.

The young botanist hero, Eugenius, has married the matronly
widow of his beloved professor and lives and works in the combination home-and-greenhouse just as he did before the professor's death, quite unaware that the adolescent Gretchen is in
love with him. Recently he has made an unwise choice of
friends in the evil Fermino Valies. In Chapter IV there is a
remarkable passage where the girl reports to Eugenius, partly
in childish fright, but more in adolescent shame, how Valies had
addressed her in the garden during the botanist's absence:

"... a strange man had suddenly stepped into the garden by
way of the gate which she thought she had bolted and had asked
after him (Eugenius). There had been something strange in the
man's air. He had looked at her with such queer, burning eyes
that she had felt an icy chill in all her limbs and for sheer anguish
and terror had not been able to stir from the spot. Then the man
had inquired about this and that in very strange words, which
she had scarcely understood, since he had not spoken correct
German, and had finally asked—here Gretchen suddenly stopped,
while her cheeks were like two fire-lilies. But when Eugenius
urged her to tell him everything, everything, she went on to relate
that the stranger had asked her whether she wasn't fond of Mr.
Eugenius. Straight from the heart she had answered, 'Oh yes,
very fond, indeed!' Then the stranger had stepped up close to
her and looked right through her again with his former repel-
lant glance, so that she had been forced to lower her eyes. What
was more, the stranger had insolently and shamelessly patted her

on the cheek, which burned from sheer anguish and terror, saying as he did so: 'You pretty, dainty, little thing, quite fond, quite fond of him!' and then he laughed sarcastically, so that her heart quivered within her. At that moment the Professor's widow had stepped up to the window and the stranger had asked whether that were Mr. Eugenius's spouse, and when she had replied 'Yes, it was her mother,' he had mockingly cried, 'Ah, the beautiful woman!—Are you perhaps jealous, little girl?'—and here again he had laughed so sarcastically and slyly, like no person she had ever heard before, and then, after he had looked the Professor's widow sharply in the eye once more, he had quickly withdrawn from the garden."

Like the conversation between Yulian Mastakovich and the little girl which the narrator of Dostoevski's story overhears from behind the in-door arbor, this scene between Fermino Valies and Gretchen in the botanical garden conveys a suggestion of covert nastiness and repugnant lust, all the more forceful for being expressed indirectly. In the German story the botanical garden is a factor of such importance that it almost becomes a character. At this point Hoffmann subtly and discreetly plays with the symbolism of the innocent girl and the tempting devil in the garden, as elsewhere he exploits the idea of rare and precious blossoms beside strange floral poisons. Dostoevski's in-door arbor may well be a carry-over from Hoffmann's botanical setting. It is curious that he seems to contradict himself as to its nature, referring to it at one point as "an arbor of flowers which filled up almost half of the room" and at another point as simply an "ivy-arbor."

Demonstration of a Hoffmann source is again not entirely possible in the case of *A Christmas Tree and a Wedding*, but a plausible suggestion would connect it with *Datura fastuosa* in combination with a recollection of the twelve-year-old Albertine Vosswinkel kissed by the absurd old Tusmann in *Die Brautwahl*.

The brevity of Dostoevski's little sketch is tantalizing. It hints much but discloses relatively little. Nevertheless it is a significant item among his early productions because it introduces the first villain in his stories. The brief data of evil embodied here will receive their amplification in *Netochka Nezvanova*, where the character of Pyotr Alexandrovich is a blood brother to the present Yulian Mastakovich. And the materials for the amplification will be found in Hoffmann.

6. WHITE NIGHTS

The last and longest of the 1848 stories, *White Nights,* was published by *National Notes* in December. It begins with an evocation of the streets of Petersburg, not the dark streets of stormy November that Mr. Golyadkin saw, not the dreary back-streets known to Ordynov and Devushkin and other unhappy urban wanderers, but the fine boulevards and canal embankments beneath a dreamy summer evening. The whole opening description reads like a prose poem in honor of a beloved city. Genuine and highly personalized as it is, it also reads like an extended paraphrase of Stanzas 47 and 48 of the first chapter of *Eugene Onegin,* the passage where Pushkin represents himself as having made the acquaintance of his hero and describes their walks together about the capital:

> Of quiet summer nights, how often,
> When with diaphanous pale light
> O'er the Neva the sky would soften
> And the smooth waters, mirror-bright,
> Would fail to show Diana gleaming,
> We yielded to delicious dreaming,
> Recalling in the soft sweet air
> Many a distant love-affair—
> The pleasures relished, triumphs thwarted;
> Like prisoners released in sleep
> To roam the forests green and deep,
> We were in reverie transported,
> And carried to the region where
> All life before us still lay fair.
>
> Onegin leaned above the river
> Upon the granite parapet,
> As did the bard—yet not aquiver
> With ecstasy, but with regret.
> Here one heard naught but echoes, dying,
> From distant streets where cabs were flying,
> And sentinel to sentinel
> Sounding the cry that all was well;
> Alone a lazy boatman lifted
> His oars above the drowsy stream;
> A horn rang out, as in a dream;
> A song across the waters drifted;
> But Tasso's murmured octaves are,
> By night, in dalliance, sweeter far.[8]

The mention of Tasso's "murmured octaves" leads Pushkin in the next stanza to a vision of "nights of golden Italy," Venice, a gondola, and the language of love, and in the stanza after that, to the expression of a desire for the Mediterranean, freedom, and the climes of his "native Africa."

The narrator of *White Nights* has just returned from a walk beyond the city gates, and if he has not exactly been "roaming forests green and deep," he is filled with a sense of the benefice of the green countryside. It is ten o'clock of just such a summer night as Pushkin describes. Passing along the canal embankment, he sees all of a sudden a girl leaning on the granite parapet overlooking the water. He catches the sound of a sob, stops to offer his assistance, but the girl, anticipating his impulse, hurries away in embarrassment. A little further on, however, she is accosted by a drunken man, and the narrator loses no time in effecting her rescue. As he escorts her home their talk becomes quickly confiding. He is a youth with idealistic dreams, she is a sensitive girl with a sorrow she will not disclose. At parting, she promises, half in jest, half in earnest, to meet him the following evening at the same place and at the same hour, adding that something requires her to be there in any case.

Next evening the two meet again. The hero tells his dreams at length. There is a recollection of *Onegin* again as he imagines a history of parted lovers who meet in Venice,

> ". . . far from their native shores, under alien skies, in the hot south in the divinely eternal city, in the dazzling splendor of the ball to the crash of music, in a *palazzo* (it must be in a *palazzo*), drowned in a sea of lights, on a balcony wreathed in myrtle and in roses, . . ."

This is only one of the dreams with which he compensates for reality. He also dreams, as he says,

> ". . . of the lot of the poet, first unrecognized, then crowned with laurels; of friendship with Hoffmann, St. Bartholomew's Night, of Diana Vernon, of playing the hero at the taking of Kazan by Ivan Vasilevich, of Clara Mowbray, of Effie Deans, of the council of the prelates and Huss before them, of the rising of the dead in *Robert the Devil* (do you remember the music, it smells of the churchyard!), of Minna and Brenda, of the battle of Berezina, of the reading of a poem at Countess V.D.'s, of Danton, of Cleopatra *ei suoi amanti*, of a little house in Kolomna. . . ."

(This is a very extensive and very interesting category in which he places Hoffmann.)

If the hero's life consists almost entirely of dreams, the life of the girl,—whose name is Nastenka,—is filled with a single concern, to see again the young man she loves. He had had lodgings at her grandmother's house where she too lives; he had been tender and honorable, but lack of money had forced him to go away to Moscow in the hope of bettering his lot; he had promised to return in a year and to meet her at this very spot by the canal embankment. The year is up. Moreover, Nastenka has learned that the young man has been in the city for three days, but he has not appeared at the meeting place. The hero suggests sending a letter. He even improvises a possible text for her,—it is very like the letter of Tatyana Larina to Eugene Onegin,—but suddenly, as they are about to part, Nastenka hands him a letter she had already written some time before and hurries away, leaving the hero to seek out the gentleman from Moscow and deliver it. The source for this amusing touch of "feminine psychology" is immediately revealed as the hero bgins to sing: "R,o—Ro; s,i—si; n,a—na" and as Nastenka chimes in with him on the word "Rosina!" The specific recollection is from the second act of Rossini's *Barber of Seville* where the quick-witted Rosina has coaxed out of Figaro most of the information she desires about her serenader "Lindoro," even to the name of the lady he loves, who is herself (as she well knows). Figaro then proposes the sending of a brief note to "Lindoro." Rosina replies first: "Non vorrei . . .," then "Non saprei . . .," then "Mi vergogno . . .," but finally 'Un biglietto? eccola qua," passing over the already composed epistle to the astonished Figaro, who will deliver it to "Lindoro," alias Count Almaviva. Nothing further, however, connects the sprightly Rosina and the wholly sentimental Nastenka, but in the matter of source-relationships it is worth noting that there has been considerable mention of *The Barber of Seville* in Nastenka's narrative, since one of her most cherished memories is of an evening when her beloved took her and her grandmother to that opera. When writing with a certain source in mind, Dostoevski sometimes refers obliquely to it, as in this instance and as with Hoffmann in the opening chapter of *The Insulted and Injured*. Hence, when the hero lists high on his list of dreams "friendship with Hoffmann," it may not be amiss to seek some Hoffmannian point of departure for the story at hand.—But to return to *White Nights*:

At their third rendez-vous the narrator announces that he has delivered the letter, but he confesses that he himself is now in love with Nastenka. Together they wait for the lover from Moscow, but he does not come.

The fourth and last colloquy shows Nastenka ready to abandon her former lover and marry the narrator. They discuss plans for their marriage. The narrator takes her into his arms. Just then a young man passes, stops, cries "Nastenka! Nastenka! It's you!" Nastenka rushes to embrace him, then runs back to give the narrator one hasty farewell kiss, then goes down the street with her lover. Next morning, a letter from her begs the narrator to be her friend always. At which he exclaims:

> "My God, a whole moment of happiness! Is that too little for the whole of a man's life?"

Once before in Russian fiction an idealistic youth had met and fallen in love with a lovely lady on the boulevards of Petersburg of a summer evening, only to discover that she was a shameless prostitute. He solaced his hurt and disillusion first with opium and dreams, then with suicide. The youth was the painter Piskarev in Gogol's *The Nevski Prospekt,* a story which is unquestionably to be ranked among the sources of the present work, along with contributory mood elements from Pushkin's *Eugene Onegin* and a touch from Rossini's *Barber of Seville.* Beyond this second of Gogol's "Petersburg Tales" lies Hoffmann's light but charming tale *Aus dem Leben dreier Freunde,* which patently served Gogol as a model.[9]

At the beginning of *Aus dem Leben dreier Freunde* three young friends, Alexander, Marzell, and Severin, seated at a table in the Tiergarten in Berlin, catch sight of a beautiful girl dining with her family at a near-by table and all three are simultaneously captivated with her charms. Two years later the three friends are once again gathered at the same spot and proceed to relate what has happened to each of them in the interval. Marzell had left the party that day and gone in search of the unknown young lady. At first his search proved vain, but eventually he had found her, fallen in love with her, then finally left her in despair, believing her to be a heartless creature solely interested in fine clothes and frivolous amusements. Severin, too, had sought her out and loved her, but he had lost her affection through his own Quixotic conduct. Alexander, as we learn at the end of the story, had likewise pursued the girl and loved her,—and married her. As his charming wife she now comes up to the table where the reunited friends are finishing the accounts of their experiences.

To Hoffmann's three-fold structure Gogol had opposed a two-fold one. As a contrast to Piskarev's pursuit of beauty and discovery of disillusion and death, he had set the adventures of Lt. Pirogov, who had left his friend Piskarev on the boulevard to follow another beauty in his own unsubtle way. The chase had brought him to the home of a porcine German named Schiller, who was carousing with a beery companion named Hoffmann, and these two worthies had soundly thrashed Lt. Pirogov for his improper attentions to the lady, who happened to be Frau Schiller.

With this bitter parody of the romantic quest for beauty Gogol had underlined the futility of Piskarev's suicide. Yet Piskarev had originally been conceived as a serious character in terms of Hoffmann's Severin. Both are marked with a hypernormal sensitivity, both ardently pursue the Ideal. Indeed, with Severin, the love of Pauline Asling is itself a main thread of illusion on which are strung the beads of his separate smaller illusions. Dreams and fancies obsess him. He imagines he understands the language of the birds. With the smell of roses he associates the sense of life, with the odor of carnations he associates death. His love is shattered by means of these very notions at a tryst which he had begged Pauline to grant him, for the girl, disliking his ways, sent her father in her stead to the meeting place, and, entering into the farce, the old man had grotesquely wreathed himself with carnations. From an upstairs window the girl herself could be glimpsed merrily laughing at the hoax. But the experience had shocked Severin into an awareness of his own absurdity. Far from slashing his throat with a razor as Piskarev does, he compelled himself to enter the Army for a two-year period and, by such exposure to reality, to rid himself of his delusions. At the end of the story his restitution to health and normalcy forms part of the general happiness.

With the regularity of Russian Hoffmannists Gogol had reversed this happy outcome. He had gone further and implied that the quest for beauty itself was an illusion ending in despair and suicide or in an ignominious drubbing. *White Nights* retains the unhappy outcome of Russian tradition but tempers it in extraordinary fashion. In so doing, Dostoevski should not be seen as "correcting" Gogol or as returning closer to the Hoffmann prototype. His story is a free variation on the theme of the love-quest resulting from chance encounter. Certain details convey the impression that *Aus dem Leben dreier Freunde* is to be related directly to *White Nights,* not merely indirectly, at one remove, through *The Nevski Prospekt.* When first we glimpse Hoffmann's Pauline Asling, for instance, she rises from her table in the Tiergarten and goes to the railing above the Spree to gaze down sadly into the waters, precisely the attitude in which the narrator of *White Nights* first glimpses Nastenka. Or again, in Dostoevski's opening prose poem about the aspect of the Petersburg streets, there is a section about a lovely girl leaning out of a window to buy flowers, a description that sounds much like the passage in which Alexander tells how he caught sight of Pauline leaning out of a window. These telltale residues are comparable to the flower-arbor or ivy-arbor in *A Christmas Tree and a Wedding,* details retained, almost unconsciously by the author, from the source of original inspiration.

For all of this, however, no more may be claimed for *White Nights* than that it is a new work *in the tradition of Aus dem Leben dreier Freunde* and *The Nevski Prospekt.* In common with Hoffmann's Severin, Dostoevski's narrator-hero is a hypersensitive youth who meets a strange girl, beautiful and sad, weeping for disappointment by a river parapet; he falls in love with her and briefly imagines that she loves him in return; he ends by losing her to another lover. That is all. The rest is Dostoevski's free invention.

Here it is worth while to anticipate a little known work of Dostoevski dating from 1861 and entitled *Petersburg Visions in Verse and Prose.*[10] It is a rambling essay embodying scenes and anecdotes about life in the capital city, one of which is cast as an autobiographical reminiscence of the 1840's and relates directly to *White Nights:*

> ". . . Formerly, in my youthful fantasy, I was fond of imagining myself now as Pericles, now as Marius, now as a Christian of the time of Nero, now as a knight at a tournament, now as Edward Glandenning in Walter Scott's novel *The Monastery,* etc. etc. And what all didn't I dream of in my youth, what all didn't I experience with my whole heart, with my whole soul, in dreams golden and glowing precisely as though from opium. In my

life there have been no moments more full, more holy, or more pure. I carried those dreams to the point where I passed up my whole youth, and when fate suddenly made me a government service man, (In 1845 Dostoevski entered the Engineering Department of the Ministry of the War as a designer), I . . . I . . . served in model fashion. But just as soon as I finished my hours of duty, I would rush home to my attic room (Dostoevski actually lived in a too-expensive apartment with his brother Andrei and the German doctor Riesenkampf), put on my ragged dressing gown, open up my Schiller and dream. I would intoxicate myself and suffer torments that are sweeter than all the delights in the world. I would love . . . I would love . . . and I would want to run off to Switzerland, to Italy, and I would imagine before me Elizabeth, Luise, Amalie. (Heroines of Schiller's *Don Carlos, Kabale und Liebe,* and *Die Räuber* respectively.)

But the real Amalie I passed up too. She lived with me, beside me, behind the screens. We were all living in corners and existing on barley coffee. Behind the screens lived a certain married man nicknamed 'Suckling.' All his life he had been looking for a position, and all his life he had been starving with a consumptive wife, with thin shoes, and with five hungry children. Amalie was the eldest. Of course they didn't call her Amalie, but Nadya. Well, she will always be Amalie for me. And how many novels we read together. I gave her books by Walter Scott and by Schiller; I subscribed to Smirdin's library but didn't buy myself shoes, just blackened the holes with ink. She and I read together the story of Clara Mowbray (Scott: *St. Roman's Well*) and . . . became so emotional that I still cannot recall those evenings without a nervous shudder. For my reading and retelling of novels to her, she used to darn my old socks and starch my only two shirt-fronts. Toward the last, meeting me on our dirty staircase, on which there were more eggshells than anything else, she would suddenly begin to blush rather peculiarly, and suddenly she would flare right up. How pretty she was, how good, gentle, with hidden dreams and repressed impulses, just like me. I noticed nothing; or, perhaps, I did notice, but . . . I found it pleasant to read *Kabale und Liebe* or the tales of Hoffmann. How pure we were then, how innocent! But Amalie suddenly got married to one of the poorest creatures in this world, a man of forty-five, with a boil on his nose, who had been living for some time in the corners with us. He had gotten a job and next day offered Amalie his hand and . . . arch-poverty. His sole possession was an overcoat, like Akaki Akakievich, with a cat-fur collar 'which, of course, could always be taken for marten.' I even suspect that, if he had had cat which it was impossible to take for marten, he would perhaps not have been able to decide to get married, but would have gone on waiting. I remember how Amalie and I parted:—I kissed her pretty hand, the first time in my life; she kissed me on the forehead and gave me a strange smile, so strange, so strange that all my life that smile has been clawing at my heart. And again I came to see a bit, as it were . . . nothing. Why did all that so painfully impress itself upon my memory! Now I recall all that with pain, although, had I married Amalie, I would most likely have been unhappy! Where then would have been Schiller, freedom, the barley coffee, and the sweet tears and the reveries and my journey to the moon. . . . For I did travel to the moon, gentlemen. (A reference to Dostoevski's Siberian exile?)

But, God be with her, with Amalie . . ."

If this could be accepted as *bona fide* autobiography, one might immediately decide that *White Nights* was written as the literary embodiment of the real "Amalie" experience and that Dostoevski quite naturally selected for it a story-type in the tradition of *Aus dem Leben dreier Freunde* and *The Nevski Prospekt.* Such may actually be the case. But, given the disconcerting mixture of fiction and fact that marks all of the sections of *Petersburg Visions in Verse and Prose,* it is at least equally plausible that the "Amalie" episode is an artistic creation as freely adapted from actual fact as *White Nights,* its cousin-piece of thirteen years before. The subtle suggestion that "Amalie's" dreamy lover was not wholly naive, that his illusion was willful, may be taken as a confessional touch, or, just as easily, construed as a new trait of Dostoevski's post-exile writing, a trait more fully exploited in *Notes from Underground* and subsequent works. Moreover, some of the details do not ring true: "Amalie's" husband-to-be is explicitly likened to Akaki Akakievich by virtue of his sole possession, a poor overcoat; but the phrase "with a boil on his nose" also applied to him, occurs in the striking final speech of Poprishchin in *The Diary of a Madman,* so that it is hard to decide whether the narrator is recalling facts or clothing dim reminiscences in Gogolian terms. No one can say whether this sketch is autobiography, literature, or a half-way stage between the two.

At best, it may be stated only that *White Nights* has a curious second version written in 1861. It is interesting that in both pieces a dreamy narrator-hero lists the subjects of his dreams and in both cases mentions Hoffmann by name.

* * * * * * *

Through the year 1848 six published works kept Dostoevski's name before the public. That was certainly an improvement over the dismal record of 1847. Had his career ended with

White Nights, we should undoubtedly say today that he began
his literary course auspiciously but soon declined in powers,
that, with the exception of *A Faint Heart,* the stories have the
quality of insufficient anecdotes.   In the light of his later works,
however, the six tales are seen as trial attempts at new subjects,
exploring the possibilities of the self-lacerating buffoon (Polzunkov), the human derelict (Emelyan Ilich), the sinister figure
of lust and greed (Yulian Mastakovich), first foreshadowings of
characters like the elder Karamazov, Marmeladov, Svidrigailov,
and Stavrogin.   In one of the six stories an important Hoffmannian element is clearly evident, in three others Hoffmannian
elements may be felt but not discerned distinctly.   But that the
tradition is erroneous which claims that after 1847 Dostoevski
abandoned his interest in Hoffmann, is demonstrated by *Netochka Nezvanova,* the large-scale creation to which he was now
eagerly to return.

NETOCHKA NEZVANOVA

In an undated letter of 1847 Dostoevski told his brother Michael that he would "soon be able to read" a new work of his, a full length novel bearing the odd title of *Netochka Nezvanova* (Nettie Nameless), but within a few lines he added that he was now working on *The Landlady*.[1] Financial pressure forced the latter project to the fore and the novel had to be laid aside. Precisely how much of it was written in 1847 is unknown, but stylistic evidence pretty clearly separates the first three chapters from the remainder, so that it may be assumed that the sequel dates from late in 1848 and from the early months of 1849.

Projected in four parts, its serial publication was begun by *National Notes* in January 1849. A second installment followed in February. In April Dostoevski found himself suddenly under arrest for seditious activities and committed to prison pending investigation of his case. The third installment of the novel appeared in May, while its author languished in the Peter and Paul Fortress, but the public was never to discover the solution of the elaborate mysteries posed by the story up to that point. The final section was never written. After return from exile eleven years later Dostoevski went so far as to revise the May 1849 installment before including the fragment in his "collected works," but gave no indication of the outcome beyond the end of Chapter VII, where the text abruptly breaks off. Least read, probably, of all his works, and least accessible in English translation,[2] it is nevertheless of great importance for the evolution of his art.

Of the seven existing chapters, the first three deal with the tenth and eleventh years of Netochka's life and involve a set of characters who, for the most part, do not reappear in the subsequent sections. The girl's step-father, the musician Yefimov, dominates the action, rather than the girl herself. A second major block of the narrative includes Chapters 4 and 5, during which Netochka is advanced to the age of thirteen. The scene is Petersburg, in the home of "Prince X," the girl's foster-father. The last pages of Chapter 5 extricate the heroine with some abruptness from her second home and transfer her to a third setting in the household of a step-daughter of Prince X, where the events of Chapters 6 and 7 are played out. The interrelation of the three sets of characters and of the three homes is far from clear. The entire narrative purports to be the memoirs of the title character and is told in first person. Though she had reached the age of seventeen at the end of the fragment, there is nothing to indicate her age at the time when she is setting down these recollections, nor are we informed as to her station in life at this time or even as to her attitude toward the events described. If the fourth installment was really to be the concluding one, Dostoevski had indeed set himself an arduous task.

Since the first three chapters constitute a story apart, it is desirable to consider them for the time being without reference to what follows. The heroine is recounting the life of her step-father, partly from her own recollections, partly from what she has heard about him from the musician "B." Her step-father, she declares, was the most important influence on her childhood.

His name, we learn, was Yegor Petrovich Yefimov, by occupation a clarinetist,—in fact, a decidedly inferior clarinetist,—in the private orchestra of a wealthy landowner. At the age of twenty-two he had become the associate of a certain Italian who "certainly was a bad man." The Italian quarrelled with his patron, lost his post as orchestra conductor, and sank into poverty and degradation. One morning peasants found him dead in a ditch. The inquest revealed that he had died of an epileptic fit.

Soon after, Yefimov produced documents in the handwriting of the deceased to prove himself sole heir to all that the Italian owned. The effects were of slight value but included "a rather ordinary looking violin," which quickly became the subject of an altercation. The first violinist of the orchestra tried to buy it from Yefimov, but the latter stubbornly refused to sell the instrument. His patron gently advised the sale, since after all Yefimov was a clarinetist and could have little use for a violin, but his words sent Yefimov into an unaccountable tantrum of insolent behavior. The would-be purchaser was just as unaccountably excited over the matter and presently he accused Yefimov of murdering the Italian. The case was brought to trial, with the result that the accuser was convicted of false witness and put in jail. There madness befell him and not long after he died, maintaining to the last that Yefimov was guilty of the Italian's murder.

Throughout the trial the patron had loyally stood by his inferior clarinetist but for his pains was rewarded with the crassest ingratitude. A distinguished French violinist had agreed to pay a visit to the landowner's estate but at the appointed time did not appear. In his stead came a letter stating coldly that he declined to visit a man who mistreated the artists in his employ,

for example, by making a gifted violinist like Yefimov confine
himself to the clarinet. The patron was flabbergasted. A confrontation of all parties was arranged, but when summoned,
Yefimov again displayed such outragious insolence that he was
thrown in jail. The grieved and conscientious patron came to
his cell by night to question him in private. Asked why he had
behaved as he did, the prisoner replied:

"God knows why I have, sir! I suppose that the devil confounded me! I don't know myself who drove me to it. . . . The
devil himself has got hold of me!"

At his patron's second inquiry he repeated:

"I tell you that the devil has got hold of me. I shall set
fire to the house if I stay with you. . . . I cannot answer for
myself now; . . . it has been like this with me ever since the
devil made a friend of me . . ."
"Who?" asked the patron.
"Why, who died like a forsaken dog, the Italian."
"It was he who taught you to play, Yegorushka."
"Yes! Many things he taught me to my ruin. It would have
been better for me not to have seen him."

All this occurs within the first seven pages of the story and
events continue at this pace.

Before leaving the cell the patron persuaded Yefimov to play
for him. Yefimov took the violin and played such heart-stirring
music,—a set of variations on Russian folk-songs,—that his
auditor was moved to tears. Then the patron left, giving Yefimov
his blessing, three hundred rubles, and the advice that a brilliant
career lay ahead, provided he could endure the hardships necessary to produce a great artist.

Thereafter Yefimov's life was a series of disasters. Successive
employers and fellow-musicians alike loathed him for his Satanic
insolence and the mistaken conviction that he was an unrecog-
nized genius. Meanwhile, his friend, the musician "B.", Netochka's principal informant concerning these events, was steadily
and loyally working to become a great artist himself.

Suddenly Yefimov announced his marriage to a certain widow,
adding that he was primarily concerned with the thousand rubles
left the lady by her first husband. For a time Yefimov enjoyed
the money, and when it was all spent, he coolly allowed his wife
to support him. Moreover he told her that she was the sole cause
of the non-fulfillment of his genius. So long as she lived, he
would never be able to play, but the day she died he would take
up the violin again.

This is the man for whom Netochka felt an unchildlike love.

One day Yefimov heard that a recital would be given by the
world-famous violinist "S——z." Extraordinarily agitated by the
news, he determined that he must attend and persuaded Netochka

to steal her mother's few savings in order to buy the ticket. Actually he went by favor of a ticket sent unexpectedly to him by a certain "Prince X," who had heard of him through the musician "B.". The concert proved a shattering experience. The playing of "S——z" revealed to Yefimov all his own worthlessness and empty pretension. With all illusions of genius wiped out, he came home, murdered his wife, and then in the presence of the corpse played wildly on the long unused violin. At a cry from Netochka he moved as if to kill her too, but relented and took her instead with him on his flight into the darkness.

With their few possessions in their hands, the man and the child made their way through the streets. They came to a canal. There was an opening in the ice. Glancing at it, Yefimov persuaded Netochka to return to her dead mother in their old rooms. The child turned back, Yefimov began to run in the opposite direction. She started in pursuit, collided with two gentlemen, fell unconscious.

Later she learned that her step-father was apprehended as a madman, taken to a hospital, and there, two days later, died.

As for Netochka herself, she awoke upon recovery from her fall to find herself in the bed of a fine room in the house of Prince X. A completely new phase of her life was about to begin. (Chapter 4.)

Over the whole of this first-person narrative of Netochka's childhood hangs the same atmosphere of terror, mystery, and dread that marked that passage in *The Landlady* where Katerina told Ordynov the story of *her* childhood. The similarity of tone is not surprising, since both works were simultaneously in composition in the summer of 1847, but it does not go beyond a similarity of tone. The evil and menacing figure of Coppelius from *Der Sandmann* has little if any connection with the present situation.

As for the Italian whose violin passed into Yefimov's possession, though nothing further is learned about him, we may conclude that he was one of those figures, numerous in fiction, who are either devils temporarily incarnate on missions of soul-destruction, or, more commonly, who are quite human but have bartered their salvation for some earthly commodity, such as fame or wealth, and can escape the penalty of their misdeed only by engaging another human soul in a similar "contract" with Hell. Though Yefimov refers to him three times as a "devil," the term should not be taken too literally. It is more likely that he belongs to the second sub-category. Presumably Yefimov bound his soul to him for the privilege of mastery of music without the necessary work and training, and received as a pledge of the bargain that "rather ordinary looking violin." Perhaps the murder of the Italian, assuming Yefimov did murder him, somehow impaired the magic of the instrument.[3] At any rate, sinister Italians are too common in Hoffmann's works to permit the identification of a prototype on the basis of the very little information we are given concerning Yefimov's friend.[4]

It is rather Yefimov himself who is of primary concern here. He is Dostoevski's only artist-hero, and from the insuccess with which Dostoevski portrayed his musicianship one may readily see that the author was not at home with music. For Hoffmann, who was a pianist, composer, orchestra director, music critic, and by temperament a musician through and through, it was a natural thing to present musical characters in his stories, but only a naive ineptitude is conveyed by the mention of those heart-stirring variations on Russian folk-themes which Yefimov plays to his amazed patron. Not only was Dostoevski himself not musical, but genuine Russian music of real worth had scarcely begun to be created in 1849.[5] The musical milieu in which Hoffmann lived was as alien to Russia as mediaeval castles and courts of chivalry.

In making Yefimov a musician, Dostoevski was undoubtedly seeking only to vary the Romantic fare, which had almost automatically cast artist-heroes as painters. In this tradition stood Gogol's Chertkov (*The Portrait*) and Piskarev (*The Nevski Prospekt*), as well as Polevoi's Arkadi (*The Painter*) and a spate of imported works from western Europe. In making Yefimov specifically a violinist, Dostoevski may simply have selected the instrument most commonly assigned to musical heroes of fiction, especially by non-musical authors. Hoffmann's works offer two violinist tales: *Rat Krespel*,[6] the title character of which is primarily a maker of violins, though he also plays, and in which there is mention of a violin with a tone like that of the human voice; and the wholly charming little story, *Der Baron von B.*,[7] about the celebrated Berlin eccentric, a pupil of the great Tartini, who paid his students to receive his priceless instruction, but who could not play himself. After showing the narrator of the story how to produce truly wonderful tones by means of quite unorthodox bowing, the Baron takes the violin himself and demonstrates exactly how it should be played, producing as he does so the most unspeakably shrill and discordant sounds. With a look of sheer ecstasy he lays aside the instrument and declares that *that* was true Tartini tone. Possibly some such instruction was imparted to Yefimov by the Italian.

But neither these two Hoffmannian violinists nor any other Hoffmannian musicians will furnish Yefimov with anything more than insignificant details of characterization, for the fact of the matter is that all Yefimov's literary ancestors are painters! These are three in number: Berthold of *Die Jesuiterkirche in G.*, who abused his wife because he believed she destroyed his genius; Franzesko the painter, ancestor of the monk Medardus in *Die Elixiere des Teufels*, who profaned art and married a witch; and Chertkov in Gogol's *The Portrait*, whose worthlessness was revealed to him when he went to see an exposition of the works of a painter of true genius. The interweaving of their three stories to make Yefimov's story shows Dostoevski in the midst of his compounding technique. Such a process of *contaminatio* is to be expected of a work that stands between *The Double* and *The Landlady*.

Most important for Yefimov of the three painter-prototypes is Berthold, the central figure of *Die Jesuiterkirche in G.* It is an interesting circumstance that this story is usually considered the companion piece to *Der Artushof*, which Dostoevski was simultaneously using as the pattern for *The Landlady*. Both Hoffmann works are in a sense problem-stories which concern themselves with the basic conflict of Art versus conventional bourgeois Life. Traugott, in *Der Artushof*, successfully avoids the fate of becoming a business man in the firm of Elias Roos and of becoming the husband of the Philistine Christine Roos; if he meets disappointment first by learning that his great painting-master Berklinger is insane and then by learning that his "Ideal," Felizitas, has herself become the humdrum wife of the Marienwerder jurist, he shakes off his disappointment and seeks new inspiration in Italy and his new love Dorina. The ambiguous close may indicate a combination of Art with married happiness or simply another source of inspiration which will in time fail and be replaced by still another. At any rate, Traugott happily proceeds, despite all mischances, to the pursuit of his artistic mission. Berthold, on the other hand, marries his ideal, thereby reducing it to the commonplace and is wretched because all inspiration has vanished amid the banality of everyday family life.[8] The question rises: why should Dostoevski have

been so concerned with these problem-tales? One does not
ordinarily think of him as troubled by such matters as the Philistine way of life in conflict with the artist's way. Nor was a
marital question involved at any point in the years 1847-49. It
would be surprising but not unthinkable that he saw himself in
those years as facing an analogous difficulty as a literary artist
if not a painter.

Coincidence or meaningful deliberateness of choice, he was
working closely at the same time with *Der Artushof* and *Die
Jesuiterkirche in G.* The latter story once again introduces the
"travelling enthusiast,"—Hoffmann himself,—as narrator. During a stay in "G." (Glogau), he has seen the mural paintings of
the local Jesuit church which are being renovated by the artist
Berthold.[9] Puzzled by the personality of the artist, he inquires
about him from a professor of his acquaintance, who, in turn,
puts into his hands a biography of Berthold written by the only
person in the town who has the painter's confidence. Berthold,
it appears, had gone as a youth, with considerable financial hard-
ship, to study painting in Italy. He preferred landscape painting, but allowed himself to be persuaded by several of his new
acquaintances that it was a genre inferior to historical painting.
He sought to conform to the arbitrary hierarchy of values, until
unexpectedly he found confirmation of his true preferences in
the master Philipp Hackert (a historical personage). His relief is short-lived. Soon he comes to realize that he is only copy-
ing what his master can do better. He is further troubled by a
remark made by an observer of his work: "Young man, you
might have amounted to a great deal." The speaker is a Greek
from the island of Malta, whom his acquaintances ridicule as a
madman, but Berthold is none the less worried by what was said
and as a result gives up his apprenticeship to Hackert.

One day, sitting in a splendid ducal garden by the sea, Berthold catches sight of a beautiful woman amid the shadows and
the sunlight of the place. Nothing will shake him from his conviction that he has beheld a vision of St. Catherine, his "Ideal."
The woman's face reappears in canvas after canvas of his work,
but when people identify her as Angiola, a kinswoman of the
Duke, Berthold refuses to believe them.

Napoleonic troops arrive at Naples and lay the city under
siege. During an attack, it falls to Berthold's lot to rescue this
very Angiola from imminent murder at the hands of maraud-

ers. Together they flee from Naples, from Italy itself, and reach Germany, where they hope to live a contented married life.

No sooner married and comfortably settled than Berthold realizes that all capacity to paint has deserted him. Though mutual love unites them, Berthold becomes dissatisfied, embittered, and desperate at the knowledge that the Ideal brought too near ceases to be the Ideal. When finally Angiola presents him with a son his rage knows no bounds. "You have robbed me of my life, infamous woman!" he shouts at her, and when she falls upon her knees and begs for mercy he kicks her aside and from that moment abandons her.

Years have passed. Berthold is now at work on the paintings of the church in "G." The fate of the wife and child are left in doubt, but the impression is left that he murdered both of them. Before leaving "G.", the "travelling enthusiast" plucks up courage to ask Berthold point-blank whether this was the case. With horror Berthold denies that there is any blood on his hands.

Some six months later, the "travelling enthusiast" receives a letter from the professor, which relates how a reconciliation had been effected between Berthold and his deserted family and how a gentle peace had come over the man after seeing them. Then one day he disappeared from "G.", and a few days after the disappearance, his hat and cane were found on the bank of the river "O." (Oder). He had apparently drowned himself.

In the opening chapters of *Netochka Nezvanova* there is no suggestion that Yefimov ever looked upon Netochka's mother as his ideal, but he is presented as a gloomy tempered artist who, like Berthold, outrageously mistreats wife and child in the name of Art. That the Hoffmann hero should only have been falsely reported to have murdered while Yefimov actually does murder his wife and comes close to murdering his child as well, may be taken as another example of the pessimism of Russian Hoffmannists. Similarly, the substitution of Yefimov's madness before death instead of Berthold's final peace of mind. The presence of the canal in the scene of Yefimov's last flight would seem to be another of those residual features from the source work such as have been pointed out before. It is curious, however, that Hoffmann's hero should ultimately drown himself while Dostoevski's Yefimov, after noticing and avoiding that ominous hole in the ice of the canal, should go to a hospital and die there two days later as a lunatic. Is it possible that Yefimov did *not* die? There are good reasons, which will be explained presently, to believe that he did not and that he was destined to make a dramatic return in the last portion of the novel.

The essential difference between Berthold and Yefimov lies in their artistic capacities. Berthold *was* a genius; Yefimov only fancied himself one. For his portrayal of the false artist with pretentions to genius Dostoevski had a ready model in Gogol's Chertkov, hero of *The Portrait*. This young man acquires one day at an auction a portrait of a sinister old man with piercing eyes. Once hung in his room, the portrait comes to life, attains a devilish power over Chertkov's will, and leads him to destruction. Gold coins spill from the frame as if by accident just at the moment when the landlord demands the unpaid rent. A lady client, dissatisfied with Chertkov's too faithful preliminary sketches of her daughter's picture, comes one day and with delight picks up a miserable painting of Psyche, exclaiming that the painter has made a magnificent portrait after all. Once Chertkov has countenanced this glaring untruth, his fame and fortune grow at fantastic speed. Knowing that his art is a delusion and that the delusion is the work of the devilish old man with the piercing eyes, he still enjoys the luxury and flattery that pour in upon him. He multiplies his works, and each one of them is an untruth.

One day he receives an invitation from the Academy of Arts to judge the works of another painter whom he knows to have suffered poverty and hunger for many years in the rigorous self-discipline of true Art. He goes to the exposition and is overwhelmed by the glory of genuine genius, by the supreme Truth of real Art. Nothing is left to him except the devastating sense of his own worthlessness. In vain he returns to his studio and tries to paint in earnest. Impossible! He can paint only trash. The rage at his own impotence passes into a mania of buying up genuine paintings and destroying them one after another. He cannot buy fast enough. The mania becomes delirium, the delirium becomes a fatal fever. He dies a raving madman.

Here is patently the origin of that concert given by the true violinist "S——z" and of Yefimov's despair after hearing him play. Here is also the basically moral conflict of the Devil's delusion versus Truth. In *The Portrait* the conflict is presented with a primitive Puritanical earnestness typical of Gogol but curiously inappropriate to an art-tale. Dostoevski is more subtle and more complex, but he is, like his fellow-countryman, more interested in character than in art. The positions of emphasis are the reverse in *Die Jesuiterkirche in G.*

Now, *The Portrait* was the first of Gogol's Hoffmannizing stories and the one in which he remained closest to his source. In this instance his model was that section of *Die Elixiere des Teufels* which presents the life of Franzesko the painter, whose sin passes from generation to generation until in the fifth generation it is finally expiated by the monk Medardus after many crimes of his own and after his final victory over the last great temptation.

This ancestral sinner Franzesko had been in his youth a disciple of Leonardo da Vinci, from whose lofty art and modest life the young man took his guidance as long as the master lived. But when the master died, Franzesko fell among evil companions and ways of dissipation. One of his godless friends tempts him until he commits the unholy deed of painting a Venus-face, lustful and unholy, into his picture of St. Rosalia. At first, his own deeper nature prevents him from finishing the features even when he tries, but then he discovers in his working-place a beautiful young woman, the very image of his Venus-vision. Encouraged by his madcap cronies he succeeds in perpetrating his blasphemous painting, meanwhile living openly with the wanton woman until, at the moment she is delivered of a child, she shrivels up before his very eyes, shrivels into a blue-spotted monster and dies with a shriek, revealing herself to have been a devil temporarily invested with human form. Thereupon Franzesko seized the new-born infant and fled with it into the wilderness, where he subsequently abandoned it. It was during his flight that he beheld a vision in the clouds and heard a voice cursing him to wander restlessly beyond the limits of a mortal life-span until his progeny, begun with this abandoned child, should be purged of guilt.

The story-outline of the Franzesko-inset from *Die Elixiere des Teufels* offers no element relative to Yefimov that is not to be found in Gogol's derivative work, *The Portrait*, but there are other ways in which it relates to Dostoevski's tale. First, it has, like the whole of *Die Elixiere des Teufels*, that breathless narrative speed, event following event so fast that, sometimes, to skip a sentence is to lose completely the thread of the story. There is nothing of this in *The Portrait*. More important is the matter of the relationship of this inset to the novel as a whole, for it was apparently Dostoevski's intention that Yefimov should be, like Franzesko, a sinning ancestor.

After the horrendous death of the female devil with whom he had cohabited, Franzesko took the child of their union and fled with it to the wilderness, much as Yefimov takes Netochka and flees into the night after the death of his wife. The child that Franzesko abandoned is discovered in a cave by a certain Count Filippo, who adopted him as his own son. The boy grows up,— his name is also Franzesko,—to repay the Count's kindness by seducing the Count's young wife, the Countess "S.", and begetting an illegitimate brother and sister pair, Pietro and Angiola. These in turn will continue the sin-marked course of their begetter, Angiola by incestuous relations with Franzesko's legitimate son, Pietro by adulterous relations with that same legitimate son's wife. Angiola's offspring, again named Franzesko, will beget the monk Medardus within wedlock and Medardus's Double, Count Viktorin, by still another adultery. One has not to look far for the purely literary origins of the incest theme as it appears in *Netochka Nezvanova*, however differently Dostoevski treated the theme once introduced. There is no indication that Dostoevski ever intended anything so complex as this five-generation scheme of *Die Elixiere des Teufels*. Evidence suggests pretty clearly rather a two-generation plan. In any event, there seems little doubt but that he aimed at a novel of complex family relationships, to which the Yefimov story was to stand as a kind of prologue analogous to the life and sin of Franzesko the painter in its relation to the career of Medardus. The point will not be clear until we shall have surveyed the remaining chapters of *Netochka Nezvanova*.

But before proceeding, it is necessary to point out a further and very specific connection between Dostoevski's novel-fragment and *Die Elixiere des Teufels*.

In Chapter 2 a character is introduced for comic relief. His incongruous buffoonery occupies the center of attention for a very few pages, after which he disappears without further notice. The corresponding passage in Hoffmann's novel is no less incongruous and quite as tangential to the main story. It is given as a story-inset and presented as a public reading by the court physician to a circle of literary amateurs at the *Residenz*, where Medardus is a guest at court. The physician claims it is an extract from his travel-journals. Taking his cue from scenes of Shakespearean farce but more particularly from the novels of Laurence Sterne, Hoffmann proceeds to relate the preposterous shenannegans of an Irishman named Ewson and an Englishman named Green. The former is a true 18th century "original."

Ewson is a most unlikely Irishman who wishes to be considered an Englishman. For twenty-two years he has lived at the inn of a German village, an odd figure with his coffee-brown coat, fox-red wig, and grey hat set at a rakish angle. He had come to this inn by chance, attracted by the sound of dance music, and in the midst of a vehement demonstration of how to dance a hornpipe he had ignominiously fallen and sprained his ankle. He remained at the inn for his convalescence, then stayed on permanently. He has innumerable eccentricities. Daily he quarrels with his German hosts for not serving roast beef and porter, packs his bags, rides away "for good," but invariably returns by dinner time, when he eats for three men. From time to time he renews his wardrobe, always duplicating the clothes in which he first arrived. His will is made out in favor of the inn-keeper's eldest daughter. Three years previously he began practicing a flute concerto, but one solo passage has consistently baffled him and day after day he may be heard in his vain attempts to master it. When the court physician left the inn, the last thing he heard was this everlasting passage from the flute concerto.

Ewson's counterpart in *Netochka Nezvanova* is Karl Fyodorovich Meyer, a pathetic little German domesticated in Russia. Too tight trousers accentuate his bow legs and his generally withered physique. He reads German poems aloud and weeps to hear himself read. Above all, he is possessed by the idea that he is a ballet dancer. He is actually a member of a Petersburg theatrical company, but his dancing is so bad that he cannot be used even in the chorus and must be relegated to the non-speaking rôles or at most to mob scenes where he is one of many who shout: "We will die for the King!" On days when Netochka's mother is not at home he comes to dance and read poems for Yefimov and the girl. Netochka finds him screamingly funny but does her best to contain her merriment. Yefimov, on the other hand, always teases him and makes a fool of him. When Meyer realizes this he always goes away in violent anger, but within two days time he is back again with a new poem to read or a new dance step to perform.

As a matter of fact, Meyer is better integrated into the novel than Ewson was into his. Dostoevski has used the comic figure to illustrate Yefimov's cruelty and at the same time to confront the self-appointed genius with a grotesque parody of himself. In other words he was making of Meyer a comic Double to Yefimov. Now, the monk Medardus had, in addition to his "serious" Double Count Viktorin, a "comic" Double in the person of the little barber known alternately as Pietro Belcampo and as Peter Schönfeld. It is not impossible that Dostoevski planned a synthesis of the "original" Meyer with Belcampo-Schönfeld.

In any case, the imitation of so insignificant a detail of *Die Elixiere des Teufels* as the Ewson episode shows how intimately Dostoevski knew Hoffmann's novel. He apparently looked upon the book as a veritable mine of useable materials and delighted in exploiting their variety and abundance.

In view of this fact, still another detail of Yefimov's career may be looked upon as deriving from the same work of Hoffmann's. When Medardus stood in peril of his life after Aurelie had identified him as the murderer of her brother and stepmother, he steadfastly maintained the falsehood that he had nothing to do with the crimes, that he was a Polish gentleman on his travels. His lies were confounded, he was convicted of his crimes and sentenced to death. Then suddenly his Double was discovered in a cell of the madhouse and evidence was adduced to show that he, not Medardus, had committed the murders. Medardus allowed the guilt to be shifted from himself, though at the last minute, as Viktorin was being led to execution, he set him free by force. Likewise, Yefimov allows the guilt of the Italian's murder to pass from himself to the orchestra violinist who has accused him. The man is not executed but dies in prison, a madman, insisting to the last that Yefimov is the guilty man.[10]

*   *   *   *   *   *   *

From the very first mention Dostoevski made of his projected novel in the undated letter of 1847 to Michael, the title was consistently given as *Netochka Nezvanova,* yet the whole of the first three chapters are devoted to the story of Yefimov. The title character does not enter Chapter 1 at all, except to announce that she is the author of these memoirs, and in the two succeeding chapters she has a wholly subordinate rôle. With the opening of Chapter 4, however, she becomes the focus of attention. The narrative pace slackens, the style is different, and we may feel confident that the text that follows dates no more from 1847, but from 1849.

Chapter 4

After a long spell of unconsciousness, Netochka awakes to find herself in the home of the wealthy and kindly Prince X. The Prince is described as an older man, a friend of the musician "B.", an amateur of music, living a somewhat solitary life in one wing of his Petersburg mansion, though on amicable enough terms with his severe wife, the Princess. The latter does not like Netochka but treats her with studied kindness. She has two children of her own, a girl named Katya, who is just Netochka's age, and a little boy named Alexander, who is living in Moscow with two elderly aunts of the Prince. Her particular worry is a third maiden aunt of the Prince, who lives upstairs in this very house and who wields a formidable influence on the lives of all members of the household.

The chapter ends with a melodramatic scene in which Netochka steals into the drawing room unobserved to listen to a recital by the famous violinist S (—— z), the same who had been Yefimov's undoing. At first she has the uncanny feeling that S. *is* Yefimov, but then she faints with a cry that S. is her father's murderer.

Chapter 5

This entire lengthy chapter is concerned with Netochka's infatuation with her foster-sister Katya. The episode is portrayed with uncanny psychological insight and represents the slow conquest of the proud Katya's love by the passive and yearning Netochka. The passion once declared is such as to upset the French governess, who reports the matter to the severe Princess. The girls are separated, first arbitrarily, to their despair, then by necessity. News comes from Moscow that little Alexander is seriously ill, and his mother sets out at once to go to him, taking Katya with her. Netochka is transferred to the household of the Princess's eldest daughter by a former marriage, Alexandra Mikhailovna, where she will spend the next eight years.

Chapter 6

Netochka is now nearly thirteen. She finds her second foster-mother, Alexandra Mikhailovna, a kind and lovable person. Alex-

andra Mikhailovna has a small child of her own, she loves music
and is clearly hyper-sensitive to it, she lives quietly, removed
from almost all society, except that of the musician "B.", adores
her egotistical husband, and is obviously suffering from some
mysterious sorrow. Pyotr Alexandrovich, her husband, is not
only a cold egotist but quite evidently the villain of the story.
He practices some abstruse kind of mental torture on his wife
under the pretext of great solicitude for her and feels a subtle
and covert lust for Netochka.

A large part of the chapter is taken up with Netochka's
theft of a key to the library and her secret self-education by
means of the books taken from there. Three years pass. In
her seventeenth year it is discovered that she has a beautiful
singing voice. Alexandra Mikhailovna consults "B.", is encouraged to find a teacher for the girl, and presently sends Netochka to take singing lessons from a well known Italian vocal
teacher in the capital.

Chapter 7

On one of her secret trips to the library, Netochka discovers
an old love-letter hidden in a volume of Walter Scott. The signature, amid tear-stains, is "S.O.", a man who declares himself
unworthy of Alexandra Mikhailovna's love because he comes from
a lower social class. Paper and ink show the letter to be many
years old.

On another occasion Netochka carefully studies the portrait
of Pyotr Alexandrovich in the library. The shifty eyes puzzle
her. She recalls that Pyotr Alexandrovich has always worn
dark glasses. The man himself enters and catches her in the act
of examining the portrait. He is much annoyed.

On still another occasion Netochka watches Pyotr Alexandrovich as he makes his way to his wife's room. He stops before a
mirror, carefully readjusts his cheerful smile into a look of sorrowful concern, then proceeds on his way. Netochka, hitherto
unobserved, bursts out laughing at the sight, for which Pyotr
Alexandrovich is naturally furious. Moreover, she noticed that
he had previously been whistling a tune, a tune reminiscent of
something in her childhood.

A major scene develops in the library when Netochka goes
to replace the old love-letter in the book where she had found it.
She is surprised by Pyotr Alexandrovich who seizes the letter
from her. She grabs it back and conceals it in her bosom. The
man then accuses her of meeting a secret lover in his house.
Despite the girl's entreaties, the matter is brought to Alexandra
Mikhailovna. Harsh things are said, among others, a bitter re-
proach from wife to husband to the effect that the latter has
looked improperly upon Netochka. In a heroic effort to protect
Alexandra Mikhailovna, Netochka declares that the letter was
indeed from a secret lover of her own. At this, Pyotr Alexandrovich demands that she leave the house within twenty-four hours.

His wife pleads for Christian mercy, but he cuts her short with a
pointed reference to some unhappy episode in her past, at the
mere hint of which she faints.   Netochka in fury then gives
Pyotr Alexandrovich the mysterious letter and denounces him
for his cruelty to his wife.   The man is taken a-back and leaves
her at once.   As Netochka herself turns to go, she meets Ovrov,
Pyotr Alexandrovich's secretary, who says he has something important to tell her.   She answers that the next day will be time
enough.   When he has gone, she stops to ponder the sly smile
with which the secretary had addressed her.

    At this point the novel breaks off.[11]

Whatever the differences between the Yefimov pre-story and
the continuation of the novel, Dostoevski must necessarily have
had in mind some plan whereby all threads of the narrative
would eventually be brought together, otherwise he would have
scrapped the early portion and begun afresh in 1849.   If Yefimov's position in the total plot is analogous to Franzesko in
Die Elixiere des Teufels, the story of Netochka proper bears no
resemblance to the career of the monk Medardus.   The complex
"family history" of Prince X's household in Petersburg involves
at most two generations and these cannot plausibly be related
to any one of the five generations from Franzesko to Medardus.
They do, however, coincide almost identically with the two generations of characters in Hoffmann's unfinished novel *Kater
Murr*.

The second of three parts of *Kater Murr* was published in
December 1821.   Within less than seven months the author died,
leaving the concluding section unwritten and without a written
note or oral hint as to its outcome.   That he should have spent
those last illness-tormented months in work on minor tales is
the grief of every Hoffmann enthusiast, for by doing so, his
generally acknowledged masterpiece was left a fragment and a
tantalizing mystery.   By and large, Hoffmann was a masterful
teller of tales, but character portrayal was generally subordinated to the interest in the action itself or to the mood of the whole.
In *Kater Murr*, action and mood are superbly presented, and in
addition there is a cast of unforgettably vivid characters that
live that permanent and unfading life found only in the greatest
literature.   The complexities of their interrelationships is not
merely an intriguing puzzle subordinate to the main theme, as
in *Die Elixiere des Teufels*, but part of their compelling destinies.   It is no wonder that Hoffmann scholars all come sooner
or later to the problem of the family-tree of the personages in

Kater Murr. Let us see what Dostoevski has done with his parallels to these characters, beginning with the heroine herself.[12]

Netochka's life has been dominated from the beginning by musicians and by music. She is the step-child of the would-be violinist Yefimov, she witnessed his spiritual annihilation upon hearing the great violinist "S.", she hears "S." play a second time in the drawing room of Prince X's house and causes consternation by her conduct on that occasion, she is a friend of "the musician B.", who is her source of information for her memoirs, she has a deep sympathy for Alexandra Mikhailovna who is profoundly devoted to music, and, above all, she is discovered to possess a beautiful singing voice. If, by virtue of these facts, she is equated to Julia Benzon, the heroine of *Kater Murr*, then her long-dead father would correspond to the long-dead Benzon, and her mother, the former governess (in some branch of the household of Prince X?) would correspond to the non-noble Rätin Benzon.

The musician "B.", who knew Yefimov from times before the story began, who in all likelihood possesses the information necessary to solve most of the mysteries of the story, and who is intimately connected with all the principal characters, occupies a position exactly equivalent to that of Meister Abraham, who likewise knew the former life of Kreisler, who was possessed of all the secrets of Sieghartshof, and who was likewise involved in the lives of all the principal characters.

Yefimov, according to this line of thought, must then correspond to Kreisler, the musician-hero of *Kater Murr*, though Kreisler, to the best of our knowledge, was not the step-father of Julia. The mutual attraction, however, between Kreisler and Julia is a thing which disquiets the girl's mother,—we do not know all the reasons why. It is certain that Rätin Benzon knows facts about Kreisler's birth and early life that are not known to Kreisler himself. When he first appears in the novel he has come unexpectedly and causes some degree of consternation by his arrival. In the last chronological section of the book he again arrives at Sieghartshof after a long absence in Kanzheim Abbey, and this time his coming is clearly the prelude to a major climax in the lives of most of the characters. Moreover, it is generally agreed that Kreisler, in the unwritten part of the novel, was to have gone mad. Music, madness, and probably a long absence followed by a dramatic return, rather than death, are factors that pertain also to Yefimov.

Still selecting parallel figures, Alexandra Mikhailovna will be seen to share several of the qualities of the Princess Hedwiga. Both are hyper-sensitive, even to a degree of clairvoyance, both are musically gifted, both are noble by birth and by the nature of their hearts.

Pyotr Alexandrovich is clearly the villain of Dostoevski's novel and while married to Alexandra Mikhailovna, casts glances of lust at Netochka. Prince Hektor was the villain of *Kater Murr* and while paying court to Princess Hedwiga, sought to seduce Hedwiga's friend Julia.

Hedwiga, in Hoffmann's work, passed for the daughter of the reigning Prince Irenäus and his spouse Princess Maria, but the reader is led to believe that the parties themselves may be the victims of a deception practiced long ago when, perhaps, there was a substitution of children. Alexandra Mikhailovna is represented as the daughter of an unidentified father, long deceased, and of the severe Princess, who has since married Prince X. By this token, Prince X corresponds to Prince Irenäus, and his wife, the severe princess, corresponds to Princess Maria.

Prince X and his wife have two children, Katya and Alexander. The latter is living in Moscow with elderly aunts and does not enter the story, though his illness announced at the end of Chapter 5 has considerable effect on the lives of the other members of the family. Irenäus and Maria also had two children, Hedwiga and the imbecile youth Prince Ignatius, and it was to the latter that the scheming Rätin Benzon was striving to marry off her daughter Julia in order to achieve nobility. If our parallel were to be followed through, Alexander would have to prove abnormal in some wise,—was his illness, say, epilepsy?—and Netochka would have to be eventually married to him, thereby becoming the Princess X.

The difficulty lies, in this instance, with the correspondence between Hedwiga and Katya, since Hedwiga has already been much more plausibly equated with Alexandra Mikhailovna. Yet even here there seems to be a quid pro quo, for Prince Irenäus had also an illegitimate daughter by the Rätin Benzon, the child known as Angela Benzoni, and to her, then, Katya would correspond.

It is necessary to schematize the foregoing information with a set of the two genealogical diagrams superimposed, with the *Netochka Nezvanova* characters enclosed in boxes and connected by solid lines and with the *Kater Murr* characters arranged, unenclosed, immediately above them and connected by dotted lines.

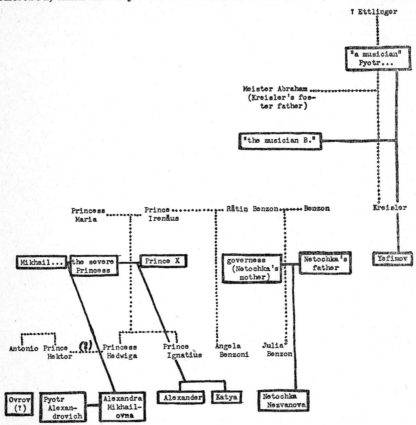

Upon examination, the discrepancy of the two diagonal lines of the diagram proves to be no discrepancy at all. They signify only that, within the framework of his own novel, Dostoevski had "solved" the mystery of Hedwiga's identity and that he had decided to bring Angela Benzoni into the story proper, rather than leave her, as Hoffmann did, to be known only through the reports of other characters. The latter step posed a problem, since very little was actually known about Angela. The matter was adjusted by dividing the traits of Hedwiga between her proper counterpart Alexandra Mikhailovna and the new Angela-figure now named Katya. To the latter were assigned the equality in age and close friendship with the heroine which in *Kater Murr* pertained to Hedwiga and Julia. The mysteriously interlocked destinies of the two girls are likewise transferred to Katya and Netochka, for at the end of Chapter 5 Netochka comments on the eight years separation from Katya about to ensue at that point and says that their two lives are to be inseparably connected and that Katya's romance is also her romance. Thus one Hoffmann figure was made to do for two.

It now becomes clear that Chapters 4-7 of *Netochka Nezvanova* represent Dostoevski's attempt to rewrite Hoffmann's *Kater Murr*. The new setting is not the "pocket-edition" principality of Sieghartsweiler, which was a peculiarly German setting, but contemporary Petersburg. The milieu, however, is that of the upper classes, as in *Kater Murr*, and represents Dostoevski's only venture into high society in the works of the pre-exile period, except for *A Little Hero* which is, in some respects, a kind of companion piece to it. None of these facts disqualifies the statements made about the literary origins and the plan of the Yefimov story. And now the realization dawns that the intention behind the whole work was to create a novel which would be an amalgamation of *Die Elixiere des Teufels* and *Kater Murr*! Since Dostoevski had made short stories with Hoffmann's short stories as models, it was natural that in composing his first full length novel he should look to Hoffmann's novels for guidance. But that he should attempt to superimpose the two extremely complex novels of Hoffmann one on top of the other, as he had superimposed short stories in *The Landlady,*—that was certainly piling Pelion on Ossa!

In the light of this concept, it is hardly to be wondered at that the work should not be finished either in 1849, when insurmountable obstacles made completion impossible, or in 1860 when those obstacles were removed. That it should remain a fragment like *Kater Murr* itself, is a striking piece of irony. Since we are confronted here with not one but two equations, both fairly bristling with unknowns, it would be folly to attempt to predict the outcome of the story. Yet, with *Kater Murr* and other works of Hoffmann as a guide, some informed guesses may be in order. It is also of interest to note what features of Hoffmann's novel Dostoevski chose to eliminate and what specific alterations may be ascertained.

Primarily, all of the gypsy characters have been dispensed
with,—an understandable procedure in 1847-49,—and with the
gypsies went necessarily the whole Italian contingent of the
family, except Angela Benzoni, who is now brought closer to the
main plot, and the wholly indispensable villain, Prince Hektor.
Some vestigial traces of the Neapolitans may be seen in the
three aunts of Prince X, two of whom live "elsewhere," that is,
in Moscow. Otherwise the cast of characters remains unal-
tered. The sole addition is the dim figure of Alexandra Mikhailovna's father, the first husband of the severe Princess, and considering the mystery of Hedwiga's origins and the past event in
Alexandra Mikhailovna's life with which her evil husband
menaces her, this father may have been a fiction of the family,
and Alexandra Mikhailovna's birth may have been illegitimate.
The transposition to Petersburg did no violence to the characters except in so far as Dostoevski insisted on locating Netochka's childhood home in the slums. Her rightful home was
undoubtedly that house with the red curtains that fascinated her
when she was small, but her rise from rags to riches, coupled
with her violent attachments of affection, give her the air of a
rather perverse and irritating Cinderella, a far cry indeed from
Julia Benzon.

Among the more likely possibilities for future developments
is the possibility that Alexandra Mikhailovna will soon die. Her
health is already undermined and she foresees her doom. Almost
certainly her husband will apply music as a deft form of mental
torment and she will succumb to its influence, as Seraphine in
Das Majorat nearly succumbed to the too great agitation occa-
sioned by music, and as Antonie in *Rat Krespel* did actually
perish.

Her death will leave Netochka wholly at the mercy of Pyotr
Alexandrovich, and her rescue will probably be effected by the
musician "B.", whose counterpart, Meister Abraham, was working so strenuously to stave off the disasters that menaced Julia
Benzon as well as others. If "B." is possessed of as much information as Meister Abraham, perhaps he will identify the
"S.O." who wrote the love-letter which Netochka found in the
library. The tearful writer who therein renounced the love that
was beyond his social class may prove to be Netochka's father;
or, since only the name "Alexandra," without patronymic, occurs in the letter, the beloved may have been Alexandra Mik-

hailovna's mother, the severe Princess, for the letter is described as being very old. In this case, Netochka might prove the daughter of the severe Princess by an early lover and hence the half-sister of both Alexandra Mikhailovna and Katya. In this or some other way, it would seem almost inevitable that Netochka's rise in the world should culminate in her becoming the new Princess X.

The identity of Netochka is actually of less concern than that of Alexandra Mikhailovna, for Netochka has already risen far and seems bound for complete success. With Alexandra Mikhailovna we should like to know what and why she has renounced and why she suffers so much with such great patience. It is curious how much mystery hangs about the Hedwiga-figure. The real-life original, Helmine Lanzendorf, was herself an international mystery;[13] Hedwiga's origins and destiny are not the least puzzling of several mysteries in *Kater Murr*;[14] and Alexandra Mikhailovna, the one character of Dostoevski's novel who is sympathetic enough to make her fate of real concern, is shrouded in mystery no less deep. One wonders whether Dostoevski achieved anything beyond the usual pessimism of Russian Hoffmannists by making her the wife of the villain and therefore actually caught in his spider-web, whereas Hedwiga was only about to marry Prince Hektor.

Most tantalizing of all the puzzles is Pyotr Alexandrovich, since he, it is startling to realize, is Dostoevski's first villain. Previous to him there was the shadowy figure of Mr. Bykov, whose sinister intentions relative to the heroine of *Poor Folk* may best be seen in his name (Mr. Bullstud), and the hardly less shadowy figure of Yulian Mastakovich in *A Christmas Tree and a Wedding*. It is noteworthy that both of these gentlemen were not concerned with mere seduction but wished to marry their victims. Pyotr Alexandrovich has already married *his* victim. His successors, Prince Valkovski (*The Insulted and Injured*) and Svidrigailov (*Crime and Punishment*), will use the same tactic. Netochka, we recall, found something oddly familiar about Pyotr Alexandrovich's features as represented without his customary dark glasses in the library portrait, just as his whistled tune revived some dim memory of the childhood which she has so inexplicably forgotten in its entirety. There are two analogous portraits in *Kater Murr*. The first is contained in the locket which Meister Abraham has given to Kreis-

ler and which strikes terror in the heart of Hektor when it is
suddenly shown to him. The subject of the portrait is not disclosed. The second is a great canvas at Kanzheim Abbey, repre-
senting a scene of the Blessed Virgin's miraculous intercession
to save the life of a man who has been stabbed. In the background is the figure of the fleeing murderer. It is Prince Hektor. That same locket of Kreisler's has also a second compart-
ment which contains a letter of vital significance for the plot.
Whether it is a love-letter or some other document we never
learn, for the novel breaks off before Kreisler has had recourse
to its contents. Dostoevski makes the letter definitely a matter
of a lover's renunciation and places its discovery by Pyotr Alexandrovich in the same chapter close to the scene where Pyotr
Alexandrovich discovers with annoyance that Netochka is examining his portrait. We guess that the two, letter and portrait,
involve the same issue. Was that issue a murder committed by
Pyotr Alexandrovich? And if so, whom did he murder? Hektor's victim was his own brother Antonio, and the quarrel was
a savage love rivalry for Antonio's wife, Angela Benzoni, but in
Dostoevski's novel Pyotr Alexandrovich has no brother, and
Katya, as Angela's counterpart, is still unmarried. If, with the
partial identity of Katya and Alexandra Mikhailovna, it was
some rival of Alexandra's whom Pyotr murdered, the logical
candidate would be the "S.O." of the love-letter. At the end of
our fragment, Netochka has just surrendered that letter to
Pyotr Alexandrovich and we may be sure its disclosure will precipitate a climax in the action. The slyly smiling secretary,
Ovrov, who approaches Netochka in the last lines of the text,
would correspond to Hektor's Adjutant, whom Hektor sent to
murder Kreisler after having been confronted with the picture
in the locket. The Adjutant, however, missed his aim when he
fired at Kreisler and was instead killed by his own intended victim. Quite possibly Ovrov comes at the behest of his master,
who has had just time enough to see the letter, on a mission of
abducting or murdering Netochka. We know that she survived,
if such were the case, but we can only guess at what happened to Ovrov and his errand.

Whatever crimes Pyotr Alexandrovich committed before he
enters the story or was scheduled to commit in the unwritten
sequel, his villainies within the reader's ken are less than impressive. Dostoevski will amend this fault when, returning

once again to the model of Prince Hektor, he will project Pyotr Alexandrovich in the new rôle of Prince Valkovski in *The Insulted and Injured* in 1860-61. His villain of 1849 falls far short of the fascinating Hektor. No small part of Hektor's fascination lay in his magnificence. More than once he is referred to as a magnificent basilisk, a splendid peacock of evil. These Romantic qualities had to be sacrificed according to Dostoevski's formula of transference from Hoffmann, just as he chose or was forced to abandon the concern with music and painting that characterizes much of *Kater Murr*. Gone, too, are the unique colors, the extraordinary evocation of moods, the lyric exaltation, and the musical prose. Gone is the incomparable technique which brought the characters out of shadow with a progressive intensification of light until they stood possessed of life itself. Reduced to its plot outlines, *Kater Murr* declines to the level of a banal story of court intrigue punctuated by the irrelevant episodes from the life of the cat Murr. Dostoevski was totally unconcerned with the cat's ironic biography, but he did work from the bare and dry outlines of the Kreisler plot. What he had to add to the stripped skeletons of these characters was at once insufficient and over-sufficient for a new work of art. A vulgar melodrama was the result. Not for its own sake, but for what it explored for use in future writing, has the work any value, and in this respect it has considerable value. The power and beauty of *Kater Murr* lured Dostoevski beyond his depth. His imitation, launched by itself, sinks like the paper model of a great ship.

VII

A LITTLE HERO

Since April 23, 1849 Dostoevski had been confined in the Peter and Paul Fortress on charges of seditious activity, specifically with having been a more or less passive auditor at meetings of the secret political discussion group known as the "Petrashevski circle" and with having given oral readings of Belinski's reproachful letter to Gogol on the subject of the latter's political and religious obscurantism. What action was to be taken in the matter remained in doubt. Much more serious was the question of whether the authorities would discover his part in the attempted establishment of a clandestine printing press. If they did, death would be certain. In spite of his worries, Dostoevski took advantage of the permission granted him to write. Either for lack of access to his notes and papers, or, perhaps, to avoid a work which might be considered unwholesome or otherwise dubious, he chose not to complete *Netochka Nezvanova* but to spend the months composing a completely new short story called *A Little Hero*. Its cheerful, even charming, quality contrasts sharply with the circumstances amid which it was written, but Dostoevski was mistaken if he thought that the government prosecutors were to be impressed by the quality of this or any other literary production. When the sentence of exile was finally pronounced upon him, sending him to Siberia, the manuscript had to be left behind. Michael Dostoevski was not allowed to publish it until 1857,—under the signature "M.——i."

By virtue of its setting in a rural manor house south of Moscow, *A Little Hero* stands as the first work of its author that was not a "Petersburg tale." It is cast in the form of the narrator's reminiscence of an episode in his eleventh year, when he was a guest at the country estate of a wealthy and spendthrift relative.

The boy recalls that he was troubled by adolescent awareness of the presence of beautiful women. One (unnamed) lady in particular seemed to sense his embarrassment and to take delight in teasing him by getting him to sit on her lap, by pinching his fingers, and by laughing at his discomfiture. Her beauty alternately attracted and repelled him, but for her intimate friend, Mme M., he felt only a worshipful awe. Mme M. was quite a different type, tenderly melancholy, majestic, grave, and her egotistic husband, a close parallel to Pyotr Alexandrovich, inspired him with instinctive resentment. On the other hand he felt impelled to abet the love affair between Mme M. and a young man identified as "N."

On the veranda the boy happens to be present while the malicious M. is subtly taunting his wife with the news that N. is leaving on a sudden and unforeseen journey to Odessa. The lady avoids his mocking invitation to come and watch N.'s departure by saying that she was about to take a walk with the boy-narrator. The latter gallantly falls in with her excuse, but the stroll proves a sad one, for the lady quickly sends him away in order to be alone with her sorrow. That day at dinner the boy becomes furious with the teasing lady when she banters M. with remarks to the effect that his wife is in love with the hero. He roundly denounces her, then flees to his room for sheer embarrassment.

The sounds of a riding party bring him forth again, but he is chagrined to find neither his own pony ready nor any seat available in the carriages. Only the vicious and unmanageable stallian Tancred is unclaimed. On an impulse of annoyance, since Tancred was somehow assigned to her escort, who now declines to ride, the teasing lady turns to the boy and says: "Well, crybaby, wouldn't you like to have a try? You wanted so much to go?" Her taunt stings him. In a flash he is galloping away on Tancred's back. All the gentlemen pursue the runaway horse and rescue the lad. When he returns, quite safe, the teasing lady is very grave and full of apologies. All the guests are loud in his praise, calling him "De Lorges" and "Toggenburg" (knights in Schiller's ballads). The teasing lady goes so far as to insist that her ill-tempered duenna yield her place to the "little hero" for the expedition.

Next day, the boy is accidentally witness to a gallant tryst in the garden. Mme M. is taking farewell of a mounted horseman, no other than young N., who has ridden back for this tender adieu. Stooping from his saddle, he kisses Mme M., then rides away. Just at parting, he slips a letter into her hands. The letter is lost by the lady in her excitement. The final episode deals with the boy's strategem of returning the letter without revealing that he was a witness of her love-meeting. He places it in a bouquet, with which the lady waves away a bee, at which movement the letter falls out. For this deed he is rewarded with a kiss as he lies on the grass near by in patently counterfeit slumber.

The sexual awareness of the eleven-year-old boy takes on a considerably more attractive form than the passion felt by the eleven-year-old Netochka for her step-father. On the other hand, the present story lacks the raw intensity of the novel-fragment. In its lightness and gaiety, *A Little Hero* reflects the lightness and gaiety of the Hoffmann tale *Die Fermate*, which served as a partial source for it.

Die Fermate is a musical tale about a pair of temperamental sisters, Italians by nationality, who travel about the country giving concerts. The vivacious Lauretta is a singer, the serene and majestic Teresina is her accompanist to the guitar. Under the spell of their influence, the nineteen-year-old hero Theodor suddenly destroys all his dry, academic compositions for organ and dedicates himself to the writing of Italian *canzone*. Miss Meibel, the spinsterish local coloratura who has rarely known competition, is much put out by the arrival of these gaudy musicians, but the public delights in them and in their music. As for Theodor, his own enthusiasm makes him decide to join the ladies on their travels.

In love with both sisters simultaneously and much concerned with the writing of music for both, Theodor is at first well pleased with his new life, but inevitably a clash of personalities ensues. At a concert one day he is seized with the irresistible impulse to pay off Lauretta's caprices by putting her out of countenance. She is singing one of the bravura arias of which she is so fond and has reached the long trill at the end of the cadenza, when suddenly Theodor, who is playing the piano accompaniment, strikes the dominant chord fortissimo, the orchestra follows tutti, and the showy finale is ruined. Lauretta screams in fury, tears up her music, and rushes from the stage. Teresina, however, calmly ignoring her sister's fury, persuades Theodor not to leave for home but to remain with the little company. Thereafter he puts all his faith in Teresina, but eventually is undeceived in her also when he overhears her ridicule himself and his music unmercifully to a visiting Italian tenor. This is more than his pride can bear and this time he does leave for home and Bamberg, without even saying farewell. Fourteen years later, while travelling in Italy, he comes quite unexpectedly upon the sisters and once again as they are giving a recital in an inn-garden. A priest is directing the performance. Just as Theodor enters the garden he is witness to precisely the same deed he himself once committed: the signal for the final chord is given before Lauretta has finished her brilliant trill and her showiest effect is nullified. Her fury, however, passes to pleasure at the sight of the long-lost Theodor and the tale ends amid general merriment. Theodor remarks that inspiration is a glorious thing but that it does not pay to fall in love with one's inspirer.[1]

Apart from the principal scene of Lauretta's unfinished trill, the most memorable incident takes place on the very first lap of the hero's journey with the singing ladies. Theodor has decided to accompany their carriage "romantically, on horseback, like a protecting paladin," and to this end has purchased an unhandsome nag which the dealer assured him was quite gentle.

"Everything went well," says Theodor, "we were already at the last station, when my horse got the peculiar notion of wanting to go back home. The realization of not being able to apply severity with particular success in such cases counselled me to try all gentle means possible, but the obstinate beast remained impervious to all my friendly coaxing. I wanted to go ahead, he wanted to go back, and all my efforts with him availed only, that, instead of bolting homewards, he kept turning in a circle. Teresina leaned out of the carriage and laughed heartily, while Lauretta, with her hands over her face, screamed aloud as though I were in the direst danger of losing my life. That gave me the courage of desperation. I dug both spurs into the nag's ribs, and in the same instant lay ungently thrown, upon the ground. The horse stood quietly and with craning neck gazed at me in downright mockery. I was unable to get up, the coachman hurried to my assistance, Lauretta had jumped out and was weeping and shrieking, and Teresina kept laughing incessantly. My ankle was sprained and I couldn't mount the horse again. How was I to go on? The horse was tied to the carriage and I was obliged to crawl in. Imagine two rather robust women, a fat maid, two pug-dogs, a dozen chests, boxes, and baskets, and finally me, all packed into a little two-seated carriage;—imagine Lauretta's lamentation over the uncomfortable seat, the howling of the pug-dogs, the chatter of the Neapolitan, Teresina's pouting, my own unspeakable pain in my foot, and you will conceive the pleasantness of my situation."

To make matters worse, Teresina got out, untied the unruly horse, mounted it side-saddle, and rode all the rest of the journey singing Spanish romances to the accompaniment of her guitar, her plumes and silken gown fluttering in the breeze as she rode.

True to his formula, Dostoevski eliminated all associations with music before placing the characters in their new Russian setting. The very slight plot of the original, as well as the major scene of Lauretta's interrupted cadenza, were of little use. What remained was the amusing scene with the unruly horse, which in the absence of Hoffmann's main episode now assumed a central position, and a set of story characters. The gaudy and Latin Lauretta he transposed into the teasing lady, who has a tantalizing physical charm not quite the same as Lauretta possessed. The beautiful and grave Teresina he made into Mme M. by the addition of more sentiment and the capacity to suffer sorrows that Teresina would have shrugged off. The Russian pair are no longer sisters, but close friends, though a casual remark late in the story refers to them as cousins. Possibly the waspish Miss Meibel accounts for the ill-tempered duenna who is thoroughly vexed at having to surrender her place in the carriage to the "little hero." Neither Monsieur M. nor the young lover N. has any counterpart in *Die Fermate*. The former, who is only moderately sinister, is clearly a carry-over from Pyotr Alexandrovich, while the latter is a purely conventional figure placed only on the outer rim of the action.

The hero is again the narrator and he still simultaneously loves two ladies, one gay, one grave, but it was in changing his age from nineteen to eleven that Dostoevski made the most radical departure from his source. In making him a kind of miniature knight Dostoevski certainly skirted the edges of the distastefully mawkish and it was remarkable deftness that prevented him from plunging into that pitfall. The boy, for instance, takes part together with Mme M. in a *tableau vivant* of mediaeval life called "The Lady of the Castle and her Page;" he understands and resents Monsieur M.'s calling him Madame's *cavaliere servente* and retorts that he is the lady's page; the riding of Tancred earns him the names of De Lorges, who in Schiller's ballad *Der Handschuh* descended into the arena to retrieve his lady's glove from among the wild beasts, and of Toggenburg, who in another ballad of Schiller's became a hermit and lived and died in a little cell that looked toward the convent where his beloved was a nun. It is the portrayal of the boy's emotions from within that makes these things acceptable. Had he been shown solely from an adult viewpoint, like a sentimentalized Little Lord Fauntleroy, he would have been ludicrous instead of sympathetic for his own sake and extremely interesting as the first of Dostoevski's magnificently portrayed boys. He prefigures Kolya Krassotkin and Ilyusha Snegirov in *The Brothers Karamazov*.

As part of the general "chivalric" atmosphere of *A Little Hero* we have that remarkably un-Dostoevskian scene near the end where the narrator is the unintentional witness of the farewell of the lovers. For this, too, there would seem to be a model among Hoffmann's works, specifically the short fragment *Die Genesung*, which Hoffmann dictated from his deathbed in the spring of 1822.[2] The narrator and unintentional observer in this case is named Theodor, as was the hero of *Die Fermate*,— an odd coincidence, if it is a coincidence. He is a painter and has gone to a particularly lovely rural spot to paint undisturbed. By pure chance this is the spot selected by the girl Wilhelmine and her lover, Doctor O., to bring her father, Baron Siegfried von S., as he sleeps. The Baron is aged and sick and from his sick room he had yearned for Nature's beneficent green, which he fancied had been withdrawn to punish mankind for its perversities. Amid the splendid trees and fresh grass he awakens and his gloomy obsession is cured. But not before the young lovers have had a tender colloquy. They will soon be married. The whole of the brief work is a kind of hymn to vernal Nature. Throughout the brief action Theodor is an unobserved spectator, who later merely reports what he saw. The original was a wistful dream-wish of a man who realized that he was on his deathbed. Is it possible that Dostoevski recalled it with a new poignancy from within his prison walls and in his turn longed for that lovely spot amid freedom and the verdure of spring? If so, his artistic objectivity was quite unimpaired by pathos when he adjusted the material to fit into his own gracious story.

VIII

EXILE AND RETURN. THE WORKS OF 1861-1862

Sentence of death before a firing squad was actually passed upon Dostoevski and his fellow-prisoners in November, though they were not informed of the fact. Nor were they informed of the fact that Nicholas I personally went through their dossiers and commuted their sentences to varying terms of imprisonment in Siberia. For Dostoevski the Tsar indicated four years of hard labor, to be followed by life-time service as a private in some Siberian unit of the Army. In the frigid dawn of December 22, 1849 there ensued the monstrous melodrama in which the prisoners were marched to Semyonovski Square, the firing squad drawn up and given the command "Aim!", and, by pre-arrangement, the messenger introduced, breathless, on horse-back, with the Imperial Majesty's gracious commutation of sentence. In the midst of the White Terror since the European revolutions of 1848 Nicholas intended to teach these men a lesson. On Christmas Eve, the prisoners, already burdened with their convict chains, were driven through the holiday streets in open sledges bound for permanent exile.

Exactly ten years later Dostoevski returned to Petersburg a free man, eager to resume his literary activity where he had left it off. The climb up out of the shadow of death had been slow and difficult. For four years, January 1850 to February 1854, he served in the chain-gangs of the prison at Omsk. The grisly experience will be reported in *The House of the Dead*, 1861-62, the book at which Alexander II is said to have wept. Well might he weep! In February 1854 he was transferred to Semipalatinsk and military service, as Nicholas I had decreed, but the life-sentence came to be altered as a result of the death of the Tsar. By October 1856 Dostoevski was given an officer's commission which brought not only greater physical comfort but the restitution of his cancelled prerogatives as an aristocrat. By 1857 he was granted permission to resume literary work, and in the course of the following two years composed two long stories, *Uncle's Dream* and *A Friend of the Family*, both of which were published in Petersburg in 1859. The same order of 1857 had made possible the publication of *A Little Hero*. In 1859 he was further permitted to return to Russia, though with restriction of residence to the city of Tver, ninety miles from

Moscow. Still more appeals to Alexander II were required before the final pardon and gloriously happy return to Petersburg in December 1859.

With might and main he then plunged into the life of the capital trying to make up for a decade of lost time. Through the year 1860 he was simultaneously working on a new novel, *The Insulted and Injured,* on the memoirs of his prison experiences, *The House of the Dead,* and on the plans for his forthcoming monthly magazine *Time* (Vremya), which was to be published under the name of his brother Michael.

Ten years of events as violent as those Dostoevski knew in his Siberian decade could not but alter a man and an author. Ten years in the middle of the 19th century could not but alter Russia and Russian literature. How and where was he to begin? Was all concern with the works of Hoffmann to be rejected as wholly unacceptable now? Of the two stories written in Siberia, *A Friend of the Family* shows not the slightest connection with Hoffmann; the other, *Uncle's Dream,* deals with a scheming mother's plot to marry off her unwilling daughter to a senile old Prince, a situation which is vaguely parallel to that of *Kater Murr,* where Rätin Benzon strives to marry Julia to the imbecile youth Prince Ignatius, but the analogy may be quite fortuitous. Certainly nothing else in *Uncle's Dream* recalls *Kater Murr* or any other work of Hoffmann, though distant echoes may be heard of Pushkin's *Eugene Onegin* and *The Queen of Spades* and at least one echo of Gogol's *The Inspector General.*[1] Had he forgotten Hoffmann altogether? The answer may be found in the fact that the initial number of the new magazine *Time,* which appeared in January 1861, contained three different works from Dostoevski's pen, in each of which Hoffmann was mentioned by name. The three works taken in sequence will show complementary aspects of Dostoevski's idea of Hoffmann at the time immediately after his return from exile.

1. Petersburg Visions in Verse and Prose

Anonymously printed in the initial issue of *Time* was an article which has since been identified definitely as being Dostoevski's.[2] In the words of N. N. Strakhov, the author's close friend in the post-exile period and his later biographer:

"F.M.Dostoevski in the first issue also took over the literary supplement (feuilleton) for himself. The supplement had really been given to D.D.Minaev, but, I don't know why, the contents he composed for the supplement did not satisfy Fëdor Mikhailovich. Whereupon he quickly wrote up an article of his own, entitled *Visions in Verse and Prose,* and in it inserted all the poems with which D.D.Minaev's supplement had been strewn, according to the fashion of the time which had been introduced, apparently, by Dobrolyubov in his famous *The Whistle* (Svistok) in *The Contemporary.*"

Perhaps Dostoevski had a reason over and above dissatisfaction with Minaev's copy for writing this rambling essay, for it reads like a review of his own pre-Siberian fiction. With the wistful recapitulation of his literary stock-in-trade he seems to be testing public reaction. "Would these themes still interest them?" he seems to be cautiously inquiring. The anonymous publication was probably an added mark of caution.

"Oh, accursed forever be my duty—the duty of a literary supplement writer! . . .," the article begins. What is to be written about? Recent news about town? Some people fancy a supplement is made up effortlessly at the writer's whim. Perhaps one should be a second Eugène Sue and write of the mysteries of Petersburg.

"For," says Dostoevski, "I am a great hunter after mysteries. I am a fantasist, I am a mystic, and, I confess to you, Petersburg, I don't know why, has always seemed to me some kind of mystery."[3]

With this remark he proceeds to some of his "visions" of the city. As a boy, for instance, he had once beheld the city in the winter twilight, when a thousand chimney smokes rose into the air and seemed to be constructing a fantastic second city above the rooftops of the real one. He adds: "From that very moment my existence began." (Dostoevski did not see Petersburg until the middle of his sixteenth year.)

Other "visions" follow. For a time the author lived among poor government clerks, titular councillors, "not Don Carloses or Posas," and knew only one of these who went mad, suffering "like Poprishchin" under the delusion that he was Garibaldi. Another, named Soloviev, was "a new Harpagon," "a new Plyushkin," and died (like Dostoevski's own Mr. Prokharchin) aged, alone, and in debt—with 169,022 rubles hidden among his papers.

There is an evocation of the Nevski Prospekt on Christmas Eve, with gay crowds on the sidewalks, flashing carriages on the pavement driven by proud coachmen and attended by haughty lackeys. In the throng suddenly appears a fantastic figure, an old man with long hair and a cane, perhaps the ghost of the miser Soloviev, and very like Pushkin's Covetous Knight. The author observes:

> "You know, I just can't get away from the fantastic frame of mind. Even in the forties they used to call me a fantasist and tease me for it. . . . Now, of course, I have grey hair, experience in life, etc., etc., yet meanwhile I have remained for all that a fantasist."[4]

Should one, for instance, write about the old miser Soloviev? To do so, would be to steal from Pushkin. Yet how had the man existed? Here Dostoevski sketches a tentative story about the miser Soloviev. It sounds like the first draft of a short story of 1848.

The scene shifts to the Gostinny Dvor. A stout lady is selecting a wooden soldier from a heap of toys. A young couple are searching for toys within their budget-range. The man likes the cannon that pops, the woman prefers a doll. A small boy begs alms. Shady characters,—one of them much like Nozdrëv in *Dead Souls*,—sidle up to the author to suggest illicit business.

A summer scene: A pair of newly-weds are kissing in a carriage while on their way to pay formal social calls. A neat, polite-spoken boy of thirteen or fourteen asks shamefacedly for money; questioning reveals that he comes of a sturdy family suddenly impoverished by loss of a position. The author digresses on the text of the boy's words: "We are very poor." The sermon trails off into literary shop-talk about the Fund for Needy Authors, Goncharov, Kraevski (editor of *National Notes*), and the like.

Just after the sketch of Petersburg beneath the winter's twilight, there occurs the quasi-autobiographical "vision" of the proletarian "Amalie," which was quoted in the discussion of *White Nights*, a story to which it reads like a real-life model. Here the narrator recalls how he read Schiller and Scott and the Tales of Hoffmann to Nadya, whom he had christened "Amalie" after the heroine of Schiller's *Die Räuber* and whose love he observed, yet chose not to observe. Of all the "visions," this is the only one to pass actually into a new literary work. In *The Insulted and Injured* the dreamer hero will once again wait, as in *White Nights*, with the beloved girl for the arrival of the man *she* loves and whom she will marry. The line of development from *Aus dem Leben dreier Freunde* is thus projected still further. Moreover, these dreamers, these readers of Schiller and Scott and Hoffmann, now take on a kind of religious quality. They become the pure of heart, the meek humanitarians, the lambs among whom the wolves prey. In *The Insulted and Injured* they are mocked at by the wicked characters for being "Schillers," impractical idealists, easy game. For Dostoevski, who before his exile avoided evil as a theme, who fumbled his portrayals of villains, the experiences of Siberia had opened an immense gulf between good and evil. The importance is not to be underestimated of the fact that, to him, the good were Romanticists, the evil were Realists. Lambs and wolves respectively. The preying of the wolves is the subject of his new novel *The Insulted and Injured*.

2. THE INSULTED AND INJURED

Precisely as if it were one of the foregoing series of "visions" stands the opening scene of the novel *The Insulted and Injured*, the first installment of which appeared in the January 1861 issue of *Time*. The time is the twilight of a cold, damp evening in March, the evening of the 22nd, to be exact, and the frost is becoming more sharp as the darkness settles in. The narrator, young, poor, consumptive, has been wearily searching all day for a room, and now comes to Müller's confectionery shop on the Voznesenski Prospekt. Inside the shop, like twin omens of doom, are a man and his dog. The man is seventy-eight years old, we learn, genuinely feeble and completely indigent.

> "His tall figure, his bent back, his death-like face with the stamp of eighty years upon it, his old great-coat torn at the seams, the battered round hat, at least twenty years old, which covered his head—bald but for one lock of hair, not grey but yellowish white—all his movements, which seemed performed, as it were, aimlessly, as though worked by strings—no one who met him for the first time could help being struck by all this. . . . I was struck, too, by his extraordinary emaciation; he seemed scarcely to have any body, it was as though there were nothing but skin over his bones. His large lusterless eyes, set as it were in blue rims, always stared straight before him, never looking to one side and never seeing anything . . ."

What can such a man be thinking of? the narrator wonders. Why is he at Müller's? And where did he get that dog?

> "That wretched dog looked as though it, too, were eighty; . . . there must be something fantastic about it, something uncanny . . . a sort of Mephistopheles in dog-form . . . Looking at it you would have allowed at once that twenty years must have elapsed since

its last meal. It was as thin as a skeleton, or, which is much the same, as its master. Almost all its hair had fallen off, and its tail hung down between its legs as bare as a stick. Its head and ears drooped sullenly forward. I never in my life met such a repulsive dog. When they both walked down the street, the master in front and the dog at his heels, its nose touched the skirt of his coat as though glued to it."

The old man sits in Müller's confectionery shop, buys nothing, reads no newspapers, says not a word, stares straight ahead. The dog lies unmoving at his feet. Bumptious Germans frequent the store in order to read the proprietor's newspapers,— the narrator has come to read the Russian ones,—to chat a bit, and to reassure each other's pride in his German nationality. Such a client, for instance, is Adam Ivanich Schultz, from Riga, who is now absorbed in the pages of the *Dorfbarbier*, but who presently becomes aware that the forlorn old man is staring at him. Schultz becomes furious and questions the man. The latter seems not to understand, not even to hear. He picks himself up and calls the dog, Azorka, preparatory to leaving. But Azorka has died. Quite peacefully and unobtrusively died on the floor of Müller's shop. The old man bends down, presses his cheek to the dog's head, then silently goes out the door. The narrator follows him, addresses him where he now sits in a fence corner of a dark alley. The old man murmurs a few words, then slumps back, dead. Dog and man have died of slow starvation.

The whole passage is a little doctored, thinks the reader, but basically what a vivid first-hand account of unheralded tragedy in the urban slums! What things must Dostoevski have encountered in his nocturnal walks about Petersburg! Let the reader then take up Hoffmann's story *Das öde Haus* at the opening scene.

The "deserted house" in question is described as being located in the city of "***n" and in the "Allee" which leads to the "***ger Gate." Read: in Berlin, Unter den Linden, near the Brandenburger Gate. No. 9, to be exact, for it was a very real house, which Hoffmann's Berlin readers could have found any day without difficulty. The narrator, Theodor, has been puzzled by the silent, closed structure located in the heart of the city and has decided to investigate the mystery. To this end he goes into the adjacent confectioner's shop and, while leisurely drinking a cup of hot chocolate, directs off-hand questions to the proprietor. The proprietor, willing talker that he is, completes a sale of bonbons to a girl customer, then leans on the counter and tells Theodor what he knows about the house. It belongs to the Countess von S., who never comes there, but for some reason refuses to sell the place. Two creatures inhabit it, an aged misanthrope of a caretaker and his sorrowful dog that sometimes bays the moon. The conversation is interrupted by the arrival of the man in question. The dog is at his heels.

> "Imagine a little wizened man with a mummy-colored face, a pointed nose, compressed lips, green-glittering cat's eyes, a fixed mad smile, his hair heavily powdered and done up in an old-fashioned manner with towering toupet and pasted curls, a large Postillon d'Amour hair-bag, an old coat of coffee-brown color, faded but well preserved and well brushed, grey stockings, and large stub-toed shoes with stone buckles. Imagine that this little wizened figure, at least in so far as the over-large hands with their long, strong fingers are concerned, is robustly built and walks sturdily up to the counter, then, still smiling and gazing fixedly at the sweet things contained beneath the crystal panes, wails out in a faint mournful voice: 'A couple of preserved oranges—a couple of macaroons—a couple of sugared chestnuts, etc.' Imagine this and judge for yourselves whether or not there was reason to think it queer."

To make conversation, the proprietor suggests that old age is creeping up on the man. The old fellow protests, first in words, then by clapping his hands and jumping into the air with a kind of entrechat that makes every glass in the store rattle. Unfortunately he brings down his foot on the dog's tail. The animal emits a frightful howl, but is quickly comforted when the old man opens the paper bag and offers it a macaroon. At once the dog sits up on its hind legs, begs, and receives the macaroon, which it crunches with gusto, sitting all the time in the position of a squirrel. The old man bids the proprietor good evening, and in parting clasps his hand so hard that the store-keeper winces at the pressure. To Theodor he then remarks that this customer comes in two or three times a month. Further conversation is ruled out by the arrival of numerous clients, for the hour of fashionable promenades is at hand and the bright noon-day has brought out unusual crowds.

Towards the end of Dostoevski's description of the old man at Müller's occurs this sentence:

> "I remember too that it occurred to me once that the old man and his dog had somehow stepped out of some page of Hoffmann

illustrated by Gavarni and were parading this world by way of walking advertisements of the edition."

They had indeed stepped out of some page of Hoffmann. But how changed! Every last detail, from the bright noon-day crowds on the main avenue metamorphosed into the dismal twilight of March 22nd, has been transposed from cheer to gloom. Hoffmann's caretaker is old, it is true, but, whatever his oddities, he is hearty, agile, and cheerful, as opposed to Dostoevski's feeble, starved, abandoned, helpless old man. The dog, far from crunching macaroons, has not even hair to keep it warm, and like its master dies in a public place. The two scenes in juxtaposition constitute a kind of laboratory specimen showing Dostoevski's methods of procedure. In such a way he must have dealt with the Chevalier Gluck to make him into the forlorn drunkard Emalyan Ilich in *An Honest Thief*, or with the mad painter Berklinger in *Der Artushof* to transform him into the non-artist proletarian Murin in *The Landlady*.

* * * * * * *

Two closely parallel plots make up the substance of *The Insulted and Injured*, one of which is taking place in the course of the novel, the other of which has reached its penultimate stage with the death of the old man with the dog and will be revealed in retrospect.

The name of the old man was Jeremy Smith. He was of British extraction, but a Russian subject. Once he had been the happy father of a beautiful daughter, but he had taken such a possessive attitude toward her that he had driven away her young suitor, a German named Heinrich Salzmann. It was perhaps by way of revenge upon her father that the girl eloped with a second suitor, Prince Valkovski, and, on eloping, had acceded to the Prince's suggestion that she take with her a large sum of her father's money. The Prince took her to Paris, where he legally married her, but, on the eve of her confinement abandoned her. In her distress, the mother was too proud to avail herself of the weapon of legal prosecution for desertion, but she did accept the help of the faithful Heinrich Salzmann, who supported her and the daughter, Nellie, as long as he lived. Left destitute a second time at his death, she came to Russia, bringing Nellie with her, sought out her father, and begged his assistance. But old Smith never forgave her. He repeated his curse upon her and left her to desperation. She died in a Petersburg slum, the charge of a family barely less destitute than herself. It is the fourteen-year-old Nellie who now comes, as she had previously come, to the lodgings of her grandfather, only to find that the old man has died and that his room is now occupied by Vanya, the narrator who witnessed his death outside of Müller's confectionery shop.

The literary provenience of Nellie is a matter of common knowledge. She is Dostoevski's adaptation of Little Nell from Dickens's *The Old Curiosity Shop* (1841). Likewise, old Smith, whose connection with the caretaker of Hoffmann's deserted house is strictly limited to the opening scene, is to be related to grandfather Trent in the novel by Dickens.

The Old Curiosity Shop was a work bound to please Dostoevski. Its two opening chapters are remarkably similar to *Petersburg Visions in Verse and Prose*; the author's concern with the existences of poor and obscure people touched sympathetic chords in Dostoevski's heart, as did the English writer's moral indignation; Quilp, as a vivid and violent character of ferocious malice, engaged his literary admiration. As the point of departure for the Smith-plot of his novel, Dostoevski apparently took Chapter LXIX, where "the bachelor" reveals his identity and narrates the history of Little Nell's family. He proves to be the younger brother of grandfather Trent and has been searching for him and Little Nell for many months. As boys, the brothers had been devoted to one another. Then they had fallen in love with the same girl. Silently and without bitterness, the "bachelor" had withdrawn his suit and left his elder brother to be happy. Old Trent *had* been happy, both in his wife and in his daughter. Ultimately the daughter had married a selfish and improvident husband, whose career is only vaguely suggested. We discern that the daughter loved the wastrel to the last and survived him by only three weeks. To the heartbroken old Trent, now beggared by his son-in-law's folly, it fell to care for two grandchildren, a boy and a girl. The boy has shown every sign of following in his father's footsteps, but the girl, Little Nell, has inherited her mother's angelic sweetness and devotion. For her sake, old Trent opens "the old curiosity shop," for her sake he borrows money from the infamous Quilp in order to gamble and win a fortune, as he mistakenly hopes, and with her he flees upon the wanderings that compose the novel. The "bachelor" on his errand of mercy, however, arrives too late to be of any help.

Fate has been infinitely more harsh to the Russian equivalents of these characters than to the originals. Smith, unlike the kindly and patient Trent, is fiercely proud and unable to forgive his daughter's treachery even in the extremes of her suffering. Quilp may have cast a glance or two at Little Nell, but the innocent child was never left friendless, as Nellie now is, among the drunken and bestial patrons of a brothel in the slums. Smith's daughter, it is true, had the solace of the loyalty of Heinrich Salzmann, who has no counterpart in Dickens, but, on the other hand, the wrongs suffered at the hands of Prince Valkovski are vastly worse than those endured by the daughter of old Trent in her life with her wastrel husband. In general, the poverty of the Russian characters has been made more desperate by far and their miseries more unrelieved.

The utter hopelessness of Nellie's situation gives evil people power over her, with the result that she is sent against her will to serve in the slum-brothel run by the harridan Mme Bubnov. From the very midst of vicious patrons she is rescued with the help of the narrator Vanya, who takes her to a decent home with his friends the Ikhmenev family. Here she will know a brief happiness before she dies. She will also bring some measure of comfort to the Ikhmenevs, who in the course of the novel are living through the same unhappy events that made up the story of the Smith family. The source of the evils that beset them is once again Prince Valkovski.

In former years Nikolai Sergeevich Ikhemev lived a happy life in the provinces with his wife and daughter Natasha. There Vanya had known them when a boy and there he had come to look upon Natasha as his sweetheart. In those days Prince Valkovski had been a friend and benefactor of the family and had even sent his son Alyosha to live with them. Without ever fully explaining his change of heart, Valkovski has now withdrawn Alyosha from them and forbidden him to set foot in their house. Moreover he has undertaken against them a complex lawsuit, which he is well aware will ruin them. For his part, Alyosha cannot understand his father's action and comes, despite his prohibition, to visit the Ikhmenevs, for he too is in love with Natasha. And Natasha is in love with him. As the book opens, they have decided to elope together. In Chapter 8, where the story proper begins, Vanya is paying a call on his friends, when Natasha asks him to accompany her to Vespers. Once on the streets away from her parents, she confesses that she is not bound for church at all but that she is on her way to meet

Alyosha, with whom she shall elope this very evening. Beneath
a street light on the canal embankment the two stand waiting
for the coming of the lover.

Even to the details of the setting, the situation reproduces
the situation of *White Nights*. Some special significance must
have been attached by the author to this basic story, since it
had been used not only in 1848 but again in the "Amalie" episode of *Petersburg Visions,* which was printed in the same first
issue of *Time* as the present installment of *The Insulted and Injured.* Its value as autobiography is reenforced by the clearly
autobiographical details given to Vanya. He is represented, for
instance, in Chapters 4 and 5 as a young novelist living much
the life that Dostoevski had lived in the years 1845 to 1848; his
first published work was a story about a poor government clerk
in Petersburg; the story was first praised, then attacked, by the
critic "B.",—obviously Belinski. (Belinski had died in May
1848.)[5] Finally, Vanya is a "dreamer," or, to apply the terms
used in self-definition by Dostoevski in *Petersburg Visions,* he
is a "fantasist," a "mystic." As such, his rôle consists in being
loyal and passive. Loyally and passively he now waits with
Natasha in the twilight on the canal embankment for the arrival of Alyosha. Loyally and passively he will love her even
after her bitter prodigal's return to her family. He will die
unmarried to her.

Alyosha arrives. He is a gay and charming youth, a creature
of momentary impulses. Right now he is passionately in love
with Natasha, but he is utterly incapable of sustained emotion
or of real understanding of the nature of his present action. He
takes Natasha joyously to the rooms he has rented for the two
of them. Prince Valkovski, upon first learning of his son's
elopement, is furious. It undoes all his plans for the brilliant
marriage to Katya, a girl of immense fortune. Then he reflects upon Alyosha's character and cynically decides to pretend
sympathy with his choice until time will destroy the alliance
without his lifting a finger. The plan succeeds. Soon Alyosha
abandons Natasha in order to marry Katya. Simultaneously
the Prince wins his lawsuit against the Ikhmenevs. Grief-
stricken, Natasha returns to her father who at first cursed her.
Vanya she still insists on considering a "brother," and in the
slowly dying Nellie she finds a sister. The parents are reconciled. At the close of the book the consumptive Vanya follows
Nellie into death.

As the two plots unfold, with their perspectives forward and backward in time, the uncanny impression is conveyed that life is repeating itself, that everything has happened before and that the outcome of the present conflict may be foreseen. Such a concept is common enough in German Romantic fiction. Novalis had extended it to a vast philosophy in his poetic novel *Heinrich von Ofterdingen.* Hoffmann, too, had used it more than once. In *Die Elixiere des Teufels,* Medardus had discovered at every step of his way that his crimes had been prefigured by his father Franzesko and by ancestors of five generations, back to the original sinner, Franzesko the painter. Even in a light story like *Die Fermate,* the central episode of Lauretta's unfinished trill is recapitulated, even in minor details, twice in real life and a third time in a painting. It was Theodor's unexpected coming upon the painting at the Berlin art exposition that served as the starting point of the story. Still more striking is the case of *Spielerglück,* where the hero is deterred from gambling by hearing the story of the Chevalier Menars, who had, in *his* time, been deterred from gambling by hearing the story of Francesco Vertua. The three parallel lives compose the total narrative of *Spielerglück.* If no work of Hoffmann's presents two family histories, one past, one present, in just the manner of *The Insulted and Injured,* the idea for such parallelization may reasonably be traced to his general practices. So, too, with the technique of the interlocking plots, a device not confined to Hoffmann but at which Hoffmann was a master.

Dostoevski has joined his two plots actually at only two points,—Hoffmann would surely have knitted them much more closely,—in the persons of Vanya and Prince Valkovski. The passive nature of Vanya makes him a little unsatisfactory for so important a function. Often he seems to do little but shuttle between the various characters to bring and take information. The vital personage from whom all action emanates is the Prince, and on him the author lavished much attention and detail.

To search for Valkovski's prototype in Quilp would be to mistake the whole course of Dostoevski's literary evolution, for the two villains have little in common beyond a frank profession of their love of evil for its own sake. Between Dickens's grotesque gnome and the suavely handsome Prince there is as much difference spiritually as physically. Quilp is almost sexless. His motivation is largely the understandable one of greed, and his meanness is instinctive and spontaneous. He is less a human being than an allegorized vice. With little change he could be transposed into a mediaeval morality play under the name of Spitefulness. His face is the badge of his character.

Not so the Prince. From his first melodramatic entrance in Part II, Chapter 2, his handsome and aristocratic bearing are repeatedly emphasized. He is tall, slim, graceful; he bears himself with innate elegance; though he is forty-five, he could easily pass for his son's elder brother. Though his face is swarthy, his lips are "beautifully chiselled" and his eyes are large and grey. His whole countenance wears an expression that is "not spontaneous, but always, as it were, artificial, delibrate, borrowed, and a blind conviction grew upon one that one would never read his real expression." Here, ten years before *The Possessed,* is the mask-like beauty of Stavrogin. Here also is a new version of Prince Hektor in *Kater Murr*.

With every entrance of Hektor, Hoffmann reaffirms his physical beauty. In Volume II, Section 4, Hektor comes in "clad resplendently in a dress uniform, handsome, strong, proud as the far-darting youthful god (Apollo)." In an earlier appearance in Volume I, Section 2, he "unfolded before the Princess (Hedwiga) the sumptuous many-colored peacock's tail of his gallantry." Yet in his eyes Hedwiga sees the eyes of a deadly basilisk with rays of fire. Beauty and evil compose Hektor's face as they compose the face of Prince Valkovski. Even the swarthiness of the latter may be a recollection of Hektor's Italian origins.

Nor is the parallel confined to their external appearance. Both have committed murder, both are unscrupulous intriguers and conscienceless hypocrites, both are aristocrats devoured by ambition, both indulge their secret lusts, both are Satanically proud. All of these things were implied in the Pyotr Alexandrovich of *Netochka Nezvanova,* who in a very real sense *was* Prince Hektor, but the author stopped with mere implication. Dostoevski now spells out his meaning.

The Prince is a wolf. His very name means "wolf."[6] Though he has Hektor's arrogant pride, fierce cunning, and savage passion, he descends to levels of depravity and bestiality undreamed of by Hoffmann's villain. And he gloats over his own nastiness and reasons toward the discovery of a new, as yet uninvented vice. In his self-declaration to Vanya in Part III, Chapter 10, he states that he longs to "flabbergast" people by his crimes, and from the recital of them, it would seem that he

might die of sheer exasperation at not being able to push his
human ingenuity any further. Besides his heartless treatment
of Nellie's mother and his gratuitous persecution of the Ikhmenevs, he has explored the violent lusts of outright sadism.
Like the sinister Kurolesov of Aksakov's *A Family Chronicle*
(1846), he has exploited his baronial authority amid the re-
moteness of his country estate to indulge in orgies of cruelty.
Like Kurolesov, too, he has had peasants flogged to death, though
even here Valkovski managed to surpass the other in bestiality.
For Valkovski had begun with the seduction of a peasant woman,
then flogged her handsome young husband for protesting the
seduction, and finally let the youth die in the model hospital
which he, as enlightened baronial master, had established. Valkovski revels in the recollections of secret orgies with a certain
lady who combined an external appearance of austere virtue
with a skill at cruelty that would have awed the Marquis de
Sade. In this instance, it was the woman's clever deception that
delighted him even more than the orgies they shared. Finally,
he has a passionate loathing for all good people,—"Schillers,"
as he calls them,—and he longs to destroy them, to obliterate
their offensive virtue, to crush, if possible, the very memory of
them. In short, he has the qualities of the cosmic Satan who
strives to turn the whole universe into the opposite of God.
Without retribution as far as the perspectives of the novel permit us to see him, he is last mentioned in the epilogue as imitat-
ing the action of Yulian Mastakovich in *A Christmas Tree and
a Wedding* by marrying a child bride with a fortune.

Thus upon the basic figure of Prince Hektor has been fastened
a veritable extravaganza of evil that would have bewildered
Hoffmann.

Thus, too, the whole of *The Insulted and Injured* offers a
notable departure from Dostoevski's previous mode of writing.
Wherein, then, is it indebted to Hoffmann? The indebtedness
may be summed under three counts: the opening scene, which
is based directly, in Dostoevski's pre-exile Hoffmannizing manner, on a passage at the beginning of *Das öde Haus*; the device
of the interlocking plots with their parallels of past and present
time; and the development of Valkovski out of Prince Hektor
in *Kater Murr*.

The impression is left, after the evaluation of *The Insulted
and Injured*, that Dostoevski's interest in Hoffmann was beginning to wane, and the impression is strengthened by his next

major work, *The House of the Dead*. Begun at least as early as
1859 and possibly earlier, the printed version appeared in ir-
regular installments from April 1861 to December 1862, with
the Russian title of *Notes from a Dead House*. Whatever artistry, and the artistry must have been considerable, went into
the composition of these prison memoirs, the book *seems* to be
sober *rapportage* without any admixture of "literature" at all.
Leo Tolstoi professed to prefer it by far to all the rest of Dostoevski's writing, precisely because it was all experience and no
art. Certainly its factual detailing of prison filth and prison
brutality, of human degradation both in prisoner victims and
their sadistic masters, is as far removed from Hoffmann as
possible. One might think Dostoevski was abandoning creative
fiction altogether. Then, in November 1862, before the last
installment of *The House of the Dead* reached the public, *Time*
carried a new short story called *An Unpleasant Predicament,*—
the Russian title: Skverny Anekdot, literally "A Nasty Anecdote," is sometimes rendered as *A Vile Tale*. In this story the
setting is Petersburg and the substance is once again a combination of Gogolian clerks and Hoffmann fantasy. With a cursory
reading, one might, in ignorance of its date, readily assign it to
the year 1848.

3. AN UNPLEASANT PREDICAMENT

The hero of the story is not himself a clerk, but rather a
gentleman. In fact, he is of general's rank. He is the forty-
three-year-old egotist Ivan Ilich Pralinski, who fancies himself
an idealist and a humanitarian. The welfare of his fellow-man,
particularly of the underprivileged, concerns him closely. He is
none the less irate on this winter's evening between eleven and
twelve when he comes from a bachelors' party with two fellow-
gentlemen, to discover that his coachman has failed to wait for
him at the door. Morosely he strikes out homeward on foot,
vowing that the fellow shall rue the hour of his desertion.

The relative mildness of the night, the bright moonlight, and
the champagne he has drunk gradually recall to him his own
magnanimity as he walks along. The fancy takes him to drop
in on a wedding party of one of his clerks, Mr. Pseldonimov, to
display his greatness of heart and, by the way, to receive some
homage, as is, after all, his due. The wedding guests are none
too pleased at his intrusion but they ply him with glass after
glass. Benevolently, Pralinski accepts the drinks as a sign of

honor, unaware either that his hosts are laughing at him or that he himself is very drunk. The rest of the night's events are described as seen by Palinski's eyes,—up to the point where his eyes fail him.

He tries at length to convey some impression of his lofty ideals and of his boundless benevolence, but the guests approach and recede strangely. The room itself is unsteady. An eerie confusion prevails. One young man unaccountably denounces him in anger for his contemptible condescension. Pralinski starts to protest but bows his head instead, bows it until it rests in a plate of blanc mange.

At the instant when Pralinski's consciousness fails him, the delirium ceases. From the absurdly disconnected conversation and the unmotivated comings and goings of the thirty wedding guests, the reader is suddenly dropped into the rational third-person account of the sorry why's and wherefore's of poor Pseldonimov's marriage. The basic reason is his new father-in-law's selection of him as a first-class subject for bullying. The latter pages of the story turn into a coarse farce, with Pralinski put to sleep off his drunkenness in the bridal bed, which he repeatedly befouls with his desperate retchings, while the unhappy newly-weds retire to a feather-bed precariously stretched over chairs. The chairs collapse and pitch bride and groom in a heap upon the floor. When dawn rouses Pralinski to consciousness, he flees without apology and for several days covers his mortified absence from the office with excuses of sickness. But he eventually returns, more convinced than ever of the magnanimity of his soul and of the dignity of his position.

The Gogolian strain may be readily perceived, though without tragic outcome for once, in the meek and bedevilled clerk Pseldonimov. His life has been as harried as his bridal night, and this is only the beginning. His father-in-law has elaborate plans for him, none of them pleasant, and his wife shows signs of being her father's daughter. As for Pralinski, he is a latter-day Very Important Personage, like the one who once oppressed the life of Akaki Akakievich.

But the drunken adventure of Pralinski recalls, though in a much modified form, the adventures which, in the opening chapters of Hoffmann's *Die Brautwahl*, befell forty-eight-year-old Privy Councillor Tusmann, the same who had arranged with his old schoolmate to marry the latter's daughter, young Albertine Vosswinkel. While Tusmann varies the unalterable pattern of his daily life only by reading, in preparation for matrimony, the tract of Thomasius, dated 1710, on the relationship of the sexes, certain persons have decided among themselves that the preposterous pedant shall never wed Albertine. These persons have determined to undertake certain "operations" which shall deter him from such a step. The "operations," however, may not be begun until the equinox. Accordingly, it is on the night of the autumnal equinox that the story begins, between eleven and twelve.

Unaccountably, Tusmann has not reached home, as he invariably does, at the stroke of eleven, but has stopped to behold a most extraordinary apparition in the tower of the City Hall. He plainly sees a woman's form in the tower window. She appears at the first stroke of the hour and disappears at the final stroke. Bemused, Tusmann stares, then unaccountably accepts the invitation of a stranger standing there to come into a wine-shop on the Alexanderplatz.

The sole client in the wine-shop is an elderly Jew named Manasse, one-time treasurer of the Brandenburg Elector but afterwards burned at the stake for sorcery in 1572. Tusmann's companion is Leonhard Turnhäuser zum Thurm, a Swiss, who frequented the court in Berlin in the 1580's as goldsmith, astrologer, and alchemist. How these two worthies happen to be alive and drinking wine in a 19th century wine-shop in Berlin is a point which Hoffmann never makes clear. Oddly enough, Tusmann cannot seem to resist the successive bumpers of wine which Master Leonhard presses upon him. He is fascinated by their talk and now feels impelled to do some talking himself. He sets forth his plans for his marriage to Albertine, but is mightily taken aback when the two gentlemen tax him with being a fatuous dotard. He has just enough wine to be belligerent, and, armed with this courage, denounces Master Leonhard as an imposter, adding that the recent apparition in the City Hall tower was a magic lantern trick. Leonhard advises him to watch his tongue. Suddenly, to the aghast Tusmann, the face of Master Leonhard turns into the face of a fox and leers at him. The Jew laughs at the sight and says he can do better than that. Whereupon, he takes from his pocket a black radish, peels and slices it, then brings his fist down on one slice after another, producing gold-piece after gold-piece. Leonhard catches the gold-pieces, which turn at his touch into dust amid showers of sparks. Tusmann has sufficient strength left to seize his hat and cane and dash out into the street.

It is midnight. The City Hall is brilliantly lighted now and people are dancing inside to gay music. Albertine may be seen among them "immoderately" waltzing. Someone running suddenly bumps into Tusmann and steals his legs. He calls for the police to catch the thief. The ball-scene in the City Hall vanishes. All lights vanish. In the darkness the thief returns and laughingly throws Tusmann the stolen legs. Tusmann begins to run, but at every turn he encounters new obstacles. For some time he compulsively waltzes with a broomstick up and down the Spandauerstrasse, but he wakes at dawn to find himself nestled in the bronze arms of the Great Elector's equestrian statue, from where he climbs down at the peril of his life.

When he comes to report the night's terrors to his old schoolmate Vosswinkel, he is dismayed to find that his friend considers the whole affair a drunken spree. To increase his terror and his discomfiture, the Jew Manasse enters and Vosswinkel receives him as an old friend. Manasse calmly states that Tusmann had been with him in the wine-shop the previous night and had continued drinking until he was barely able to reel out into the street.

Tusmann's protests that he is an abstemious man prevail, however, and for the time being his father-in-law-to-be is reconciled. The marriage plans remain in effect and Tusmann continues his suit. Needless to say, the "operations" likewise continue. Their sequel is less amazing and wonderful than their beginning, but ultimately they work the desired effect. That part of the story has nothing to do with Pralinski.

It is Vosswinkel, the lowliest rationalist in *Die Brautwahl*, who believes that Tusmann's wild night in the Berlin streets was an alcoholic spree. Tusmann knows better. So does the reader. It was the spirit world with which he had come in contact, and the magic of his opponents was mighty. Pralinski, on the other hand, owed his illusion solely to champagne and vodka, as the night of nausea proved only too literally. This is not to say that Dostoevski's understanding was as crassly rationalistic as that of Vosswinkel or that he did not appreciate the tempestuous sweep of imaginative invention, the dazzling virtuosity, and breathless scherzo-like quality of these pages which would be hard to equal anywhere in literature. His purposes were entirely different from Hoffmann's, but the technique used in *Die Brautwahl* served those purposes.   Here was a model to show how the world looked to the eyes of a drunken man.   He used the model to present the middle portion of his story as it looked to the eyes of Pralinski.   How well he succeeded may be tested by the shock the reader feels when Pralinski's eyes close amid the plateful of blanc mange and the style reverts to rational procedures.   The differences between Dostoevski's story and *Die Brautwahl* are very great.   They are differences not only in degree, but in kind.   Yet basically they both present as central figure, a staid and fatuous gentleman in his forties who, by some chance, oversteps his normal drinking limits during a congenial chat with two gentlemen acquaintances, and as a result finds himself around midnight in the midst of a bizarre adventure in the most familiar streets of his native city.   Each is swept along in an ever increasing tempo of emotions and events until he reaches a state of quasi-delirium.   In the course of the night each broadly expounds his most fatuous notions to hostile ears, each is told the bitterest truth about himself, and each refuses to pay the truth any heed.   Each awakes in the sober dawn to an acute humiliation.

Once Pralinski's eyes close amid the blanc mange and the parallels with Hoffmann's story cease, the Gogolian tradition carries the tale to the end, though it, too, is much modified.   The poor-devil clerk is actually a subordinate theme.   It is Pralinski who occupies our attention primarily.   He is a detestable person.   His adventure begins with moral nastiness and ends with the physical nastiness of his retchings.   Yet he learns nothing from his experience, any more than Gogol's Lt. Pirogov in *The Nevski Prospekt* learned anything for being thrashed by the brutish merchant Schiller and his beery friend Hoffmann for improper advances to Frau Schiller.   Within a brief time Lt. Pirogov is dancing again.   Just so, Mr. Pralinski.   Within a brief time he is again dancing the cancan of his fake humanitarianism and admiring his steps as he dances.

It would be an error to look upon *An Unpleasant Predicament* as simply a work in the pre-exile manner and to place it as a belated seventh story in the 1848 series.   Not only does it look downward toward the lowly clerk's position from above, rather than upward from where he views the world, but by its preoccupation with evil, it stands apart from the earlier productions. Its inward-directed analysis and its "nasty" hero are marks of a transitional development leading into *Notes from Underground,* its successor story of 1863, which will open up entirely new perspectives of Dostoevski's art.

But we have already anticipated events by coming up as far as the publication of *An Unpleasant Predicament* in November 1862. Before concluding the review of the exploratory works composed in the years immediately following the exile's return, it is worth while to go back to the third piece that mentions Hoffmann by name in the first issue of *Time* in January 1861. This is not a creative work, but rather a brief essay in which Dostoevski is led to make a few comments directly relative to Hoffmann.

4. "THREE TALES OF EDGAR POE"

The initial number of *Time* carried three translated stories of Poe (1809-1849),—*The Black Cat, The Tell-tale Heart,* and *The Devil in the Belfry,*—to which there was affixed an unsigned editorial preface which has since been identified as Dostoevski's.[7] As with scores of critics before and after him, the subject led Dostoevski to a comparison of Poe with Hoffmann. Through a long first paragraph he gropes his way toward a definition of Poe's original and distinctive type of imagination, without quite finding the words. In the second paragraph he hits on the phrase: "materialistic fantasy." Today he might use the ready-made rubric: "science fiction." Opposed to it, is Hoffmann's "secret, enchanted world" in which the author believed as in a "higher thing." Dostoevski leaves no doubt as to where his own preference lies, for all that he may admire Poe's unique talent:—

> "People call him (Poe) the equal of Hoffmann. We have already said that this is not true. Moreover, Hoffmann is immeasurably greater than Poe as a poet. With Hoffmann there is an ideal, indeed not always explicit, but in this ideal there is purity, there is real beauty, genuine, peculiar to the man. This is most evident in his non-fantastic stories, such as, for example, *Meister Martin,* or that most graceful and charming tale, *Salvator Rosa* (i.e. *Signor Formica*). We have not yet spoken of his best production, *Kater Murr.* What genuine, mature humor, what vigor of realism, what malice, what types and portraits, and with all of these—what thirst for beauty, what bright ideal! If there is fantasy in Poe, it is a kind of materialistic fantasy, if one may speak of such a thing. It is obvious that he is wholly American even in his most fantastic tales."

Brief as the comment is, it is nevertheless striking in several ways. The genuine enthusiasm for Hoffmann's work is apparent not only for what is actually said, but from the very fact that he should say anything of the sort at all in a little foreword ostensibly devoted to the three translations from Poe. That he should select *Kater Murr* for special praise, is understandable, but the counts on which he bestows his praise are surprising. First he speaks of "genuine and mature humor," which he himself never sought to imitate, and which is so remote from the wistful absurdity, never very far from tears, of Gogol's humor, which he did try to imitate. He rightly sees *Kater Murr* as Hoffmann's "best production" and hits on the very quality, its "vigor of realism" which separates it from most of the Tales, at least in degree. Above these excellences hovers the lofty idealism and beauty, which, he says, are part and parcel of Hoffmann's very nature. With these remarks, we may feel sure that, whatever his intention in writing *Netochka Nezvanova*, it was not an attempt to "correct" *Kater Murr*.

The two other titles which he singles out for specific mention are, in themselves, surprising. Nothing in Dostoevski's writing would lead one to suspect that he would admire the somewhat stylized and artificial *Meister Martin* or any of the little group of tales which glorify mediaeval Nürnberg and prepare the way directly for Wagner's *Die Meistersinger*.[8] Certainly he never imitated this aspect of the Tales. It was Hoffmann as "poet of Berlin," the modern metropolis and capital, whom Dostoevski and Gogol paralleled in their composition of "Petersburg Tales." Equally far from Dostoevski, one would think, are the merry pranks of "signor Formica," which are surely a far cry from the tasteless jests of *A Novel in Nine Letters* or, more particularly, of *Another Man's Wife and The Husband under the Bed*. But one may admire the "graceful and charming" in literature and write in quite another vein.

More surprising, however, than the titles mentioned, are those which go unmentioned. In recalling works of Hoffmann, surely *Die Elixiere des Teufels* should have occurred to him, or, if this was not apt for a comparison with Poe, one would expect him to speak of *Der Sandmann* or *Der Magnetiseur*. But he passes over in silence all the "tales of horror and imagination" and indeed all the tales from which he had derived his own earlier works. An over-hasty conclusion would be to say that he wished to avoid such mention as would invite a scrutinizing comparison and disclose his indebtedness to them. A likelier explanation is that he had, by 1861, outgrown his enthusiasm for such works as *Der Sandmann* and *Der Magnetiseur,* or, more precisely, that he had absorbed into himself the virtues they contained, so that he was no longer so impressed by them. Certainly he will never draw on them again for materials to make any further works of his own. The brief remarks quoted suggest two significant things: first, a certain objectivity and distance relative to Hoffmann in general, an admiration for a writer who no longer encroaches on Dostoevski's own literary domain; and second, an enthusiasm for aspects of Hoffmann's writing which he had *not* absorbed into himself, which, perhaps, he has no intention of trying to absorb. Since Dostoevski's Hoffmannism is about to undergo a major change after 1862, the present moment may best be used to review the categories of tales from which he had drawn inspiration in the past, as well as the categories left untouched.

At the head of the list may be placed Hoffmann's two novels, *Die Elixiere des Teufels* and *Kater Murr.* The immense resources of the former have lent only a few touches to *The Double* and to the Yefimov episode of *Netochka Nezvanova,* but we shall have cause to consider its further influence. The latter has contributed one episode to *The Double* and provided the important model of a villain in Prince Hektor, from whom two villains, Pyotr Alexandrovich and Prince Valkovski, have already been created. To the same line will belong Svidrigailov and Stavrogin, though with further vast modifications. Dostoevski's first attempt at a novel was actually an attempt at reworking *Kater Murr.*

A second and surprising category of used works is made up by the Art-tales, which were usually centered in the problem of the artist torn between the urge toward conventional life and marriage on the one hand, and undivided dedication to his art on the other. *Der Artushof* formed the over-all scheme for *The Landlady.* Its pessimistic companion-piece, *Die Jesuiterkirche in G.,* was fundamental to the first long section of *Netochka Nezvanova,* to which *Rat Krespel* added minor details. From *Die Fermate* was made a totally different kind of story, *A Little Hero.* The fifth and last of the **Art-tale group, *Das Fräulein von Scudery,*** will have some bearing on *Crime and Punishment.*

The "horror" tales, which are not very aptly named and which have always received more attention than was their due, form a third category of Dostoevski's borrowings. Here belong the twin stories *Der Magnetiseur* and *Der unheimliche Gast,* as well as *Der Sandmann,* all of which were ingeniously interwoven with *Der Artushof* to make *The Landlady.* It is interesting to note in passing that Dostoevski never made use of an actual ghost story such as *Der schwebende Teller* (otherwise called *Eine Spukgeschichte*) or of the ghost episodes in *Das Majorat* or in *Aus dem Leben dreier Freunde.* Here, too, if not wholly appropriately, may be grouped *Die Abenteuer der Sylvesternacht,* in which not the quasi-supernatural Dapertutto, but rather the motif of the lost mirror-image and the adventures of the "travelling enthusiast" were used in writing *The Double.* And finally, *Das öde Haus,* from which only the opening scene is concerned in the opening scene of *The Insulted and Injured.*

The musician tale *Ritter Gluck* lent an important motif, no longer connected with music, to *A Faint Heart,* while the central figure may possibly be involved in the conception of *An Honest Thief.* The violinist tale *Der Baron von B.* was probably involved, though the connection is debatable, in the life of the would-be violinist Yefimov.

The remaining works are as heterogeneous as the Russian stories with which they are related. The scheme of *Haimatochare* served as a model for the epistolary mystifications of *A Novel in Nine Letters.* The fragment *Die Genesung* was probably the inspiration of the love scene unintentionally witnessed by the narrator amid the lovely garden at the close of *A Little Hero.* A striking passage from *Datura fastuosa* seems to relate to *A Christmas Tree and a Wedding,* while the latter's immediate successor story, *White Nights,* is derived from a section of *Aus dem Leben dreier Freunde,* both directly and at one remove through Gogol's *The Nevski Prospekt.* Lastly, *Die Brautwahl,* which is to be connected certainly with *An Unpleasant Predicament,* lent also a few details to *The Double* and possibly suggested some part of the idea of *A Christmas Tree and a Wedding.* Such a group of Hoffmann works can hardly be labelled anything other than "Miscellaneous."

The inventory includes eighteen titles, including the two novels, from Hoffmann's total output. There will be occasion to add only two, or perhaps three, more in the course of further discussion. It is interesting to observe that the choices fall indiscriminately among the three major collections into which Hoffmann gathered his scattered stories during his life-time, as well as among the posthumously published group of the *Letzte*

Erzählungen. Yet, in contrast to the approximately twenty titles, stands the complete list of Hoffmann's works of fiction, which includes well over sixty items even if the various pieces of *Kreisleriana* are counted as one; if they are reckoned as separate works, the list comes roughly to seventy-five titles.

Distribution of this remarkable output (of approximately a dozen years!) into categories is a perplexing task, involving necessarily much over-lapping of motifs from story to story. Among some of the readily identifiable groups which have no connection with Dostoevski are two which have already been mentioned, the tales of mediaeval Nürnberg and the actual ghost stories. Nor does Dostoevski show any interest in the fairy-tales for children, such as *Nussknacker und Mausekönig* (the inspiration for Chaikovski's *Nutcracker Suite*) and *Das fremde Kind.* The concept of "Meisterschaft," which occupied Hoffmann in the Nürnberg tales and elsewhere, finds no counterpart in the Russian works. Except for the very slight short story *The Crocodile* (1865), which will be discussed in the next chapter, there is no suggestion of the many speaking animals, in the creation of which Hoffmann was exceedingly dextrous, especially with the felines and canines of *Kater Murr.* One feels that Dostoevski was probably well advised in this omission. Quite possibly it was his own very subtle artistic instinct that kept Dostoevski away from those stories where Hoffmann had worked somewhat too close to the productions of contemporaries he admired:—*Ignaz Denner,* which, for all its good points, cannot help but suffer from comparison with Kleist's *Michael Kohlhaas*; *Das Gelübde,* which pales indeed beside Kleist's *Die Marquise von O.*; *Die Räuber,* which infelicitously parallels the situation in Schiller's famous drama of the same name; or that section of *Der Zusammenhang der Dinge* which advances a new version of Goethe's Mignon. In avoiding a unique and striking story like *Die Bergwerke zu Falun* Dostoevski may simply have been deterred by the elaborate Nature-symbolism with which Hoffmann overwove the basic historical anecdote, but it is more probable that the anecdote itself did not recommend itself to him for further treatment,—as it did recommend itself to more than one German author. Despite avid interest in real-life events as he found them in newspapers, at least during the latter half of his career, he preferred to use only those where the human will could be seen to operate, not one like this famous, utterly answerless, happening at the Swedish mine-village of Falun, where the corpse of a young man, perfectly preserved and petrified by mineral acids, is discovered inside the mountain; the villagers can neither identify the youth nor exactly date his old-fashioned attire, until an ancient crone comes up on crutches and beholds her fiancé precisely as he looked on the morning of their wedding day when he went to the mine on an errand and never returned. Finally, Dostoevski never imitated the device,—essentially un-realistic in nature,—of the frame-tale which had been made famous by the "Serapion brethren" in the great four-volume collection of 1819-1821.

But the really significant omission of Dostoevski is that of the long Märchen, which, after *Kater Murr*, represent Hoffmann's most original and most durable creation. These are four in number: *Der goldene Topf,* earliest written, simplest, and most popular, which forms part of the *Fantasiestücke* (1814); and the three independent works which enter into none of the collections, *Klein Zaches* (1819), *Prinzessin Brambilla* (1820), and *Meister Floh* (1822). Yet it is apparently to these that Dostoevski has reference in the first paragraph of his foreword to the three translations from Poe, when he says:

> "(Hoffmann) personifies the forces of Nature in forms: he introduces into his stories sorceresses, spirits, and sometimes even seeks his ideal beyond the earth, in some extraordinary world, accepting this world as a higher thing, as if he himself believed in the actual existence of this secret, enchanted world."

If these words are interpreted to mean that Hoffmann devoted long pages to the profitless exposition of things "which simply do not exist," the omission is understandable enough. But such shallow rationalism is hardly to be credited to Dostoevski, and it is practically inconceivable that he should have missed their purport. These Märchen, it is true, are intimately involved in the complexities of German Romantic philosophy, aspects of which they portray in the form of grandiose "myths," somewhat in Plato's sense of the term. The philosophical ideas in question had yielded precedence, by Dostoevski's time, to newer modes of thought, such as those of Hegel and Karl Gustav Carus. Yet Dostoevski evinced particular interest in these latter writers in the years immediately after release from the Omsk prison, and, what is more, the new writers were sufficiently akin to their predecessors to make for a better understanding of the Romanticists proper. The elaborate "myths" did require a variety of inventive combinations totally alien to Dostoevski's genius.

Often of a cosmic scope, and sometimes concerned with the mystical concept of the annihilation of time, they tended to merge individuals into types which have an allegorical function amid various personified aspects of Nature. From the whole course of Dostoevski's evolution as an artist and from the cursory allusions to *Kater Murr* in the present essay, it is clear that he is greatly concerned with the literary methods of portraying characters. When, in his latter novels, he comes to deal with ideological matters, these will be of quite another sort from the Romantic thought underlying, say, *Meister Floh,* and the methods he will employ in their literary expression will be completely at variance with those of Hoffmann's mythologizing Märchen.

For all of this, the Märchen are far from being complicated philosophical allegories with lifeless characters. On the contrary, the personages live independent and vivid existences, bearing their "philosophical" meanings quite effortlessly amid an atmosphere of wit and humor that precludes all heaviness. It is a puzzle how Dostoevski could have avoided using a character like the delightful heroine of *Meister Floh,* Dörtje Elverdink, who, with her tantalizing ambivalence of emotions, is more *like* a Dostoevskian heroine than any character in the stories actually used in his adaptations from Hoffmann.

In the next chapter it will be necessary to examine, under the heading of "Acis and Galatea," a curiously anomalous passage which recurs in no less than three of Dostoevski's mature novels and which may, after all, reflect some influence of the great Märchen upon his writing. For the present, however, it is of more concern to take some general view of Dostoevski's attitude toward his German predecessor at this crucial stage of his post-exile career.

5. DOSTOEVSKI'S OPINION OF HOFFMANN

However one reads the little foreword to the Poe translation, it is impossible to construe the remarks as the objections of a doctrinaire realist to a Romantic author and his work. Nor was Dostoevski any such. Like the "classicism" of Brahms, his "realism" is Romanticism in a new guise. He was a kindred spirit to Hoffmann. The differences between them are not so much differences in kind as in generations. Dostoevski understood Hoffmann's nature and appreciated his art fully. If, after 1862, he worked very little from Hoffmann models, there is no question of a thankless rejection of an author hitherto much admired—and much used. It is simply a case of dynamically changing thought along with changing times, and of having absorbed all of Hoffmann's techniques that he was able to absorb. And that was a great deal. In fact, the amount is so great that we now come soberly to accept Dostoevski's statement of 1838, when he claims to have read "all of Hoffmann," rather than to smile and consider the words as an excited youth's exaggeration.

Nor is there any reason to believe that the years after 1862 made any alteration in Dostoevski's opinion of Hoffmann. Only twice after this date does he refer to him by name.[9] One occasion comes in *The Possessed* (1870-72), where the character Karmazinov, a caricature of Turgenev, reads his rather silly rhapsodic "paper" entitled *Merci* to the persons assembled at the "fête." The "paper" does present a preposterous medley of things German and things Romantic, but the ridicule is directed at Karmazinov-Turgenev, not at the compound factors of his silly medley, though it must be confessed that Dostoevski at the time of *The Possessed* was in an ill humor with everything and everybody that was German. However, if he wished even then to ridicule Hoffmann, we would expect something worse than the following lines in the rhapsody *Merci*:—

> "Hoffmann appears on the scene, the wood-nymph whistles a tune from Chopin, and suddenly out of the fog appears Ancus Martius over the roofs of Rome, wearing a laurel wreath."

A final reference is made in a journalistic article of December 1876, called *An Anecdote from Children's Lives,* in which the author is commenting on truancy as a prelude to juvenile delinquency.[10] Formerly, Dostoevski fondly opines, "one or two generations back," truancy resulted from too-vivid day-dreams,—

> "well, for example, to escape to Venice after having read about Venice in the novels of Hoffmann or George Sand—I knew one such fellow. . . ."

A curious *lapsus memoriae* is involved here, since among all Tales of Hoffmann only one, *Doge und Dogaresse,* takes place in Venice.[11] Perhaps "Venice" is an odd synecdoche for "Italy," but, if so, it comes as a surprise. The "one such fellow" whom Dostoevski recalls was undoubtedly himself. Even in 1876 he still thought of himself as the dreamer-hero of *White Nights,* whose reveries included, among dozens of other things, "friendship with Hoffmann" and the glorious reunion of parted lovers "in a *palazzo* (it must be in a *palazzo*)" in "the divinely eternal city" of Venice.

Even in so casual and indirect an allusion, Dostoevski indicates that Hoffmann signified to him some fervor of aspiration, some Romantic ideal.

IX

THE TURNING POINT AND AFTER

With the year 1863 a major change begins to make itself felt in Dostoevski's life and in his writings. There is an acceleration in the tempo of his existence, and one after another those characteristics now most commonly associated with him put in their appearance. It was, for instance, the year in which he made his first European trip. To finance the journey, he borrowed, as he will repeatedly borrow, from the Fund for Needy Authors. The gambling mania takes possession of him. The pursuit of Polina Suslova, the bespectacled lady medical student, adds a grotesque quality to his travels. His consumptive and perhaps unfaithful wife dies in his absence. His animosities become vociferous, against all nationalities except his own, against revolutionaries in general. His antipathy towards Turgenev begins to assume a rabid tone. Financial distress becomes chronic with him. The dreamer aspect of his personality acquires a religious cast, while, opposed to it, a kind of ruthless aggressiveness makes him assert his will and opinions as never before. When, in this same year 1863, his magazine *Time* is suppressed as the result of an editorial blunder, he immediately replaces it with a new magazine, *The Epoch* (Epokha), which reflects his changed attitudes.

It was quite appropriately *The Epoch* which in January and February 1864 carried his new story, *Notes from Underground.* It is a story in which structure and plot are abandoned to make way for untrammeled and passionate outpourings of a troubled and exasperated heart. More essay than story, more confession than essay, the work seethes with the "underground man's" suffering and delight in suffering, with the conflicts of his inordinate pride and his deliberate self-abasement. Its heat is the heat of a forge where all the ores of self and art are now molten. These are about to pour together into a great new mold where Dostoevski's first world masterpiece will form:—*Crime and Punishment.* Into the new alloy has passed, along with many other substances, the metal of Hoffmannian art.

It will be futile to search in *Crime and Punishment* or in any subsequent work for an application of the well-used formula of Gogol plus Hoffmann plus Dostoevski himself. There are no further cases of superimposition of Hoffmann plots and episodes to construct a new work.   Yet the Hoffmannian element persists, transformed and many times undemonstrable.   But it is there.   It is part of the alloy.   An example in point may be seen in the case of *The Crocodile,* the very slight short story of 1865 immediately preceding *Crime and Punishment.*

1. THE CROCODILE

Again appropriately, it was *The Epoch* which printed this little story in February 1865.   The author roundly denied that the piece was intended as a satire, but the general opinion holds in spite of his statements that its purpose was a parody of the recent arrest of the revolutionary critic Chernyshevski and his exile to penal servitude for fourteen years in Siberia.   However far to the right Dostoevski's political opinions had veered and however much he might personally dislike Chernyshevski, it is difficult to see how he could have made a jest of the man's precipitation into the torments of the living hell from which he himself had not so long before escaped with such profound relief.   Yet such seems to be the purport of the fact that Ivan Matveich, the hero of the story, is one day swallowed up by a crocodile at a Petersburg zoological exhibit.   From within the belly of the beast, which he declares to be perfectly hollow and of the consistency of gutta-percha, Ivan Matveich explains his plan to be kept in a tank in his wife's salon and to expound philosophical systems for the enlightenment of the curious who will undoubtedly flock to behold the marvel of the speaking crocodile.   His skittish wife has already begun a new flirtation, however, and is not at all pleased with her husband's plan.   The outcome of the matter is left in doubt as the story closes.

The mock-serious humor, particularly in the case of the official, Timofei Semyonovich, is partly in Gogol's tradition, while the caricature of the seedy German owner of the crocodile amounts to sheer xenophobia.   Readers of *Kater Murr* may be reminded of the "unseen maiden" whose voice spoke from the transparent crystal ball for the audiences who attended Severino's exhibitions of occult devices.   The "unseen maiden" was actually the Mignon-like gypsy girl Chiara, whom Severino cruelly confined in a small chest, whence he managed to project her voice to the crystal ball.   Meister Abraham, himself a skilled practitioner of occult skills, was at first deceived by the device, but later discovered the secret and set the captive free.   *Kater Murr* also offers talking animals in plenty, beginning with the inimitable Murr himself and including all his feline family and canine acquaintances. Ivan Matveich is, of course, quite a different creature from either Chiara, the "unseen maiden," or from Tom-cat Murr, yet a combination of the two is the likeliest source for this piece of Dostoevskian grotesquerie.

2. CRIME AND PUNISHMENT

At the opposite pole of literary creation from this cruel jest stands the monumental *Crime and Punishment* of 1866. The origins of the novel are manifold and complex. The earliest impulse toward its creation was received, as we know, from Dickens's *David Copperfield*, from which the figure of the improvident Mr. Micawber was adapted into the character of Marmeladov. Notebook jottings of Dostoevski's reveal that the subject of the projected work was to be a study in the effects of drunkenness on a family. A tentative title of *The Drunkards* was chosen. This initial scheme was soon subordinated to larger plans, in which the hero Raskolnikov soon emerges as an infinitely more complex version of Pushkin's Hermann, the central character of *The Queen of Spades*,—through which Raskolnikov is ultimately traceable to Hoffmann. Then was added the figure of Sonya, the saintly prostitute, the holily sinning embodiment of the principle of Good, and after her the figure of the tiger-like Svidrigailov, Evil itself stalking its prey. With each addition the hero, his motivation, his course of action, the plot as a whole, increased in complexity, until the completed work stood as a grand portrayal of sin and the struggle with conscience, of ultimate submission and redemption.

Assimilated, too, into the final composite is many a motif from Hoffmann. The whole novel, for instance, is a "Petersburg Tale" on the grand scale. The very intensity that marks scene after scene of the work suggests a Hoffmannian atmosphere, though at no point is it possible to ascertain a specific source. The intensity is surely effected in part by the use of dream sequences. Raskolnikov's horrible vision of the horse beaten to death by drunken peasants has about it a totally un-Hoffmannian ferocity, yet the artistic use of a dream to illustrate a soul-state is quite Hoffmannian. Svidrigailov's memorable nightmare is even further from the spirit of Hoffmann and at the same time still more Hoffmannian in its deceptive interpenetration of waking and sleep, of reality and irreality, for within his dream Svidrigailov fancies that he wakes from dreaming and therewith

confronts a new set of dream illusions.   Even when he is awake
and about, there is a Hoffmannian quality about Svidrigailov.
He comes and goes mysteriously, his past veiled in mystery, he
has an air of being not entirely human, like some of the sinister
old men whom Hoffmann depicted.   The Coppelius of *Der Sandmann* is an example taken at random.   Svidrigailov is also subject to dreams and hallucinations.   He insists that his late wife
has visited him three times as a ghost.   Dostoevski's notebooks
clearly indicate that he was modelled on two fellow prisoners
in his own chain-gang of the Omsk prison, the famous Orlov
and Petrov.   That Svidrigailov's intense self-will derives from
this source is incontrovertible, but his visions, his hallucinations,
his mystery have another origin.   His crime of child-rape relates him to Prince Valkovski of *The Insulted and Injured,* with
whom he also shares the crime of beating a peasant to death,
and to the Yulian Mastokovich of *A Christmas Tree and a Wedding.*   His heart is also afflicted with many of the exasperations
of the Underground Man.   In short, he is a concentration of
evils from all corners of Dostoevski's experience, both from life
and from books.   Through Valkovski, his kinship may be traced
to Prince Hektor of *Kater Murr.*   Through Yulian Mastakovich,
the line goes back to Fermino Valies of *Datura fastuosa.*   Ultimately he is a composite of traits from all of Hoffmann's Mo-
linari-villains, who among them duplicate several of his crimes:
Berthold of *Die Jesuiterkirche in G.,* who was believed to have
murdered his wife and who did commit suicide; Franzesko the
painter and his descendant Medardus in *Die Elixiere des Teufels,*
who between them left few stones of evil unturned; Fermino
Valies of *Datura fastuosa,* who tempted the adolescent girl; and
Prince Hektor of *Kater Murr,* who simultaneously wooed a wife
and a mistress, untroubled by the murder which he had committed.   Yet, with all his crimes, Svidrigailov proves more humanly credible than Prince Valkovski.   He speaks more softly,
he is marked by a certain pathetically lost quality,—in spite of
the author's intention of making him a veritable "tiger,"—he
rants less, he has less "cosmic" intentions.   His human scope
makes his evil the more intense, his fierce will more terrifying.
    At the opposite pole from Svidrigailov stands Sonya, the
wholly passive, Madonna-like figure, who patiently watches and
prays.   Squarely between them is Raskolnikov.   On the one hand,
he sees himself mirrored, even caricatured, in the man of many
evils.   Each has committed murder.   Each in his alienation from

society and in his own way, seeks love, Svidrigailov in Dunya, Raskolnikov in Sonya. After the crisis, each comes to terms with his fate, the evil man by despair and suicide, the man mixed of evil and of good, by suffering and atonement. For if Raskolnikov partakes of the nature of Svidrigailov, he also shares Sonya's aspiration toward holiness. He is the wavering sinner placed between the saintly girl and the unredeemed villain. How like the pattern of *Die Elixiere des Teufels*! There Medardus hesitated repeatedly amid his sins, now leaning toward the unredeemed Viktorin, now leaning toward the holiness of Aurelie, who in the climactic scene is actually recognized as a saint. In the parallels of Raskolnikov's and Svidrigailov's lives and crimes lies a residue of the Medardus-Viktorin Double-relationship, and in the struggle through sin toward redemption there is more than a chance reflection of Hoffmann's purpose in *his* novel of crime and atonement.

One further work of Hoffmann's may have some connection with *Crime and Punishment*. This is the well known *Das Fräulein von Scudery*. Its setting, unique among German Romantic stories, is the Paris of Louis XIV, and at the outset we learn that the city is in the grip of a frightful terror. A ruthless band of murderers is abroad by night and no one's life is safe. The truth of the matter proves to be that there is no band of murderers at all, but one sole though deadly killer, the master goldsmith René Cardillac. He is a great artist in jewels and metals, and once having produced a masterpiece, he cannot bear to part with it to the purchaser. When he does part with it, the purchaser becomes a marked man. With method and caution, Cardillac observes his habits and customary walks, then chooses a place and time of ambush, and slays the owner with a thin stiletto. Thus the work of art returns to its artist maker, who loves it best, unmindful of the blood shed for its sake. One night Cardillac is himself murdered by an unknown assailant and circumstantial evidence throws the guilt upon his innocent assistant, Olivier Brusson, who is also the fiancé of his daughter Madelon. It is the latter's grief which first moves the elderly and noble Mlle de Scudéry to champion the cause of Olivier. She undertakes no easy task, for she has opposing her the astute police official, La Régnie, who has been appointed by the king himself to seek out the parties guilty of terrorizing the capital.

La Régnie is represented as a man of ugly physical appearance and with a devotion to duty that leads him to be ruthless to the point where people are as frightened of him as of the supposed murdering band. His efforts are ably seconded by his subordinate, Desgrais, whose energy is boundless. When the innocent Olivier falls into the hands of these two, all seems lost, and only with the greatest efforts is he finally extricated from their toils. Both these representatives of the law are kept more or less in the background of the story, the prime interest being centered in the artist-criminal Cardillac and in Mlle de Scudéry's rescue of the lovers, yet here are ready-at-hand models for Porfiry Petrovich and "the explosive lieutenant" Zametov in *Crime and Punishment*. Porfiry Petrovich is, of course, far more important a character than La Régnie and much more carefully delineated. Some of his astuteness may well derive from Poe's C. Auguste Dupin, the immediate ancestor of Sherlock Holmes and, through him, of an unending series of cunning detectives; his tenacity, and probably other qualities, owe even more to Gervais in Victor Hugo's *Les Misérables*. Yet certain factors speak for the connection with Hoffmann's story. Raskolnikov's crime is itself a kind of art-crime and he himself, with his hyper-sensitive nature, is a kind of artist, somewhat in the way Ordynov "had the soul of an artist," though with no connection whatsoever with either the elderly Cardillac or the rather colorless Olivier. In both works, too, the police officer is a solid bourgeois for whom art,—or hyper-sensitivity,—count as nothing and the apprehension of the criminal counts as everything. An irreconcilable clash of Romanticist and Realist underlies the duel of wills between police officials and hero in both instances.

At best, however, *Das Fräulein von Scudery* may be said to contribute certain details to Dostoevski's novel. It is with the central trio of characters from *Die Elixiere des Teufels* that the real analogy with *Crime and Punishment* lies.

3. THE ETERNAL HUSBAND

After the impressive gathering of forces that produced *Crime and Punishment*, Dostoevski seems to have been set free from the past. Certainly the work made a far more effective summary of his development than the symbolic act of 1860, when Dostoevski reedited his "collected works" in two volumes. As an artist he could now create at will, and set models, not follow them; as a man, he frequently found his art harried by the demands of creditors. Thus, before *Crime and Punishment* was

even completed, he saw himself forced to produce a new work to
meet the terms of a wretched publisher's contract which he had
signed in a reckless moment of need. The hastily composed short
novel *The Gambler* was the result. A large share of autobiography in the story made it possible for him to finish the dictated
manuscript in twenty-six days. Had there been less pressure of
time, some touch of *Spielerglück* might have appeared in it, but
as it stands, there is not a trace of Hoffmann. Nor is there any
perceptible trace of Hoffmann in *The Idiot*, the next of the great
novels, which appeared serially in *The Russian Messenger*
through the months of 1868. Then, most unexpectedly, in the
interval between *The Idiot* and *The Possessed*, comes a work
with a partial source in the Tales of Hoffmann.

Since April 1867 Dostoevski had been living in Europe, where
he found the need for money no less pressing than at home.
From Dresden in 1869 he mailed the manuscript of a short novel
for publication in N. N. Strakhov's magazine *Dawn* (Zarya) in
order to raise some ready cash. This minor production between
two great novels was called *The Eternal Husband*.

Originally planned as a comic work, *The Eternal Husband*
never quite loses the sense of the ridiculous amid the more
serious matter which the author introduced as the manuscript
grew beneath his pen. In the rather slow-paced opening chapters the reader is acquainted with Alexei Ivanovich Velchaninov,
a good looking scapegrace whose prime of youth has passed, and
with the mysterious individual who for some time has dogged
his footsteps. The latter is Pavel Pavlovich Trusotski, the
"eternal husband." Some six years previously, Velchaninov had
been a frequent guest at the home of Trusotski and his wife.
Subsequently, after Velchaninov's departure, a certain young
officer had been a frequent guest in the Trusotski household,—
for a five-year period. Only after the death of his beloved
Natalya Vasilevna this past March, has Trusotski discovered, in
the reading of his wife's papers, that his wife had always been
unfaithful to him and that his adored child is not his, but Velchaninov's. He has sought out the young officer, but the latter
had died just before he found him. But Velchaninov, the
greater enemy, is still alive, and Trusotski has come for revenge. A duel of wills develops in a series of episodes, some
serious, some comic. At one point, the ineffectual Trusotski,—
the very name is based on *trus*, the Russian word for "coward,"—
does actually try to murder Velchaninov while the latter lies

asleep and ill, but the scene ends with Trusotski disarmed by the sick man and tied up with a window-shade-cord until dawn, when Velchaninov turns him loose in the street.

Only with the final chapter (17), which is a kind of epilogue, does the hint of a Hoffmannian source occur.

Two years later, Velchaninov is travelling to Odessa when he unexpectedly encounters Trusotski anew in a provincial railway station. An overdressed lady is trying to settle a handsome young officer in the train, but she is beset with a two-fold difficulty: first, her officer friend is thoroughly drunk, and second, another drunken individual is making offensive remarks at her. Velchaninov intervenes and drives the latter away. The overdressed lady is profuse with her thanks and with her complaints about her husband, who, she says, is never on hand when needed. Just then the husband appears. It is Trusotski. He is once again married, and even now he is in the act of accompanying his wife's lover, the drunken young officer, to the train. As a final drop of bitterness, he must now stand silent while his wife offers the intimacy of his home to the always attractive Velchaninov in an unmistakable way. Almost tearfully he inquires whether Velchaninov intends to accept the invitation. To his inexpressible relief, the answer is: No. At the close of the story he runs to obey the shrill summons of his wife, the train bears him away, and Velchaninov waits for a different train.

Absurdity and pathos characterize Trusotski, the "eternal husband," just as they do Ludwig in Hoffmann's *Der Zusammenhang der Dinge*. From the beginning of the story he is shown under the spell of a pretentious society beauty named Viktorine, but the long middle section is occupied with the adventures of his friend Euchar, who has volunteered to fight in the Spanish forces during the peninsular campaign against Napoleon. Euchar, like Velchaninov, is handsome, gracious, and popular wherever he goes, while the footling Ludwig makes himself a parody of gallantry in his pursuit of Viktorine. The final chapter, which is a kind of epilogue, brings the two friends together again after a separation of two years. Euchar's travels have once again brought him to the town of W. As he alights from the coach, the first person he spies is Ludwig. Amid mutual expressions of delight at meeting again, Ludwig urgently invites Euchar to his home, adding that for a little more than a year he has been married to the beautiful Viktorine. Upon ar-

rival at the house, the behavior of the maids gives sure indication that Ludwig is a cipher in his own home. He occupies the
difficult interval until Viktorine makes her appearance by telling at length the story of his wooing. It is obvious to the reader,
as it is to Euchar, that the wooing was a preposterous pursuit
by an unwanted suitor. He digresses in a tirade of adoration of
his wife, only to be interrupted by the impertinent maid, who
says that her mistress is shocked that her husband should bring
a caller when he knows perfectly well that she is ill to the point
of death. Euchar tries to withdraw gracefully, but Ludwig is
intent on continuing his story. On the eve of his marriage, he
says, he chanced on Viktorine's diary and found that all entries
were concerned with a passionate and hopeless love affair. As
Viktorine entered the room he cried out that he had never loved
another as her diary claims. With a scream, Viktorine fled from
him, crying, "Unhappy man, I didn't mean you!" Just whom
she did mean becomes apparent when she now comes in, sees
Euchar, and faints. That evening she confesses everything to
Euchar and assures him that her love is long since dead.

The embarrassing scene in Ludwig's home is extraordinary
with Hoffmann, who otherwise never dwelt on the comic aspects
of marriage or on household humor. The scene is an isolated
episode in a story devoted to quite different matters, but within
the brief space Hoffmann managed to concentrate considerable
humor and also to imply a certain pathos, without breaking the
pleasant mood of a graceful comedy of errors. Neither con-
jugal infidelity nor revenge enters into consideration for a moment, and Euchar, perhaps a little implausibly for such a man
of the world, has never so much as guessed Viktorine's passion
for him, much less taken advantage of it.

Dostoevski's transformation of the material must have begun
with the question: But what if Euchar *had* been guilty? Euchar, guilty and aware of his guilt, is already Velchaninov, to
all intents and purposes. Ludwig, aware of his plight, is only
half way to becoming Trusotski. All the rest is Dostoevski's invention. Where Ludwig read Viktorine's diary and remained as
unenlightened as before, thus keeping the tone of pure comedy,
Trusotski found the bitter truth in Natalya Vasilevna's papers
and felt conflicting impulses of love and hate which strain the
comic mood to the breaking point. The strain is further increased by Dostoevski's further amplifications, such as Trusotski's obsession with revenge, his neglect of his daughter which

is the partial cause of her death, and his fantastic competitive wooing of the daughter of Zakhlebinin. Omitted, of course, in compensation for these developments, are all the elements that make up the bulk of Hoffmann's story, the peninsular wars and the romance of Euchar with the Mignon-like Spanish girl. This material offered little attraction to Dostoevski. It was the amusing scene at Ludwig's house in the final chapter that caught his eye. How effective a close he thought it made, is evidenced by his own final chapter, which parallels it closely, even to the two-year interval since the preceding action. It is a curious and striking fact, that, even in an instance of comedy, the spirit of Hoffmann has been rendered more somber in Russian adaptation.

4. "Acis and Galatea"

The kind of relationship that exists between *The Eternal Husband* and *Der Zusammenhang der Dinge* suggests a contact with Hoffmann more recent than a recollection of readings from a decade previous or from the years before exile. Just before he wrote the story, Dostoevski had moved from Italy to Germany, and the actual composition was done in Dresden. The possibility exists, then, that in 1869 he had come upon some collection of Hoffmann's work and was reading in it, probably at random, and chanced on the out-of-the-way story *Der Zusammenhang der Dinge*, which gave him the notion for his new work. Perhaps, in running through various Tales of Hoffmann, he was reminded of other ideas conceived long ago and since relegated to the back of his mind, for it was precisely at this time that he made his first plans for a supreme novel with which to crown his career, *The Life of a Great Sinner*. This subject will be the concern of the following chapter, but before it is discussed there is one further detail to be considered in the matter of Hoffmannian elements in the works of the 1870's prior to *The Brothers Karamazov*. These works include the two major novels *The Possessed* (1870-72) and *A Raw Youth* (1875), as well as five rather undistinguished short stories, all of which were written for Dostoevski's newspaper column called *The Diary of a Writer*. The latter are all remote from the spirit of Hoffmann, and, as for the novels, they too have no connection with the German tales except in so far as they draw on the materials accumulated in preparation for the master-novel, *The Life of a Great Sinner*. Yet running through these works is a motif which has puzzled more than one attentive reader of Dostoevski, the uncharacteristic dream passage which may be designated as "Acis and Galatea."

Three times it appears, with only minor modifications, once in the famous suppressed chapter of *The Possessed*, entitled *At Tikhon's*, again in Versilov's vision in *A Raw Youth*, and a third time in the short story of 1877 called *The Dream of a Ridiculous Man*. Stavrogin, who relates the vision in the first instance, identifies the source specifically as a painting by Claude Lorrain in the Dresden art gallery, bearing the title "Acis and Galatea," though he himself always called it "The Golden Age." The setting is "a corner of the Greek archipelago" and the time "some three thousand years ago." In that place and time dwelt a primaeval race of men, happy, innocent, inspired by general love, uncorrupted—yet. At sight of this pagan Utopia, Dostoevski makes Stavrogin exclaim:

> "Oh, marvellous dream, lofty illusion! The most improbable of all visions, to which mankind throughout its existence has given its best energies, for which it has sacrificed everything, for which it has pined and been tormented, for which its prophets were crucified and killed, without which nations will not desire to live, and without which they cannot even die!"

Here lived, Stavrogin insists, "beautiful men and women," and the element of sensuous loveliness is emphasized by details like "caressing azure waves, rocks and islands, a shore in bloom, afar a magic panorama, a beckoning sunset. . . ." Then he adds: "Words fail one." Words probably did fail Dostoevski, whose gigantic powers as a writer did not include the power to evoke convincingly any visions of rapturous beauty.

Such concepts of lovely and sinless Hellas are common enough in western European literature since the time of Rousseau, but one normally thinks of them as alien to Dostoevski, the prophet of "the Russian Christ." Nor are they to be found in the works of German Romanticists, who, as a group, were hostile to Hellas as an ideal. Yet visions of ideal lands and ideal states are among the most characteristic features of their works. The most exalted of them is to be found at the conclusion of the Märchen (Chapter IX) of Novalis's *Heinrich von Ofterdingen*, where nothing less is conceived than the end of time itself and the full realization of the perfected universe. Not quite so vast and not quite so logically derived from a progression of philosophical thought, but quite as beautiful in a different way, are the ideal lands proposed in those four long Märchen of Hoffmann enumerated in the previous chapter. The most simply conceived of them is the "Atlantis," to which Anselmus, the hero of *Der goldene Topf,* escapes at the end of the story. It is clearly a land of ideal art and ideal artists, where stupidity and ugliness no longer exist. It is also eternally coexistent with the present moment and attainable by anyone who has the will and the sensitivity to perceive it. The noblest in conception is the "Famagusta" of *Meister Floh,* the last of the series (1822). "Famagusta" is the pristine world of beauty and wonder which is eternal and indestructible but which has been lost from view. It is most nearly to be defined as a state of eternal childhood, though without the faintest trace of mawkishness about it. The entire Märchen consists of a progressive revelation to the characters themselves of their own true identities within the land of Famagusta, which is in turn reestablished with the guidance of the human heart when these identities are fully revealed. It is not only the realm of the individual's own childhood, but also of the childhood of the human race and of the earth itself. It is the time when Nature, unhampered by human perversity and false intellectuality, was still freely creative and with sheer joy multiplied the forms of matter. It is this very activity which the hero, Peregrinus Tyss, beholds when, putting Meister Floh's magic lens in his eye, he gazes into the depths of Dörtje Elverdink's mind and memory. He sees plants transforming themselves at will into minerals, minerals turning into men, men into animals, animals into flowers, and so on infinitely, and every change is toward a stronger and more beautiful form. It is the state of affairs which will be resumed when the heart will have reasserted supremacy over the meddlesome and erring intellect,—when the Romantic ideal will have triumphed over shallow 18th century Rationalism. In other words, Peregrinus beholds the process of Nature of which Novalis in *Heinrich von Ofterdingen* ventured to conceive the conclusion.

It was to such aspects of Hoffmann's writing that Dostoevski referred in the passage previously cited from his foreword to the "Three Tales of Edgar Poe":—

> "(Hoffmann) personifies the forces of Nature in forms . . . and sometimes even seeks his ideal beyond the earth, in some extraordinary world, accepting this world as a higher thing, as if he himself believed in the actual existence of this secret, enchanted world."

The bold, and frankly undemonstrable, hypothesis is hereby

advanced that the thrice-repeated "Acis and Galatea" vision in Dostoevski's works is the *equivalent* of the "secret, enchanted worlds" of Hoffmann's Märchen, and that it occurs and recurs because Dostoevski, either since readings or rereadings of Hoffmann in Dresden, or from earlier readings, or from both, was profoundly impressed with the "thirst for beauty" and the "bright ideal," and by the essential truth of these splendid passages in Hoffmann's writing. The Claude Lorraine painting is unquestionably the source of the Hellenic terms in which the three-fold dream is expressed, but the literary function of the dream is more plausibly related to a literary inspiration. As a glimpse of the true and beautiful world from amid the ugliness of the real one, the vision is most likely to have its inspiration in Hoffmann, and the nearest analogues may be sought in *Der goldene Topf* and *Meister Floh*.

X

THE LIFE OF A GREAT SINNER

Almost from the very beginning of Dostoevski's career as a writer there recurs the intention to create the grandiose, to produce the effect that will positively stagger the reader. *The Double* was such a work. Even the jest of *A Novel in Nine Letters* was meant to give such an impression within the scope of a mere anecdote. Through the decade of the 1860's a progression may be observed which widens the horizons of each successive major composition, and if smaller works make their appearance side by side with the greater ones, they come as diversions or as money-makers until sufficient breath is acquired for the next and still greater effort. Toward the close of the decade there came to Dostoevski's mind a plan for the mightiest creation of all, a plan to rival and to parallel the Christian epic itself,—the epic of innocence, temptation, fall, sin, a welter of crimes, desperate actions, visions, promptings to grace, repentance, and ultimate salvation in ineffable ecstasy. The plan required the strenuous task of inventing modern-day, realistic equivalents for the theological concept of the soul's progress from the hands of God into the crucible of life, its testing and purification, and its final retransmission in clarified state back to the hands of God.

It is impossible to say when this gigantic project first began to form in Dostoevski's mind. Quite possibly the first impulse came amid the hell-on-earth of the Siberian prison. Perhaps it even antedates those terrible years. However these things may be, the plan surely remained amorphous until the latter 1860's. The first hint of it occurs in a letter of December 1868 written from Dresden to his friend Apollon Maikov,[1] wherein Dostoevski speaks of

> ". . . a huge novel, to be called *Atheism* (for God's sake between ourselves), but before undertaking it I must read a whole library of atheists, catholics, and orthodox believers. It will materialize, even with complete security for the work, in no less than two years. The chief figure is a Russian, of our own social standing, mature, not very well educated, but not uneducated, and not without rank—*suddenly*, in his maturity, he loses faith in God. All his life he had been occupied only with his job, had never altered his routine, and up to his 45th year had done nothing extraordinary. (The psychological solution: a profound feeling, a man and a Russian.) His loss of faith in God acts

upon him in a colossal way. (The action itself in the novel and the environment are extensive.) He pokes about among the new generation, among atheists, Slavs, and Europeans, among Russian fanatics, hermits, and priests. Among other things, he is thoroughly caught on the hook of a Jesuit, a propagandist, and a Pole; from this he falls to the very depths of self-abasement, and in the end he returns to find both Christ and the Russian soil, the Russian Christ and the Russian God. (For God's sake do not tell anyone); but my hope is to write this last novel, and then I can die—I shall have said all."

Despite the obvious excitement underlying these words, the plan of the novel *Atheism,* so far as we perceive it here, seems not so very "huge" after all. Beyond the sober theme of a man beset with troubled doubts "nel mezzo del cammin di nostra vita," it suggests little more than a distasteful combination of sectarian prejudice and Russian nationalism. The mystical junction of these elements in "the Russian Christ" is a theme which does indeed dominate long stretches of the novels of the 1870's, but we are probably fortunate in that the figure of the wily Polish Jesuit never materialized in Dostoevski's fiction.

During the year 1869 the plan was deferred perforce while *The Idiot* was being completed and while *The Eternal Husband* was being hastily put together to cover the costs of day-to-day existence. For well over a year it remains in abeyance, and when it is next mentioned, it is greatly altered and enlarged. Radical and elaborate transformation of an initial idea is a procedure familiar to anyone who has investigated the genesis of Dostoevski's novels. It was from Dresden that he wrote to Nikolai Nikolaevich Strakhov on April 5, 1870 concerning the project of his master-novel:[2]

"I have been meditating the idea of this novel for three years; till now I have not been able to make up my mind to attack it in these foreign lands: I wanted not to begin until I was in Russia. But during these three years, the whole conception has matured within me and I think that I *can* begin the first part (which I intend for the *Zarya*) even here, for the action of that part is concerned with many years ago. You need not be uneasy when I speak of a 'first part.' The idea demands great length, at least as great as the Tolstoyan novels. It will be a cycle of five distinct stories; these will be so independent of one another that any one of them (except the two that come midway) could perfectly well be published in different journals as completely separate works. The general title is to be: *The Life-Story of a Great Sinner,* and each separate tale will have its own title as well. Each division (that is, each single story) will be about fifteen sheets at most in length. To write the second story I *must* be in

Russia; the action of that part takes place in a Russian monastery; although I know the Russian monasteries well, I must nevertheless come back to Russia. I should like to have said much more about it to you, but what can one say in a letter? I repeat, however, that I can't possibly promise the novel for this year; don't press me, and you will get a conscientious, perhaps even a really good, work (at all events I have set myself this idea as the goal of my literary future, for I can't hope at all to live and work more than six or seven years longer)."

However much more Dostoevski would have liked to say about his plan to Strakhov, he cautiously limited himself to remarks just sufficient to convey that he had a really tremendous idea. To his more intimate friend Apollon Nikolaevich Maikov he committed himself on the very next day[3] in much more specific terms:

"The job for the *Russki Vestnik* (The Russian Messenger)— (Dostoevski means *The Possesed*)—will not particularly tax me, but I have promised the *Zarya* (Dawn) a real piece of work, and I want *really* to do it. This latter has been maturing in my brain for two years past. It is the same idea about which I have already written once to you. This will be my last novel; it will be as long as *War and Peace*. I know from our one-time talks that you will approve of the idea. The novel will consist of five longish tales (each fifteen sheets; in these two years my plan has fully ripened). The tales are complete in themselves, so that one could sell them separately. The first I intend for Kachpirev; its action lies in the 'forties. (The title of the whole book will be *The Life-Story of a Great Sinner*, but each part will have its own title as well.) The fundamental idea, which will run through each of these parts, is one that has tormented me, consciously and unconsciously, all my life long: it is the question of the existence of God. The hero is now an atheist, now a believer, now a fanatic and sectarian, and then again an atheist. The second story will have for its setting a monastery. On this second story I base all my hopes. Perhaps people will admit at last that I can write something but pure nonsense. (I will confide to you alone, Apollon Nikolaevich, that in this second story the principal character is to be taken from Tikhon Zadonski;[4] of course under another name, but also as a Bishop who has withdrawn to a monastery for repose.) A thirteen-yeared boy, who has been concerned in a serious crime, a lad intellectually mature, but utterly corrupt (I know the type), and the future hero of the novel as a whole—has been sent by his parents to the monastery to be there brought up. The little wolf, the little Nihilist, there comes in contact with Tikhon. In the same monastery is to be found Chaadaev[5] (also of course under another name). Why should not Chaadaev have spent a year in a monastery? Let us suppose that Chaadaev, after that first article which caused him to be weekly examined by physicians as to the state of his mind, had been unable to refrain from publishing a second article somewhere abroad (say, in France; it is quite conceivable;) and for *this* article he gets banished for a year to a monastery. But he is allowed to receive visitors there—for example Belinski,[6] Granovski,[7] even Pushkin, and others. (Of course it is not to be the actual Chaadaev; I only want to display the type.) At the monastery there is also a Paul the Prussian,[8] a Golubov,[9] and a monk Parfeny.[10] (I know the milieu through and through; I have been familiar with the Russian monasteries from childhood.) But the principal figures are to be Tikhon and the boy."

Dostoevski cautions Maikov not to breathe a word of this to anyone, and then adds:—

"Perhaps I shall succeed in creating a majestic, authentic saint. Mine is to be quite different from Kostanzhoglo,[11] and also from the German in Goncharov's *Oblomov*.[12] I shall probably not *create* at all, but present the real Tikhon, who has long been shrined in my heart. But even a close, faithful delineation I should regard as a great achievement to succeed in. . . . The first part deals with the childhood of the hero. Of course there are other characters besides children; it is a real novel. This part fortunately, I *can* write even here; I shall offer it to the *Zarya*. Will they refuse it though? . . . ."

From these two letters written on consecutive days, a general notion of Dostoevski's plan may be deduced. The contemplated work is to be his last and greatest novel, one that will compel the admiration even of his detractors; it is to approximate the length of Tolstoi's *War and Peace*; it is to have five separate and distinct parts, though the second and third of these may not be independent of each other; and the over-all title is to be *The Life-Story of a Great Sinner*. It may be schematized as follows:

Part I—*can* be written without the author's return to Russia, "for the action of that part is concerned with many years ago" (letter to Strakhov) "its action lies in the 'forties" (letter to Maikov)

Part II—the essential part; it will deal with the problem of the existence of God; its setting is a Russian monastery.
Primary characters:
a saintly Bishop to be faithfully modelled on Tikhon Zadonski
a thirteen-year-old criminal and nihilist
Secondary characters:
personages based on prominent Westernizers of the 1840's: Chaadaev, Professor Granovski, Belinski
genuinely "Russian" personages: Pushkin (Dostoev-

ski's ideal Russian), religious sectarians (Old Be-
lievers)

Part III—essentially a sequel to Part II and not to be separated
from it (?)

Part IV—?

Part V—?

It is clear from both letters that all of Dostoevski's enthusiasm
is directed toward the monastery sequence in Part II, while
Part I would seem to be in the nature of a prologue, and all the
rest of the plan is so vague as not to be mentioned at all.

Supplementary information about the plan is to be found
among the mass of Dostoevski's notebooks, which were made
public by the Soviet government late in 1921, particularly in the
one now labelled "Notebook No. 2 (Lenin Library N-22)," which
was used by the author during the last month of 1869 and during the first half of 1870.[13]   Here one entry reads: "20/8 December LIFE OF A GREAT SINNER."   Beneath it follow several pages of disconnected jottings, some of them obscure, most
having to do with Part I, only a few relating to the later stages
of the five-fold plan.   The last note, dated May 3/15 (1870),—
i.e. about a month after the letters to Strakhov and Maikov,—
bears a heading all in capital letters: "THE MAIN IDEA" and
reads as follows:[14]

"After the Monastery and Tikhon the Great Sinner comes out
into the world in order to be the *greatest of men*. He is sure that
he will be the greatest of men. And in that way he behaves: he
is the proudest of the proud and behaves with the greatest
haughtiness towards people. The vagueness as to the form of
his future greatness coincides perfectly with his youth. But he
(and this is cardinal) has *through Tikhon* got hold of the idea
(conviction) that in order to conquer the whole world one must
conquer oneself only. Conquer thyself and thou shalt conquer
the world. Does not choose a career, but neither has he the time:
he begins to watch himself profoundly. But along with this there
are also certain contradictions:

(1) Gold (amassing) (a family on his hands); amassing
money was suggested to him by a usurer, a terrible man, the
antithesis of Tikhon. (2) Education (Comte—Atheism—Friends).
Education—He is tormented by ideas and philosophy but he
masters that which is essential.

Suddenly youth and debauchery. A martyr's act and terrible
crimes. Self-reunciation. But out of mad pride he becomes an
ascetic and pilgrim. Travels in Russia. (Romance of love. Thirst
for humiliation), etc., etc., and so on.

(The canvas is rich.)

Fallings and risings.

Extraordinary man—but what has he done and achieved.

Traits.—Out of pride and infinite haughtiness towards people he becomes meek and charitable to all because he is already higher than all.

He wanted to shoot himself (a child was exposed at his door).

He ends with establishing a Foundling Hospital and becomes a Haase.[15]   Everything is becoming clear.

He dies confessing a crime."

Here, then, is the clue to Parts III, IV, and V of the work. The hero was to leave the monastery and the saintly Bishop, presumably at the end of Part II, to go forth on a spiritual pilgrimage "in Russia," in the course of which he would come through sin to repentance and to true humility. The scheme of the whole *Life of a Great Sinner* may now be reconstructed in its main outlines:

Part I—Childhood and youth; the beginnings of sin and depravity through pride; entry into the monastery

Part II—The monastery; inspiration from the true saint, Bishop Tikhon, and simultaneously the conflict of ideologies from philosophers and sectarians
Departure from the monastery (?)

Part III—The wide world; wealth, love, family; struggle with ideologies
Crimes
A spiritual contest within the hero between his own mad pride and Tikhon's doctrine of humility

Part IV—The same continued

Part V—The crisis: impulse to suicide
The inner triumph of humility over pride and self-will
"He dies confessing a crime."

This plan, for which Dostoevski optimistically estimated two years' time to carry out, calls for a true epic sweep of sin, fall, and redemption, compared to which the similar scheme of *Crime and Punishment* would necessarily seem a mere forestudy, and for a broad panorama of the earthly state of man. Reduced to its simplest formula, the subject is: the evolution of a saint.

What is this plan other than a Russianization and a "Dostoevskianization" of the plan of Hoffmann's *Die Elixiere des Teufels?*

Hoffmann's novel was likewise the story of a boy placed in a monastery by his parents; who grew up under the tutelage of a saintly monk; who was inwardly divided between powerful forces of Good and Evil; who was possessed of a fierce pride that caused him to pose prematurely as a saint when his spirit was closer to Satan than to God; who was tempted, succumbed to temptation, deserted his vocation, went forth into the world, committed the worst crimes, struggled with his conscience, eventually repented, achieved true sainthood, returned to the monastery, and died after confessing his crimes.

Externally, this complex matter is divided into two parts, with four and three subdivisions respectively, but, as Harich points out,[16]—and this would surely seem to be more than a matter of coincidence,—the novel imposes upon itself a more organic structure in a "Prologue" and five "Acts," as follows:

Prologue —The monastery; childhood and youth of the monk Medardus; his temptation through "the devil's elixirs;" his departure into the world, ostensibly on a commission to Rome

"Act"   I—Medardus's apparent "murder" of Viktorin and his subsequent assumption of Viktorin's identity and evil life

The disastrous events at the rural estate of Baron von F., ending with Medardus's flight after his murder of the evil Euphemie and the Hamlet-like Hermogen

"Act"   II—The sequence at the "mercantile city," where Medardus is identified as the fugitive murderer and escapes with the help of the barber Pietro Belcampo

"Act" III—The confrontation of Medardus and Viktorin at the forester's house

The long series of adventures at court, including Medardus's concern with state economics, gardening, art, literary clubs, fashions, public mores, princely genealogy, as well as his own spectacular trial for the murders he had committed and his successful efforts to unload all guilt on Viktorin

The sequence ends at the scene where Medardus, alone for a moment with Aurelie just before they are to be summoned to their wedding rites, suddenly proclaims his guilt, stabs Aurelie, sets free the mad Viktorin as the latter is being carried to execution, and flees into the open country. (End of Part I)

"Act" IV—Rome and repentance

The interpolated memoir about Franzesko the Painter, Medardus's sinning ancestor

"Act"   V—The return to the monastery in East Prussia; the murder of Aurelie by Viktorin as she is taking her vows as the nun Rosalia; her manifest sainthood; the saintly death of Medardus one year later.

Obviously conceived as a novellized saint's legend, *Die Elixiere des Teufels* is unique among Hoffmann's productions by its skillful portrayal of the various estates of society,—the rural manor, the simple cottage of the forester, the "mercantile city," the *Residenz* city, and the life in monastic circles. Hoffmann, too, intended a panorama of "the world," and his "canvas is rich." Against the rich background he set not only the struggle of the "Doubles," Medardus and Viktorin, but the rather dense population of a whole family sinning through five generations and achieving ultimate redemption through the hero, who sins worst of all but accomplishes his own purification.

Above all, it was the sustained intensity of emotions amid the astonishing plenitude of characters and events of this novel which must have fascinated Dostoevski. Twice before he had drawn upon its materials to make works of his own, in *The Double* (1846) and in the opening section of *Netochka Nezvanova* (1847), but in both instances he had selected isolated episodes for specialized treatment. In *Crime and Punishment* (1866) he had created a trio of central characters roughly approximating the three major persons of *Die Elixiere des Teufels*. But only now, with the plan for the *Life of a Great Sinner* did he take the scheme of the novel as a whole for his model. There is no mistaking the earnestness with which he considered his projected work. He solemnly intended that it should be his final and supreme creation. Yet his calculations went somehow amiss, and the supreme work was destined never to be written in the form in which he wished. Circumstances of time and money determined matters otherwise.

First, *The Possessed*, that "job for the *Russki Vestnik*" which he had told Maikov "would not particularly tax him," proved much more taxing than he had anticipated. All through 1870 it engaged his best energies until the month of August, when with a resoluteness nothing less than heroic he destroyed some three hundred pages of manuscript in order to begin afresh on the basis of a wholly new idea. Into the already heavily burdened plot he now poured no small quantity of the materials accumulated for the childhood story of the Great Sinner, so that the original hero, Pyotr Verkhovenski, was displaced by the new figure of Stavrogin. The presence of the Great Sinner under this name attracted the character of the saintly Bishop, who in the novel is called Tikhon directly from the real Tikhon Zadonski. Likewise there is a "lame girl," who, according to the jottings of "Notebook No. 2," was to have been associated with the Great Sinner; a theft of jewels from an icon corresponds to another jotting from the same source to the effect that "Albert and he steal a star from the crown and escape successfully." But Tikhon's rôle in the novel is relatively slight, and a host of characters from the first draft still demanded their place in the book. Stavrogin himself makes a very belated entrance into the story and when he does appear, he is seen to have borrowed the mental superiority and moral depravity of the Great Sinner only to proceed through a career of unrelieved sinning to end in despair and the ignominy of suicide by hanging. For all his possession of aspects of the Great Sinner, he is still far from *being* the Great Sinner.

Meanwhile Dostoevski had returned to Russia in July 1871, thanks to the generosity of the publisher Katkov, but *The Possessed* was still unfinished. After finally completing it in 1872, political and editorial duties engaged the author's energy and time. By 1874, still another novel was in progress, *A Raw Youth*, and once again the hero took on aspects of the Great Sinner, this time under the name of Dolgoruki. Between them, Stavrogin and Dolgoruki pretty well exhaust the supply of ideas that Dostoevski had amassed for the childhood and youth of the Great Sinner, but the "essential" monastery story still remained untouched.

By the time *National Notes* had completed the serial publication of *A Raw Youth* in December 1875, Dostoevski had come to enjoy some measure of long delayed financial security and some degree of tranquillity in his home life. From his newly acquired villa in Staraya Russa he could also go up to the capital as occasion demanded, and when he went, he could rely on receiving deferential invitations from persons in high places, for his reputation not only as a literary man but also as a political pundit was outdistancing the cries of his detractors. But if fame and leisure had come to him at last, the work nearest his heart remained an unfulfilled ambition. It is with some surprise that we find him beginning, at some point in 1877, a new novel entitled not *The Life of a Great Sinner* but *The Brothers Karamazov*. As in previous cases, multiple and diverse are the strands that went into the making of this last and longest and greatest of his works, but among them, as scholars now generally recognize, was a major strand from the unrealized master-novel. Despite much alteration and adaptation, *The Brothers Karamazov* represents to all intents and purposes the "essential" Part II, the monastery sequence, of *The Life of a Great Sinner*.

XI

THE BROTHERS KARAMAZOV

A lucidity not always customary with Dostoevski enhances the grandeur of his final novel, *The Brothers Karamazov*. Its diverse elements are so ordered as to produce the effect of a vast world surveyed from a lofty eminence, where serenity is untroubled precisely because the view encompasses not only the intense strife below, but also the ultimate limits beyond which that strife may not go. The book is quite as crowded with persons and events as *The Possessed*, though the reader feels less strain than in that former work. Magnificent grouping of material concentrates much of the action into three days and leads to a mighty climax on the night of the third day, when a detestable libertine and scoundrel, Fëdor Pavlovich Karamazov, is murdered. On that night the man's eldest son, Dmitri, who intended to murder him but did not, finds salvation and ruin simultaneously in ecstatic love; his second son, Ivan, who morally willed the murder in his heart, absents himself from home so that the deed may be done; his third son, Alyosha, a novice monk, after some hours in the company of a woman of dubious reputation, returns to his monastery, more preoccupied with the death of his spiritual father, the monk Zossima, than with the danger threatening his father according to the flesh. It is the fourth son, an illegitimate offspring, a coward, and a base rascal, who deals the death blow. After an interval of two months the story resumes in order to show the decisive effect of the central event on the destinies of the several characters. The actual murderer conceals the evidence of his crime, then reluctantly confesses and thereafter hangs himself from despair. Dmitri stands a formal trial for the deed he intended to commit but did not, and when the court finds him guilty, he bows to its decision in acknowledgement of its essential justice. In the epilogue there is talk of plans for his escape. Ivan, too, comes to realize the nature of his own moral guilt and for a time collapses into insanity. His physical and spiritual recovery are plainly indicated for the future. Only the fate of the youngest brother, Alyosha, is left unclear at the end. For this apparent inconclusiveness there is a very good reason: Aloysha *is* the Great Sinner, and the present story presents only the beginning of his career.

1. ALYOSHA KARAMAZOV AND MEDARDUS

Alyosha's childhood, spent as a kind of orphan charge among distant connections of his mother's, is only sketchily described in Part I, Chapter 4, either because the scope of the novel precluded longer treatment, or, more likely, because the ideas accumulated by the author for the Great Sinner's early life had already passed to the previous heroes Stavrogin and Dolgoruki. One striking occurrence of his boyhood did, however, linger in his memory. Though his mother died when he was four, he recalled her "as though she stood living before him," and one recollection in particular was very vivid.

> "He remembered one still summer evening, an open window, the slanting rays of the setting sun (that he recalled most vividly of all); in a corner of the room the holy image, before it a lighted lamp, and on her knees before the image his mother, sobbing hysterically with cries and moans, snatching him up in both arms, squeezing him close until it hurt, and praying for him to the Mother of God, holding him out in both arms to the image as though to put him under the Mother's protection . . . and suddenly a nurse runs in and snatches him from her in terror. That was the picture! And Alyosha remembered his mother's face at that minute. He used to say that it was frenzied but beautiful as he remembered. But he rarely cared to speak of the memory to any one."

This scene of premonitory dedication has its close parallel in *Die Elixiere des Teufels,* where Medardus recalls having been taken at the age of two years by his mother to visit a certain Cistercian cloister, the Abbess of which has the rank of Princess. The Abbess-Princess is actually his aunt, half-sister to his sinful father. At sight of the child, she senses the evil which threatens his life and in sorrowful emotion clasps him to her bosom.

> "But at that moment (Medardus relates) a sharp pain which I felt on my neck forced me to utter a loud cry, such that the Princess in fright let me go, and my mother, in utter dismay at my conduct, hurried up to take me away at once. This the Princess did not permit. It proved that the diamond cross which the Princess wore at her breast had so sharply wounded me in her violent embrace that the spot was all red and covered with blood."[1]

Thus, through all his career of crimes, Medardus bears the mark of the Cross on his throat until his ultimate death in holiness.

Medardus specifically mentions that this event took place in his second year. Alyosha Karamazov received his dedication some time before the age of four. Yet, oddly enough, Dostoevski adds a comment in the matter of the child's age:

"Such memories may persist," he says, "as everyone knows, from an even earlier age, even from two years old, but scarcely standing out through a whole lifetime like spots of light out of darkness, like a corner torn out of a huge picture, which has all faded and disappeared except the fragment. That is how it was with (Alyosha)."[2]

While still a boy, Medardus was sent by his mother and the Abbess-Princess to study in the Capuchin monastery of a near-by city. There he came to be so attracted by the happy tranquility of the monks, by the beauty of the ritual, and above all by the personality of Prior Leonardus, that at the age of sixteen he announced his intention of entering the order. Forthwith he entered upon his novitiate.

Alyosha is described at the beginning of the novel as being aged nineteen or twenty. Only recently he has left his guardians and come to his native village to seek out his father. Scarcely arrived, he announces his intention of entering the local monastery, where he has been profoundly impressed by the saintly character of the Elder, Father Zossima.

Prior Leonardus and Father Zossima are parallel figures in more respects than saintliness and a particular interest in a gifted disciple. Both are distinguished by an acquaintance with worldly things beyond the normal range of monks. Prior Leonardus, for instance, is a master of the French and Italian languages, in addition to his native German, and in former days had been entrusted with important missions outside the monastery, while Father Zossima, son of a family of land-owners, is described as having served as an Army officer in the Caucasus in his youth. Both men have about them a certain worldly charm, not at all inconsistent with the serenity and extraordinary goodness of their characters. A cheerfulness, even gaiety, marks both men, and nothing like gloomy fanaticism or harsh severity is to be found in either of them. Both are knowers of men. It is with the greatest sympathetic insight that Leonardus permits the eloquent Medardus to preach, even when he senses the oratory to be vain display of rhetoric, and when the young novice's restiveness has reached the breaking point, he sends him out into the world on a mission to Rome. By "Rome" he understands, as Medardus does not, something much more than a certain city of the Italian peninsula. From afar he traces the sinner's every step and eventually he welcomes the prodigal's return. Father Zossima, too, has uncanny insight into human

nature and a marked predisposition in favor of persons given to
sin. Suffering through sin awes him. It is to the future suffering of Dmitri that he makes his famous bow down to the
ground. Like Leonardus, he perceives the necessity of his
disciple to go forth into the world, well aware that many things
must be endured before a return is possible. To Alyosha he
says:

> ". . . This is not your place for the time. I bless you for
> great service in the world. Yours will be a long pilgrimage.
> And you will have to take a wife, too. You will have to bear *all*
> before you come back. There will be much to do. But I don't
> doubt of you, and so I send you forth. Christ is with you. Do
> not abandon Him and He will not abandon you. You will see
> great sorrow, and in that sorrow you will be happy. This is my
> last message to you: in sorrow seek happiness. Work, work
> unceasingly. Remember my words, for although I shall talk
> with you again, not only my days but my hours are numbered."

On the night of the following day, Father Zossima dies, as he
had foreseen.—The farewell of Leonardus to Medardus is pitched
less in prophet-tones and more like deep but purely human
wisdom:

> "I understand you and do firmly believe that the world, if
> you travel through it in piety, will better cure you of your con-
> fusion than will the solitude of the cloister. . . . Betake yourself
> now to your cell. Pray with fervor for the salvation of your soul.
> I shall do likewise. . . ."[3]

On the other hand, his words to the older, returned Medardus
have a more exalted tone:

> "I could have destroyed you, but, far from imagining myself
> chosen for the office of judge, I left you and your fate to the
> everlasting power of Heaven. You have been preserved in miracu-
> lous fashion, and this fact convinces me that your earthly de-
> struction had not been determined upon."[4]

The temptations which had made Medardus unfit for longer
stay within the monastery had been varied and gradual. Once,
five years previously, he had suppressed a momenary impulse
of lust at sight of the buxom sister of the choir director. A
subtler temptation of the flesh had come in the form of a beautiful lady who, in the very confessional itself, had revealed her
passionate desire for him. His faith had also been somewhat
undermined by the reckless mockery with which a visiting nobleman and his tutor had belittled the monastery relics. The relics
themselves had proved his final undoing. Most famous of them

were the vials of liquor with which Satan had tempted St. Anthony and these Medardus one night tasted to their wild dregs.

On a far grander scale is the three-fold temptation undergone by Alyosha. He is tempted in his faith by a long series of unhappy jealousies, rivalries, and unedifying fanaticism among his fellow monks before the humanly stinking corpse of Zossima makes him doubt the very goodness of his spiritual Mentor. He is tempted intellectually by daily contact with the cynical "career-monk" and essential atheist, Rakitin, (a parody of Kraevski, the editor of *National Notes*) and by his contacts with Miusov, his father's brother-in-law by a first marriage. (Miusov corresponds to Chaadaev.) But the supreme challenge to his intellect comes from his brother Ivan, whose talk with him in the tavern (Book V, Chapters 3, 4, and 5) is one of the most amazing conversations in all of literature. With irresistible logic Ivan denies, not the existence of God, but the justice of God, and unfolds to his brother a monstrous panorama of the chaotic cruelty, suffering, and evil which God permits in the world, until Alyosha is compelled to agree, at least in one essential point, with his argument. Finally, Alyosha is tempted sensually by the daily spectacle of his father's and Dmitri's competitive lust for the woman Grushenka, until, on the very night of his father's murder, he himself goes to the harlot's house and allows himself to submit to her capricious caresses.

Tempted, then, thrice,—in heart, in mind, and in body,—Alyosha is ripe for the fall. But the actual fall does not take place. Through the rest of the novel he plays a rather passive rôle, as friend and helper to all the distressed members of his family, to friends, and the group of neighborhood boys, who make up a separate story, almost a novel within a novel. It seems as though Dostoevski was loath to carry out his plan to send "the chief, *though future*, hero of my story," as he calls Alyosha in Book VII, Chapter 1, out upon his career of sin and crime through the world.

Yet the preparations are all made for that career even before the book closes: not only has Alyosha undergone the three-fold temptation, but on one night he lost in death both his spiritual father, Zossima, and his actual father, and lost his brothers, who are swept away by their separate destinies. And in still another respect the preparations are made. This is a matter of detail, but nevertheless interesting.

Almost all of Dostoevski's tales and novels have Petersburg

as their setting, but *The Brothers Karamazov* is significantly
not a "Petersburg tale." The locale is not identified, though the
shadowy narrator (what reader remembers him?), after many
references to "our town" and "our village" and "our monastery,"
does actually mention the name of the place in two instances.[5]
The town is called "Skotoprigonevsk,"—"Cattle Jump." This
stray bit of Gogolian humor is not to be taken seriously, of
course. The town is all Russian towns, just as their locale is the
whole of Russia. The Great Sinner, it will be recalled, was to
"travel through Russia." Similarly, Hoffmann did not identify
the sites of any of Medardus's adventures except the two extremes of his wanderings, the home monastery of the Holy
Linden in East Prussia and Rome, both for symbolic, not for
geographical, reasons. The setting of both novels is the whole
world as far as it is within the ken of their readers; it is *sub
divo,* as the Romans would put it; and geographical delimita-
tions would in both cases be as inappropriate as in a mediaeval
Morality play. It is striking that in this detail Dostoevski is not
only at one with the Hoffmann of *Die Elixiere des Teufels,* but
also with the Gogol of *Dead Souls.*

None of the foregoing parallels between *The Brothers Karamazov* and *Die Elixiere des Teufels* precludes the validity of
other known influences or associations. It is common knowledge
that the monastery which Dostoevski had in mind as he wrote
was the famous cloister of Optina Pustyn', south-west of Moscow, and that Father Zossima repeats words which Dostoevski
had heard at that monastery from the lips of Father Amvrosi.
The historical Bishop, Tikhon Zadonski, is surely also to be connected with Zossima. These and many other things are merely
examples of the author's amazing skill at combination. Even
more fundamentally, it may be asserted, Zossima is to be equated
with Prior Leonardus, just as Alyosha recapitulates on a grander
scale the early stages in the life of the monk Medardus. Dostoevski worked from life *and* from books.

The novel ends with Alyosha wavering just before his fall,
somewhat as Viktorin sat in precarious balance on the edge of
the Devil's Chasm so that the merest touch of Medardus's hand
sent him tumbling down. The final published installment of the
book appeared in the pages of *The Russian Messenger* in November 1880, containing Alyosha's speech of farewell, in which
he says he is going away *for a long time.* If contemporary
readers sensed the necessity of his journey and looked forward

to a sequel from the author, they were soon aware that no sequel
would ever appear. For within two months, on January 28,
1881, Dostoevski was dead.

2. IVAN KARAMAZOV AND MEDARDUS

The prototype of Dmitri Karamazov may be found as an unnamed character in *The House of the Dead* but whose name in
real life was Ilinski. Dostoevski knew him as a fellow convict
in the prison at Omsk, and in his prison memoirs reports how
this man from the Siberian town of Tobolsk, north-west of
Omsk, had been convicted of slaying his own father for the
sake of some badly needed money and how, only after serving
many years in the chain-gangs, it was discovered that he was
not guilty of the crime of which he had been convicted.[6] Alyosha, as we have shown, is the Great Sinner, whose literary
ancestry leads directly back to the monk Medardus of *Die Elixiere des Teufels*. But what of Ivan Karamazov and his spiritual
Double, Smerdyakov?

Like all the other principal characters of *The Brothers Karamazov*, Ivan is a creation of great complexity, but by virtue of
the very fact that he is a "split personality," he is to be associated with all the divided selves of Dostoevski's fiction and in
particular with the first of the series, Mr. Golyadkin. Upon
reflection, his connection with Mr. Golyadkin is seen to be more
specific than mere membership in a broad category of Dostoevskian types. Precisely coincident with the formative stages of
The Brothers Karamazov is an article which Dostoevski wrote
for his independently published newspaper-pamphlet *The Diary
of a Writer* in November 1877, in which he digresses for a comment on his own early story *The Double*. While deploring his
own inability to manage the material adequately in 1846, or even
in 1860, when he revised the piece for inclusion in his *Collected
Works*, he adds:[7]

"... and were I now to expound and express this idea, I should
adopt an altogether different form."

If one were to state concisely the "idea" as it was expressed
in 1846, it might be put thus:—the sympathetic analysis of a
schizophrenic man, who, under the stress of humiliation and
suffering, projects a second self or Double, at first friendly but
soon turning hostile, until the hallucination turns into actual
madness and destroys him. What "altogether different form"
would this idea assume in 1877, if the author were to treat it

anew? A thorny question! Yet, in general terms an answer may be given. We may be sure that the new form would be more complex, and on the basis of many possible analogies in Dostoevski's writings, we may feel reasonably sure that the antitheses of the personality would take on ideological significance, both religious and political. The description precisely fits Ivan Karamazov. He is a Russian, divided in his loyalties between the irreconcilable poles of 19th century Russian thought, Westernism and Slavophilism. In so far as he is a "Westernizer," Ivan puts his trust in the corrosive intellect and in Reason, which (in Dostoevski's opinion) have already led Europe, and will, if unchecked, lead Russia, to Socialism, Atheism, and Anarchy; to his brother Alyosha he ardently pleads the cause of Atheism, and, since without God "all things are lawful" and parricide may be tolerated, he morally consents to the murder of his father, cynically absenting himself from the scene so that the killer may have unimpeded access to his victim. In so far as he is a Slavophile, Ivan's heart is only temporarily estranged from "the Russian Christ," and the promptings of his heart rend his conscience until he collapses into brain fever and transitory madness. This very collapse into madness, even though temporary, relates Ivan to the heroes of Dostoevski's early fiction, for that theme, so common in the stories of 1846-48 as to be almost a mannerism, has not recurred since *A Faint Heart* (1848). Unlike those early heroes, however, Ivan is clearly destined to recover, and in his recovery he will most certainly swing wholly over to the side of "the Russian Christ."

In short, Ivan is the much modified "new form" of Mr. Golyadkin, and in a sense his share of the total *Brothers Karamazov* is the long deferred, though repeatedly contemplated, rewriting of *The Double*. By the same token, his story is to be traced to *Die Elixiere des Teufels* which underlay the concept of *The Double*, and his literary ancestor is, as is Alyosha's, the monk Medardus. But not in the same aspect. Alyosha reflects Medardus the false saint sinning and striving his way toward true sainthood, in other words, the over-all concept of Medardus; Ivan reflects Medardus the Double.

The *alter ego* of Medardus was his half-brother Viktorin. Between them, they share a life, Viktorin wholly bad, Medardus torn between bad and good until the final victory of the good. Ivan's *alter ego* is likewise a half-brother, Smerdyakov, and Smerdyakov, like Viktorin, embodies all the evil aspects of the

hero's divided self.   For Smerdyakov is, in his own unintel-
ligent way, a "Westernizer."   He affects European manners,
acts the dandy, plays the guitar, and on the eve of his suicide
begins learning French in the hope of one day seeing Paris.
He has, as far as his lights permit, followed the corrosive
principle of Reason down to the depths of Socialism, Atheism,
and Anarchy, and, having rejected "the Russian Christ," finds
that "all things are lawful," including parricide.   With unflinch-
ing calculation he does what Ivan's heart would not let *him* do:
he murders his father.   When his conscience belatedly awakes,
it prompts him to tie a rope and hang himself from sheer
despair.

But beyond being the all-evil *alter ego* and half-brother of
the hero, Smerdyakov bears little resemblance to the debonair
and quasi-Voltairean Viktorin.   This Russian Double is physically repulsive, absurdly dandified, craven, epileptic, and a
lackey, both literally in that he is a servant in the Karamazov
household, and figuratively,—as Dostoevski frequently uses the
term,—in that he is a base imitator of Western Europe.   Some,
but not all, of these qualities he derives from quite another
character in *Die Elixiere des Teufels*, the barber Pietro Belcampo.

The fact of the matter is that Medardus had not one, but two,
Doubles, one on a thoroughly serious plane of Good-versus-Evil,—
Viktorin; and a second who was non-serious and even whimsical,—Belcampo.   The latter is one of Hoffmann's most charming creations.   Himself a Double, with an Italian and a German
aspect, as evidenced by his alternate names: Pietro Belcampo
and Peter Schönfeld, his prime purpose is to relieve the *terri-
bilità* of the novel as a whole by a comic travesty of the Double
theme itself.   In his Italian aspect he is patently of the Com-
media dell' Arte, and his antics and grimaces reduce all the components of life, however serious, to the cries and gesticulations
of a Punchinello.   Man, by implication, becomes no better than
a Punchinello himself, destinies are rôles played either well or
badly, only God is real, and time and life are a dream.   (Friedrich Schlegel would have cried Bravo! to such a creation—in
1798.)   In his German aspect as Peter Schönfeld, he had to be
more sentimental, and he does indeed shed tears and at the end
of the novel enters Medardus's monastery as Lay-brother Peter.
He also serves another function, as Professor Hewett-Thayer
points out,[8] that of the Shakespearean clown.   In his speaking

of the bitter truth to his master Medardus, and in his grotesque formulations of exact analyses, he most nearly resembles the Fool in *King Lear*. His very existence is only half real, and his comings and goings are mysterious and unexplained. His whole story is a kind of whimsical arabesque along the margin of the real narrative. It is in one of his earliest appearances, in the "mercantile city," that he says:[9]

> "Reverend Sir, inside me exists an infamous sinful fellow, and he says, 'Peter Schönfeld, don't be a monkey and believe that you exist, but I am really you, by name Belcampo, and am an original idea (eine geniale Idee) . . .' This Belcampo has made me, Peter Schönfeld, quite confused and all mixed up."

The words are at one and the same time an example of Romantic Irony undercutting the reality of all things, a travesty of Medardus's own thoughts, and a species of Shakespearean buffoonery. A few pages prior to this he has made a fantastic entrance, absurdly bowing and scraping, and bearing in his hands the shears and combs with which he will barber Medardus out of monkishness into the form of a man of the world. In the midst of his clown's farrago he says:

> " 'But you shall nevertheless admire my glance which pierces to the depths, yes, worship the genius in me, Sir. In vain I sought to match up all the contradictions that lie in your whole being, in your movements. There is something in your gait that points to the cleric. *Ex profundis clamavi ad te, Domine— Oremus—Et in omnia saecula saeculorum. Amen!*'
>
> These words the little fellow sang with a hoarse, quavering voice while he imitated with the most exact verisimilitude the position and gestures of monks. He turned around as before the altar, he knelt down and got up again; but now he assumed a proud, defiant stance, knit his brows, opened wide his eyes and spoke:
>
> 'Mine is the world!—I am richer, cleverer, wiser, than all of you, you moles; bow down before me! You see, Sir,' said the little fellow, 'those are the chief ingredients of your external bearing . . .' "

How aptly he has caught the essentials of Medardus's external *and* internal bearing, the reader well knows. The two extremes are meekness and self-will, to use the familiar antitheses used in speaking of Dostoevskian Doubles.

Belcampo is not only the humorous ape of Medardus. He is also a fantastic and finicky barber, something of a dandy, a parody of good manners. His gait is mincing, his speech is affected. Smerdyakov, the ape of Ivan, shows the usual "darkening process" of Russian Hoffmannists, but he parallels Belcampo

by brushing his clothes twice a day, by cleaning his smart calf
boots with a special brush and English polish so that they shine
like mirrors, by spending most of his salary on clothes and
pomades and perfumes, by playing the guitar, and the like.
Smerdyakov is also given to grandiose arguments, but these are
a clown's farrago in another sense: Dostoevski means them as
outrageously bitter parodies of Western ideologies. Smerdyakov
does not analyse Doubles but rather parrots the cant he has
heard about Socialism, Atheism, and Anarchy. He is Belcampo
turned realistic, pessimistic, nasty, and satirical.

In *Die Elixiere des Teufels* Medardus stood flanked by two
Doubles, Viktorin and Belcampo. Dostoevski has assigned to
Smerdyakov the genuinely evil nature of the first and his relationship of half-brother to the hero; from the second he has
adapted the humor and grotesquerie to new purposes, making
the capering and lowly barber a "lackey" in quite a new sense.
But further: Ivan, in *The Brothers Karamazov*, stands flanked
by two Doubles, one "serious" and one whimsical and half-real.
Besides Smerdyakov there is the Devil.

From Belcampo, Ivan's Devil inherits his sly humor and his
penchant for speaking the painful truth. His half-reality is
reinterpreted in a wholly new way. He is the projection of one
part of Ivan's mind, his form is incorporeal. He is a hallucination, both literally and in the subtler sense that he is the very
embodiment of the "European" mentality. He is corrosive intellect itself. He is the very image of disbelief. In his emerg-
ing from the mind of Ivan he resembles the plaguing, mocking,
tormenting Mr. Golyadkin Junior, but this time the Double
materializes, not for the hero's destruction, but rather as a
felicitous isolation and identification of evil,—like poison erupt-
ing in a single major sore instead of permeating the whole blood
stream; now that it has been found, it can be treated.

Ivan first encounters him in his own room. There the Devil
sits waiting for him to come back from his third and last conversation with Smerdyakov. The description of him is memorable:[10]

"(he was) a Russian gentleman of a particular kind, no
longer young, *qui faisait la cinquantaine*, as the French say, with
rather long, still thick, dark hair, slightly streaked with grey and
a small pointed beard. He was wearing a brownish reefer jacket,
rather shabby, evidently made by a rather good tailor though, and
of a fashion at least three years old, that had been discarded by
smart and well-to-do people for the last two years. His linen and

his long scarf-like neck-tie were all such as are worn by people who aim at being stylish, but on closer inspection his linen was not over clean and his wide scarf was very threadbare. The visitor's check trousers were of excellent cut, but were too light in color and too tight for the present fashion. His soft fluffy white hat was out of keeping with the season."

Quite as unexpectedly Medardus first encountered Belcampo in his inn-room in the "mercantile city." He had ordered a bottle of wine to be brought, and scarcely was the servant gone to fetch it when

> ". . . there was a knock, and a face peered in at the door like a comic mask, such as I had often seen. A pointed, red nose, a pair of glittering eyes, a long chin, and a towering powdered wig, which, as I afterwards discovered, terminated most unexpectedly in the rear as a Titus, a large jabot, a fiery red vest, from which two heavy watch-chains hung down, trousers, a frock-coat which was sometimes too tight and then again too loose, in short which fitted properly at no point!"[11]

The humorous external description is unusual with both authors, neither of whom had anything like a Balzacian interest in costume or appointments, and the stress placed on it in these instances is for a calculated effect. "Character" parts are being undertaken. And the two have much in common. Both launch directly into talk, both are garrulous, with a penchant for the extended anecdote, both love argument and quibbling, both enjoy a philosophical debate. Belcampo talks of "holy art"; he applies ideas of the Age of Enlightenment to dismiss the mysterious painter (Franzesko, the sinning ancestor of Medardus) as a disgusting spook (schnöder Revenant); he travesties Medardus's ideas and person. Ivan's Devil likewise plays with philosophical ideas, tells back to Ivan all the metaphysical speculations that have ever passed through the latter's mind, and in a more subtle sense analyses Ivan's character. The external description of him, however, goes beyond mere picturesqueness or comedy. The details of his dress are all meaningful. He is seedy, he is sleazy, he is a shady character. He is *contemptibly* amusing. He is an outmoded Idea. He is the liberal Idea of the 1840's (to which Dostoevski had once subscribed),—frayed, threadbare, received by second-class people. He is out of date, behind the times without realizing it. In fact, he fancies himself quite modern. He has refused to grow old decently and insists on appearing younger than he is. He is a wrinkled youth. He is,—Oh, laceration of self-pride,—a poor relation. "On the middle finger of his right hand (is) a massive gold ring with a cheap opal stone in it."

Much later in *Die Elixiere des Teufels* Belcampo makes another appearance. It was he who found Medardus in his frenzied state after the attempted murder of Aurelie and who brought him to the Italian monastery where he painfully awakes into a new phase of his life. On this occasion he makes a passing comment on Medardus's former looks. If only he, Belcampo, could have chosen Medardus's clothes, things would have been different. Clothes make the man. But as it was, the world took Medardus for

"... a mean *glebae adscriptus* (peasant) and the Devil for (his) *cousin germain.*"[12]

The remark may possibly have caught Dostoevski's eye.—This appearance of Belcampo immediately precedes the dread moment when the broken Medardus begins his horrendous confession of crimes. Then follow the scenes of remorse and fierce, self-imposed physical torments, which pass in turn into mental torments and hallucinations of meetings with his murdered victims. The whole section ends in a phantasmagoria of guilty dreams.—Ivan's interview with the Devil likewise ends in delirium. When the talk is interrupted by the coming of Alyosha with the news of Smerdyakov's suicide, Ivan receives the news, then collapses in a fit of brain fever. The spiritual crisis has become a physical crisis. The expulsion of a devil from a possessed man rends both soul and body.

Thus Belcampo is made to contribute characteristics both to Smerdyakov and to the Devil, who may be described as physical and spiritual embodiments of the same evil, while Viktorin offers only a little of the matter that forms Smerdyakov. In this procedure Dostoevski remained faithful to the pessimistic manner of the Russian Hoffmannists, for, where Medardus stood between a good Double and a bad Double, Ivan Karamazov is attended by two Doubles *both* of whom are *evil*.

XII

DOSTOEVSKI AND THE TRADITION OF
RUSSIAN HOFFMANNISM

At the end of *The Brothers Karamazov* the spiritual crisis has passed for Ivan, as it has for Dmitri. By separate paths both have returned, after strayings afar, to the Russian Christ. But the ordeal of Alyosha lies in the future. Of the specific details of this ordeal nothing definite is known. It seems probable that he will marry "the lame girl," Liza Khokhlakova, and that the marriage will bring him both bliss and torment. It is likely that he will encounter still further representatives of the ideologies of Socialism, Atheism, and Anarchy, but that in the end he will return like his brothers before him to the Russian Christ. That he is destined for a career of many crimes seems beyond doubt. And if we had the sequel, we should in all probability find more than one parallel to the life of the monk Medardus on his sinning way to "Rome."

The persistence of *Die Elixiere des Teufels* in Dostoevski's inspiration is itself a fascinating phenomenon, both literarily and psychologically. From *The Double* of 1846 to *Crime and Punishment* of 1866 to *The Brothers Karamazov* at the very end of his career in 1880, Hoffmann's novel proved a touchstone for his genius. It was indeed a rich source and Dostoevski by no means exhausted its store, but the astonishing thing is the transformation of the material in Dostoevski's hands. *Die Elixiere des Teufels* is an admirable work but of the second order of greatness. It is of silver; Dostoevski turns it into gold. Both the process and the result set Dostoevski apart,—and far above,—all preceding Russian Hoffmannists. He was the only one of them who had the insight and the genius to dominate so large a model and to conceive so vast a plan of transformation.

In his manipulation of the shorter tales and of *Kater Murr* the same superiority of insight and genius is to be observed. Even in a relatively infelicitous case such as that of *The Landlady*, the concept underlying his adaptation is admirable. He saw Hoffmann's tales as totalities and treated them as such, quite in distinction to the other Russian Hoffmannists who almost invariably borrowed motifs or detached sections of tales for special development, usually with artistic mediocrity as a result. His method of procedure was precisely the contrary of theirs, a multiplication, not a division.

The case becomes all the more remarkable when one takes into account the fact that the source stories for Dostoevski and for the preceding Russian Hoffmannists were, by and large, identical. *Der Sandmann, Der goldene Topf,* and the twin stories, *Der Magnetiseur* and *Der unheimliche Gast,* served both "Pogorel'ski" and Prince Odoevski in the construction of their own tales; Polevoi had recourse to *Der Artushof* and *Die Jesuiterkirche in G.,* as well as to a portion of *Meister Floh;* the literary oddity called *The Lonely Cottage on Vasilevski Island,* conceived by Pushkin but written by "Tit Kosmokratov," derived in part from *Datura fastuosa;* Gogol's Petersburg tales drew successively on the Franzesko-inset from *Die Elixiere des Teufels,* on *Aus dem Leben dreier Freunde,* and on certain motifs from *Kater Murr.* Every one of these titles occurs anew in relation to Dostoevski's early stories, but with results so different that the common origins have passed all but unnoticed.

Different as those previous Hoffmannists were, one from another, they were in total agreement on two counts: first, in the borrowing of parts rather than entities; and second, in the writing in what each one of them fancied was "the Hoffmann manner." This amounted to challenging Hoffmann on his home-ground but with borrowed and ill-adapted arms. Failure was inevitable. Gogol, who sensed the disparity between his own high talents and the spirit of his model, turned resentful of the elusiveness of Hoffmann's secret and ended by reducing all "Hoffmannism" to an inane parody in *The Nose.* Only the inimitable Pushkin in *The Queen of Spades* penetrated to the inner areas of Hoffmann's art and wrote, independently and without specific borrowings, as Hoffmann might have written. The story matches Hoffmann at his best, and in his own terms. But *The Queen of Spades* stands unique even in Pushkin's own repertory.

It was with the notion of Hoffmann's solemnity that the Russian writers made their major error. So long as they persisted in seeing philosophy where there was only imaginative fiction, they were bound to miss his splendid wit and humor; so long as they persisted in taking his juxtaposed real and ideal worlds in a sombre religious sense, they were bound to miss his subtle and wonderful irony. His steadfast optimism was apparently inacceptable to their collective temperaments. To Dostoevski likewise the optimism proved alien, but for personal reasons, not because he misread the texts. He perceived the whole of Hoffmann much more clearly than his predecessors, perhaps because of a greater remove of distance. Not for a moment was he deceived into thinking of him as fictionalizing philosopher. Rather, he rightly saw him as a creative artist of great range and depth and his works as sources abounding in characters and narrative invention. Dostoevski had urgent need of both, and it was as apprentice to master that he approached Hoffmann. He borrowed freely but he also adapted freely, for he had a strong artistic will of his own. He used the borrowings, not like his predecessors in a pseudo-Hoffmannian manner, but in Dostoevski's manner. They imitated, he created. There is a world of difference between the two processes.

The new conception of Hoffmann was entirely Dostoevski's own, the insight of one great artist into the nature of another great artist. His utilization of the borrowed elements, despite unevennesses and infelicities at first, was always original and striking. If the wit and irony of Hoffmann eluded him, and above all the element of beauty, as they had eluded his predecessors, Dostoevski had other purposes quite as valid and justifiable to pursue, and for all their differences, the new master proved himself fully worthy of the old, and the old master was fully worthy of the new. Ultimately, by means of processes learned from Hoffmann and with materials derived from Hoffmann, *The Brothers Karamazov* came into being, close to the very summits of world literature.

NOTES

I — INTRODUCTION

1. *Das Fräulein von Scudery* (Devitsa Skiuderi) in the *Son of the Fatherland* (Syn Otechestva), Supplement, Part III, 1822.

2. *Doge und Dogaresse* (Dozh i Dogaressa) in the same magazine, Part XII, 1823.
   Spielerglück (Schast'e igrokov) in the *Messenger of Europe* (Vestnik Evropy) 1823.

3. *Eine Spukgeschichte* (sometimes entitled *Der schwebende Teller*) translated as *The White Apparition* (Beloe prividenie) in the *Moscow Telegraph* (Moskovski Telegraf), Supplement, 1825.
   Die Marquise de la Pivardière (Markiza de la Pivard'er), ibid.

4. *The Poppy-seed-cake Woman of the Lafërtov Quarter* (Lafërtovskaya Makovnitsa) by "Antoni Pogorel'ski," whose real name was Perovski, though he was the natural son of Count Razumovski. The story derives from the episodes involving Old Liese and her cat in Hoffmann's *Der goldene Topf*. The story first appeared in *News of Literature* (Novosti Literatury) in March 1825, and later was placed as the tale of the *Fifth Evening* in the collection called *The Double, or My Evenings in Little Russia*, 1828.

5. *Datura fastuosa*, translated as *The Botanist* (Botanik) in the *Moscow Telegraph* (VIII), 1826.

6. *Der Magnetiseur* (Hoffmann's original title was *Träume sind Schäume*) translated as *As Foam in water, so (are) dreams in the head* (Chto pena v vode, to sny v golove) in the *Moscow Messenger* (Moskovski Vestnik) (III), 1827. Dmitri Vladimirovich Venevitinov (1805-1825) was a lyric poet of great promise and a close friend of Pushkin. He died of consumption not long after his twenty-first birthday.

7. *The Double, or My Evenings in Little Russia* (Dvoinik, ili moi vechera v. Malorosii) 1828. See Note 4 above. "Pogorel'ski" is said to have coined the Russian word "dvoinik" in this work in order to render the German "Doppelgänger" or "Doppeltgänger."

8. *The Improvisor* (Improvizator) in *Halcyon* (Al'tsion) 1833 by Prince V. F. Odoevski, organizer of the "Lovers of Wisdom" group (Lyubomudry) for the discussion of Romantic, chiefly German, literature and philosophy.

9. *The Felicity of Madness* (Blazhenstvo Bezumiya) in the *Moscow Telegraph* 1 and 2, 1833; and *The Painter* (Zhivopisets) in the same magazine, 9-12, 1833, by Nikolai Alexeevich Polevoi, general man of letters and founder of the *Moscow Telegraph* (1825-1834) as an international Review in the manner of the *Revue Encyclopédique*. He was also a novelist, amateur philosopher, and historian.

10. *The Portrait* (Portret) 1834, but included in Vol. I of *Arabesques* (Arabeski), published January 1835.

11. *The Nevski Prospekt* (Nevski Prospekt) and *The Diary of a Madman* (Zapiski sumasshedshego) (originally planned as *The Diary of a Mad Musician*), both in Vol. II of *Arabesques*.

12. *The Nose* (Nos), written early in 1836 and published in the first number of the new magazine founded by Pushkin, *The Contemporary* (Sovremennik), September 1836. This was the most famous of all 19th century Russian journals.

13. *Russian Nights* (Russkie Nochi), a collection of tales in book form, published 1844.

14. In general, Russian Romanticists of the English-French persuasion carried on their activities in Petersburg, considered Pushkin as their leader, and were averse to "mysticism"; those of the German persuasion tended, on the other hand, to center their lives in Moscow, had no specific leader, and were devoted to philosophy, such as Schelling and Hegel, as well as to literature. The home of Prince Odoevski was a gathering place for them.
15. See the selection *From the Reminiscences of D. V. Grigorovich* included as pp. 247-255 in the book of *Letters of Fyodor Michailovitch Dostoevsky to his Family and Friends*, translated (from the German versions of Alexander Eliasberg) by Ethel Colburn Mayne, London 1914; also Macmillan Co., New York.
16. Ibid., p. 248.
17. Ibid., pp. 3-5.
18. Ibid., pp. 9-15; p. 11.
19. Ibid., pp. 251 ff.
20. Ibid., pp. 31-33; p. 33.
21. Ibid., pp. 33-36; pp. 34-35.
22. See N. Brodsky's essay, *The Unfulfilled Idea: Note on "The Life of a Great Sinner,"* pp. 145-169 of the book entitled *F. M. Dostoevsky: Stavrogin's Confession and the Plan of "The Life of a Great Sinner,"* translated by S. S. Koteliansky and Virginia Woolf, Hogarth Press, Paradise Road, Richmond, 1922. On page 150 Brodsky says:
"In Dostoevski's note-books there remain traces of his creative ideas, 'ideas for new stories,' plans of unfinished works, 'memento. For my whole life.' Thus on one page I found a note: *'In 1860,* (1) The Darling, (2) Spring Love, (3) *The Double (to re-write it),* (4) Memoirs of a Convict. . . ."
See also *The Diary of a Writer*, translated by Boris Brasol, New York, Charles Scribner's Sons, 1949, Vol. II, p. 883, article of November 1877. Speaking of the history of the verb "stushevat'sa" (to efface oneself), which Dostoevski claims he invented and used for the first time in *The Double*, he says of the story itself:—
"Most decidedly I did not succeed with that novel; however, its idea was rather lucid, and I have never expressed in my writings anything more serious. Still, as far as form was concerned, I failed utterly. Fifteen years later, I made considerable improvement in it for the then *Complete Collection* of my works; however, also at that time I came again to the conclusion that in this work I had not succeeded at all, and were I now to expound and express this idea, I should adopt an altogether different form. But in 1846, I failed to find it, and was unable to master the novel."

II — THE DOUBLE

1. This famous tale of the luckless fellow who sold his shadow to the "man in grey" originally appeared as *Peter Schlemihl's wundersame Geschichte* mitgetheilt von Adelbert von Chamisso und herausgegeben von Friedrich Baron de la Motte Fouqué, 1814. Its fame was almost instantaneous. Hoffmann's *Sylvesternacht*, which introduces Schlemihl into a new setting together with a patently imitated figure who has lost his mirror-image, was composed in the first week in January,—hence directly after New Year's Eve,—in the year 1815. On the night of the 13th Hoffmann gave a reading of the new work to a group of friends, of whom Chamisso was one.
2. *Kater Murr*, Erster Band, zweiter Abschnitt; the 8th "Makulaturblatt."
3. For a notable instance of such procedure, which may not be unrelated to this chapter-close, see *Die Elixiere des Teufels*, end of the Erster Abschnitt des zweiten Teils, where the pair of Doubles wrestle all night in deadly combat in the forest until Medardus loses

consciousness. It is never explained how he managed finally to elude his antagonist. The beginning of the following section (Zweiter Teil, Erster Abschnitt—*Die Busse*) describes Medardus coming to consciousness—three months later.

4. See Notes 4 and 7 to the preceding chapter.

5. Yasha is the diminutive of Yakov (James). The hero's full name is Yakov Petrovich Golyadkin.

6. Note the interpenetration of the lives of Medardus and Viktorin. This confession reads like the experiences of *Medardus* seen through the medium of a deranged mind.

7. Medardus, in a passage previously quoted, describes his waking in the Italian monastery by saying ". . . my Self was divided hundred-fold."

In this connection, another Tale of Hoffmann may be mentioned, *Die Brautwahl*, the opening chapters of which deal with the adventures of the hapless Privy Councilor Tusmann in the streets of Berlin on the night of the autumnal equinox. Tusmann has for opponents certain persons who control very potent magic and who have undertaken certain "operations" to forestall his marriage to the heroine, Albertine Vosswinkel, who is thirty years his junior. At one stage of the "operations" he finds himself compelled to waltz up and down the Spandauerstrasse with a broomstick (Chapter 3). Suddenly the place around him "teemed with Privy Councillor Tusmanns," all of them waltzing with broomsticks.—A page or two previously he had tried to enter his own house, but there at the door he met "himself" and "stared wildly at himself with the same large black eyes as are located in his own head."

Tusmann's adventures will be used by Dostoevski as the partial basis for *An Unpleasant Predicament*, a short story of 1862, and it is quite likely that *Die Brautwahl* is to be included in the various Hoffmann works which contributed details to *The Double*. The primary point of connection would be the bizarre nocturnal adventures of the middle-aged hero in the streets of the capital.

8. It should be observed that this passage is paralleled *within* Hoffmann's novel by the scene where the would-be bridegroom Medardus looks down from the palace window to behold his Double being carried in the hangman's cart to execution. Undoubtedly both scenes are to be related to the final pages of Dostoevski's story.

9. Complex as this analysis has been, it has not wholly exhausted the elements that went into Dostoevski's story.

See V. V. Vinogradov: *Evoliutsiya russkago naturalizma*, Leningrad, 1929, a series of six articles; Article 5: *K Morfologii natural'nogo stilya. Opyt lingvisticheskogo analiza Peterburgskoi poemy "Dvoinik*," pp. 239 ff., fills four pages with linguistic and stylistic parallels between *The Double* and Gogol's *Dead Souls*.

See also S. Rodzevich: *K Istorii russkago romantizma* in *Russki Filologicheski Vestnik*, LXXVII (1917), pp. 194-237. On page 223 Rodzevich mentions that Hoffmann's *Klein Zaches* and *Prinzessin Brambilla* have bearing on *The Double*, but does not elaborate his statement. The case for *Prinzessin Brambilla* is dubious except in so far as it deals with the interlocked worlds of reality and "higher reality," in which respect it would run competition from various other works of Hoffmann. From *Klein Zaches* could very plausibly come the motif of Zaches's fateful fairy-gift of receiving credit for every good thing said or done by anyone in his presence. This would apply to the passages where Mr. Golyadkin Junior gets credit at the office for the work done by the staid Mr. Golyadkin Senior.

III — A NOVEL IN NINE LETTERS

1. Quoted on p. 12 above. See Mayne: *Letters of Dostoevski*, op. cit., pp. 33-36; p. 35.

2. Ibid., pp. 38-40. On page 39 he says:
   "Now they are spreading it about that I'm off my head with
   conceit, and have sold myself to Kraevski, because Maikov praises
   me in his paper. Nekrasov henceforth means to drag me down.
   But, as to Belinski, he is so pliable that even about literary matters
   he changes his view five times a week. With him alone I have kept
   up my former happy relations. . . ."
3. Ibid., pp. 37-38; p. 37.
4. For the perception of the relationship between *A Novel in Nine Letters* and *Haimatochare* I am indebted to Professor Dmitri Čiževski
   of Harvard University, who mentioned it to me in private conversation.
5. Though there is no more relationship of *contents* than there is with
   Haimatochare, one cannot help wondering whether Dostoevski did
   not intend this literary jest to be *his* literary equivalent of Gogol's
   delightful Ukrainian tale: *How Ivan Ivanovich Quarelled with Ivan
   Nikiforovich*.

IV — THE LANDLADY

1. Gerhard Gesemann in *Der Träumer und der Andere*, p. 14, contrasts
   Dostoevski's dreamer heroes with figures like the painter Piskarev in
   Gogol's *The Nevski Prospekt* (1835) and defines them as Gogolian
   heroes with finer nerves. He also comments on the taboo of painter-
   heroes in the 1840's in Russia and points out that when Dostoevski
   does introduce artists into his stories, he makes them either musicians or poets.
   See Gerhard Gesemann: *Der Träumer und der Andere*, Ein Kapitel
   zur vergleichenden Dostoevskij-Forschung, in *Veröffentlichungen
   der Slavistischen Arbeitsgemeinschaft an der Universität Prag*, I.
   Reihe: Untersuchungen, Heft 8 (1931) (Dostoevskij-Studien).
2. Compare for instance a passage like the following from the early
   pages of *Die Elixiere des Teufels*, where Medardus is recalling his
   childhood:
   "But as soon as the monastery bell sounds, the noise is suddenly hushed—as far as the eye can see, everyone, pressed in ser-
   ried rows, has fallen to his knees, and only the indistinct murmuring of the prayer breaks the holy stillness. . . . The Bishop himself . . . used to hold solemn service and his choir used to perform
   the music on a platform erected at the side of the high altar and
   draped with rich and rare tapestry. . . . I vividly recall a Gloria
   which was frequently performed. . . . When the Bishop had intoned
   the Gloria and now the mighty tones of the choir poured forth:
   Gloria in excelsis Deo!—was it not as if the cloud-halo above the
   high altar were opening? yes, and as if by a divine miracle the
   painted cherubim and seraphim glowed forth into life and moved
   and stirred their strong wings and floated up and down, praising
   God with song and wondrous music of lyres? . . . After the High
   Mass the nuns used to pass in solemn procession through the pas-
   sageways of the monastery and through the church, the Abbess at
   their head invested with the miter and the silver crozier. . . ."
   Similar passages can be found at various points in the novel.
   Curiously enough, the opulent Orthodox ritual had never been introduced into Russian fiction. The strict censorship undoubtedly made
   the subject taboo. At any rate, Dostoevski, for all his religiosity,
   describes a church only in this passage. The monastery scenes in
   The Brothers Karamazov take place in the residence quarters of
   the monks.
3. *Der Magnetiseur*, originally entitled *Träume sind Schäume*, Hoffmann's
   first horror tale, was written in 1813 and published as part of Vol.
   II of the *Fantasiestücke in Callots Manier*, Easter, 1814.

4. On page 9 above; see Note 17 to the Introduction.

5. For a lucid and fascinating account of these concepts, see Ricarda Huch: *Ausbreitung und Verfall der Romantik*, Leipzig, 1902; pp. 95-98 take up the matter of hypnosis; pp. 228-229 mention Baader's question and Hoffmann's *Magnetiseur*.

6. *Der unheimliche Gast* was written in 1819 and published 1820 in Volume III of *Die Serapionsbrüder*. It may be noted that a third variation of the basic situation forms the story of *Der Elementargeist*, written by Hoffmann in 1822, the last year of his life, and that its central figure, the Danish Major O'Malley, is even less plausible than Count S——i. See Harvey W. Hewett-Thayer: *Hoffmann: Author of the Tales*, Princeton University Press, 1948; p. 176.

7. See Note 8 to the Introduction. Odoevski's story is related to various works of Hoffmann, notably to *Der goldene Topf, Klein Zaches*, and *Der Sandmann*.

8. *Der Sandmann*, written in November 1815 and placed as the opening story in Vol. I of the *Nachtstücke*, published in the spring of 1817, enjoyed considerable popularity in Russia as elsewhere, though we would not now consider it one of the author's best productions. "Pogorel'ski" unblushingly lifted the whole central section about the mechanical doll to make his own story, *The Baleful Consequences of an Unbridled Imagination* (Pagubnye posledstviya neobuzdannogo voobrazheniya), which he then assigned to the *Third Evening* of *The Double, or My Evenings in Little Russia*, 1828. The *Moscow Telegraph* published a translation of *Der Sandmann* in 1830, entitled *House-spirit Sand* (Domovoi Pesochnik), and in the following year *The Telescope* carried a second translation called *The Sand Man* (Pesochny Chelovek). Its influence, as has been mentioned, may be observed in Prince Odoevski's *The Improvisor*, 1833.

9. The "unchildlike passion" inspired in the boy Ordynov by the evil old man of his dreams is passed over with a mere mention, but in Katerina's case it is expanded to considerable length. She represents herself as her mother's rival for Murin's love and guilty of some serious crime relative to her mother in this matter. The mother, in her fury of defeat, turns on her daughter and threatens to tell the girl's father "whose daughter you are, whose bastard child." If by this she means Murin, then the Romantic theme of incest is involved, and that is precisely the theme introduced into the contemporary work *Netochka Nexvanova*, where the young heroine has a most "unchildlike passion" for her stepfather.
   Dostoevski could not but have been aware that he was here introducing a note never struck in Hoffmann's works. Observe his remark about the essential "purity" of Hoffmann in the brief essay entitled *Three Tales of Edgar Poe* (1861), quoted below on p. 133.

10. Gerhard Gesemann: *Der Träumer und der Andere*, op. cit., p. 7.

11. *A Terrible Vengeance* (Strashnaya Mest'), included in Vol. II of *Evenings on a Farm near Dikan'ka* (Vechera na khutore bliz Dikan'ki), more commonly called "The Ukrainian Tales," is not Ukrainian except in so far as Gogol altered the externals of the story. The plot is borrowed from Ludwig Tieck's *Pietro Apone*.

12. Rodzevich: *K Istorii russkago romanitzma*, op. cit., (Note 9 to the chapter on *The Double*), discusses the sources of *The Landlady* pp. 231-236. He compounds Murin out of Coppelius, Alban, and Count S——i; makes Ordynov parallel to Nathanael; and makes Katerina equivalent to Maria in *Der Magnetiseur*. But he offers no explanation for the contradictions thus raised. No one, apparently, has recognized the crucial relationship with *Der Artushof* or the concept of the two stories "incapsulated" within a third.

V — THE SHORT STORIES OF 1848

1. Mayne: *Letters of Dostoevski,* op. cit., p. 254.
2. *Ritter Gluck* was first published February 15, 1809 in the *Allgemeine musikalische Zeitung* and later incorporated into Vol. I of the *Fantasiestücke,* Hoffmann's first story-collection, Easter 1814.
3. Georg Ellinger, in the *Einleitung des Herausgebers* to his edition of Hoffmann's works, Vol. I, p. 3, categorically states that the strange musician of the story is the departed spirit of Gluck himself, who, with his uncompromising ideals of art, is introduced into the Berlin of 1807 with its wretched music and wretched musicians. Many readers have jumped to this erroneous conclusion unprompted by Ellinger.
    Harvey W. Hewett-Thayer: *Hoffmann: Author of the Tales,* op. cit., p. 149, less dogmatically and more plausibly says:
    "Hoffmann leaves the reader in doubt whether this chance acquaintance is merely a pathetic lunatic who imagines himself to be Gluck or is in reality Gluck reincarnated."
    The first difficulty encountered by the unsuspecting reader is the absence of any specific dates in the story. When the work originally appeared in 1809 readers would be aware that Gluck had been long dead, even if they did not recall that the precise year was 1787. They would also recognize the details of the story, such as the description of the Tiergarten, as distinctly contemporary with themselves. Since the whole understanding of the story depends on the perception of the discrepancy in time and in costume, the lapse of a century and a half since 1809 has brought difficulties to the modern reader.
    The narrative tone certainly gives the impression of an event recently transpired. Scholars therefore have unanimously inferred some experience of Hoffmann's during his year's stay in Berlin from June 18, 1807 to mid-June 1808, presumably in the autumn of 1807, since the story begins on an autumn afternoon. (His only previous visit to Berlin was from August 1798 to March 1800.)
    As to when the work was actually written, and where, and in what circumstances, there is wide difference of opinion. These things would be most useful to know, first to help in the elucidation of *Ritter Gluck* itself, and second, to help explain how Hoffmann, now in his early thirties and a jurist and a musician by training, made the transition to literature, the field in which he was to achieve his true fame.
    Hewett-Thayer, op. cit., p. 61 (footnote),—after avoiding the issue of the date himself,—mentions that Hans von Müller assigns the composition to the summer of 1808 in Glogau, where Hoffmann, financially desperate since the dissolution of the Prussian civil service by Napoleon, was spending the summer with his friend Hampe, a musician; whereas Rudolf Köppler, *E. T. A. Hoffmann am Bamberger Theater,* Bamberg, 1927, claims that the work was written before Hoffmann left Berlin in mid-June 1808. It may be added that Ellinger, in the same introductory article mentioned above, p. 2, says that the composition is definitely to be assigned to the autumn of 1808 after Hoffmann had settled down in his new post as music director of the theatre in Bamberg. Walther Harich's biography, *E. T. A. Hoffmann,* Berlin, 1920, Vol. I, p. 111, wavers between agreement with Hans von Müller and Ellinger.
4. The most conveniently available edition of Dostoevski's shorter prose works, *The Short Stories of Dostoevsky,* edited by William Phillips, Dial Press, New York, 1946, has unexplainably omitted the last page of the text of *A Christmas Tree and a Wedding.* Since much of the significance of the story depends on this final page, the reader must have recourse to *The Novels of Fyodor Dostoevsky* translated by Constance Garnett, New York, Macmillan, 1918, Vol. X, p. 207.

5. See p. 133 below.

6. *Die Brautwahl* will later serve as a source for Dostoevski's story *An Unpleasant Predicament*, 1862.

7. *Datura fastuosa*, one of Hoffmann's latest stories, was first published posthumously in the autumn of 1822 and subsequently included in the collection *Die Letzten Erzählungen*. Unjustly neglected of late years, it is one of the better Tales. In Russia it was translated as early as 1826 in the *Moscow Telegraph*, with the title of *The Botanist* (Botanik). Three years later Pushkin used it as the source for his orally improvised tale, *The Lonely Cottage on Vasilevski Island* (Uyedinenny domik na Vasilevskom), which he then abandoned to the young amateur writer V. P. Titov, in whose version alone the work survives. Titov, with Pushkin's permission, published the story in the 1829 *Almanach*, or special issue, of Baron Delvig's journal *Northern Flowers* (Severnye Tsvety), with his regular *nom de plume*, "Tit Kosmokratov" as signature. For a number of years the Pushkinian authorship was unknown, and not until 1879 did Titov make the matter fully clear in a written statement. The text, not to be found in many editions of Pushkin's complete works, is included, together with notes by Professor S. A. Vengerov, in *Biblioteka Velikikh Pisatelei: Pushkin*, Petrograd, 1915, Vol. VI, pp. 181-192.

8. Babbette Deutsch translation.

9. Hoffmann's story was actually an early work (1813) called *Szenen aus dem Leben zweier Freunde* (i.e. Marzell and Severin), reworked some three years later to include the third friend, Alexander. Under the title of *Fragment aus dem Leben dreier Freunde* it forms part of Vol. I of *Die Serapionsbrüder*, published in the spring of 1819. The Russian translation, *The Life of Three Friends* (Zhizn' trëkh druzei), was printed in the *Moscow Telegraph*, 1831, three years prior to Gogol's *The Nevski Prospekt*.

10. *Petersburg Visions in Verse and Prose* (Peterburgskie Snovideniya v stikhakh i proze) was printed anonymously in Dostoevski's magazine *Time* (Vremya), January 1861, but identified as being unquestionably his writing both by statements of N. N. Strakhov and by evidence from the author's account books. The text, from which the present quotation was translated by me, is printed in *Sobraniya Sochinenii F. M. Dostoevskogo v 13 tomakh*, Moscow-Leningrad, 1930, Vol. XIII, pp. 154-172.
The *Visions* will be considered later in more detail in their proper chronological position. See pp. 115-118 of the present text and Note 2 to the Chapter "Exile and Return. The Works of 1861-1862."

VI — NETOCHKA NEZVANOVA

1. Mayne: *Letters of Dostoevski*, op. cit., pp. 40-43; p. 42.

2. The novel fragment *Netochka Nezvanova* and, somewhat oddly, *Poor Folk*, have not been included in either of the latest reprints of Dostoevski's fiction, *The Short Stories of Dostoevsky*, Dial Press, New York, 1946, and *The Short Novels of Dostoevsky*, Dial Press, New York, 1945. The English translation of *Netochka Nezvanova* is accessible only in the 12-volume *Novels of Fyodor Dostoevsky* translated by Constance Garnett, Macmillan Co., New York, 1918; Vol. XII.

3. The motif of the illusoriness of the Devil's gifts is common enough in folklore, but, if a parallel is demanded, it may be found in the gold which the hero of Gogol's *St. John's Eve* acquired at a fearful price from Basavryuk (Basa—Turko-Arabic for "Pasha," plus Russian *vrun*—"liar," *vran'yo*—"lies"; hence: "Prince of Liars," "Father of Lies"), and which ultimately proved to be mere shards of pottery.

4. Perhaps no character in Hoffmann is wholly supernatural like a devil in a morality play, but partially supernatural are certainly Coppelius, alias Giuseppe Coppola, in *Der Sandmann*, Dr. Dapertutto in *Die Abenteuer der Sylvesternacht*, and probably the pseudo-Spaniard of *Datura fastuosa*, Fermino Valies. (The name is decidedly un-Spanish and "Fermino" is definitely in the Italian form.) As opposed to these, there is the group of purely human Italian villains or partial villains, whose prototype was a real person. When Hoffmann was twenty-one and away on his first journey from home, he met in Glogau the young Italian painter Molinari, who was engaged in redecorating the Jesuit church of that city. His handsome, dashing person, and his stories of student life in Rome, impressed young Hoffmann as both fascinating and sinister. Almost twenty years later he wrote *Die Jesuiterkirche in G.* (Glogau) with Molinari in mind, though the hero of that tale was made to bear the German name of Berthold. Subsequently Molinari served as model for Franzesko the painter, sinning ancestor of the monk Medardus in *Die Elixiere des Teufels*, for Medardus himself in part, whose ancestry was Italo-German, and above all, for the master villain of the Tales, the Neapolitan Prince Hektor of *Kater Murr*. In discussing this matter, Walther Harich (*E. T. A. Hoffmann*, op. cit., Vol. I, pp. 53-54) adds that Fermino Valies may also belong to the Molinari group.

5. Glinka, the "father of Russian music" (1804-1857) had begun his *Ruslan and Lyudmila* in 1838, and this first Russian opera of any intrinsic merit was not presented to the public until November 27, 1842, five years before Dostoevski wrote the opening section of *Netochka Nezvanova*. The work of Dargomyzhski (1813-1869) belongs to the latter 1850's and the decade of the 1860's. The following birth-years of composers indicate the lateness of Russian musical development: Cui 1835; Musorgski 1839; Chaikovski 1840; Rimski-Korsakov 1844; Rakhmaninov 1873.

6. *Rat Krespel* is the editor's title for this famous story which is placed by Hoffmann without title in the midst of the conversations of the frame-tale in Vol. I of *Die Serapionsbrüder*. In English translation it has been known as *The Cremona Violin*, the title also assigned to the Russian translation (Kreminskaya skripka) which appeared in *The Messenger of Europe* in 1830. The French have known the story as *Antonie*, from the name of the heroine. With radical changes, it forms the basis for Act III of Offenbach's opera.

7. *Der Baron von B.* and *Der Schüler Tartinis* are alternate editor's titles for this little story which is, like *Rat Krespel*, to be found without title in the midst of the frame-tale conversations of *Die Serapionsbrüder*, Vol. III.

8. Most scholars agree in making *Die Jesuiterkirche in G.* the pessimistic counterpart of the optimistic *Der Artushof* and in seeing in them alternate outcomes of the conflict between Art and Life. Hewett-Thayer: *Hoffmann: Author of the Tales*, op. cit., pp. 203-204, discusses the ambiguous ending of *Der Artushof* and holds that Dorina will make Traugott an admirable wife without intruding on his artistic career. This explanation then makes the father of Dorina a kind of practical mean between the Philistine Elias Roos and Berklinger, just as it makes Dorina a practical mean between the Philistine Christine Roos and the excessively idealized Felizitas. Possibly the two "Sorrentos" are further symbols of the extremes, for Traugott goes neither to the well known city in Italy nor to the "Sorrento" estate near Danzig, where the Berklingers live.

9. Hoffmann's visit to Glogau in 1796, his inspection of the Jesuit church and of the paintings then in process of renovation, and the "sinister" quality in the painter Molinari are matters of historical fact. See Note 4 above.

A diagram will perhaps make clear the connection between the real Molinari and his literary descendants:

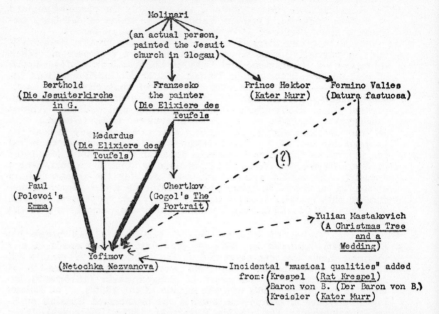

The line of connection between Yefimov and the villain of *Datura fastuosa* is dubious, but if it is assumed, it establishes an interesting *literary* origin for the recurring theme of sexual attraction between an adolescent girl and a middle aged man, as we find it in Dostoevski's works.

10. When Professor Ernest J. Simmons (*Dostoevski, The Making of a Novelist*, Oxford University Press, 1940, p. 52) suggests that *Netochka Nezvanova* may derive in part from Balzac's story *Gambara*, 1837, he undoubtedly refers to the Yefimov section. An influence here is possible, though it can at most be of a contributory nature. The crazy musician of that story is never undeceived as to his genius and goes on living quite happily. Moreover the story as a whole concerns Gambara's wife rather than the insane husband. The text may be found among the *Études philosophiques* in the Pléiade edition of Balzac's collected works, Paris, 1935, Vol. IX, pp. 415-473. In brief outline its action is as follows:

On January 1, 1831, Count Andrea Marcosini, a Milanese nobleman living in Paris, follows a beautiful young woman to the rue Froidmanteau, where she enters one of the ugly houses and disappears. Marcosini then goes into a poor restaurant run by a bonhomme named Giardini, who fancies himself a culinary artist of distinction. As the nobleman is sitting there, the beauty herself appears. She is the devoted wife of a half-crazy musician named Gambara. The count presents himself and proceeds to devote some time to a process of gradual insinuation into Gambara's household, where he pretends to be fascinated with the insane operas and fantastic musical theories of the husband. He encourages Gambara in his delusion of genius and simultaneously finds time to work on the sympathies of the beautiful wife, until he finally persuades her to run off with him.

Six weeks later the wife reappears at Giardini's restaurant, abandoned, starving, and prematurely aged.   Gambara takes her back with joy, and henceforth she spends her days guiding the old man about the streets of Paris, where he ekes out a living by playing music from memory, for which passers-by give him alms.

11. The relationships of the two families is best clarified by a diagram. Characters in Chapters 4 and 5 are all located to the left of the dotted line; characters in Chapters 6 and 7 are located to the right of it.

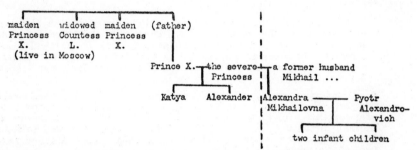

The little that is known concerning the immediate family of Netochka herself may be summarized as follows:

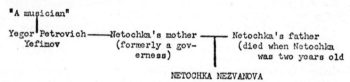

NETOCHKA NEZVANOVA

The remaining characters (not including the "sinister Italian," the landowner, Karl Fyodorich Meyer, etc., who are solely connected with Yefimov) are:

1. "the musician B."—Netochka's informant concerning her own childhood, a friend to Yefimov, to Prince X. and to Alexandra Mikhailovna.

2. the violinist "S."—a true artist; the cause of Yefimov's undoing; Netochka, upon seeing him at Prince X.'s house, first thinks he *is* Yefimov, then cries out that he is Yefimov's murderer.

3. Ovrov—secretary of Pyotr Alexandrovich; appears only in the very last lines of the text; the only named character since Chapter 3.

4. "S.O."—the writer of a love-letter, presumably to Alexandra Mikhailovna, at some previous time; he renounced his love because he came of a lower social class.

12. Dostoevski, in the letter to Michael August 9, 1838, previously cited on p. 9, specifically mentions *Kater Murr* when he says he has read "the whole of Hoffmann in Russian and German (that is, *Kater Murr,* which hasn't yet been translated) . . . ."

A Russian translation did appear in 1840.   Meanwhile, of course, the French version was available.

In 1861 he will single out *Kater Murr* from among Hoffmann's works for special praise in his Foreword to *Three Tales of Edgar Poe*. See pp. 133-134 of the present text.

There is some question as to the amount of German Dostoevski knew in 1838, when he claims he read *Kater Murr* in the original for lack of a Russian translation. In the memoirs of Baron Alexander Vrangel there is a casual remark concerning Dostoevski's knowledge of German as of 1854, just after his release from the prison at Omsk and his transfer to military duty at Semipalatinsk. Vrangel says:

> "I subscribed to three papers: a Petersburg one, a German one, and the *Indépendance Belge*. Dostoevski delighted in reading the Russian and the French ones; he took no particular interest in the German paper, for at that time he did not understand much German, and he always disliked the language." (See Mayne: *Letters of Dostoevski*, op. cit., p. 276.)

A little further on (p. 280), Vrangel speaks of helping Dostoevski translate Hegel and Carus in daily sittings, and it was undoubtedly for this project that Dostoevski asked Michael to send him a German dictionary in the very first letter he was permitted to send from Siberia, the letter of February 22, 1854. (See Mayne: *Letters of Dostoevski*, pp. 51-65.) On p. 61 he says: "Remember, above all things, I need a German dictionary."

Even a quite respectable knowledge of German might still require some bolstering with a dictionary in order to cope with Hegel and Carus, but Vrangel's remark about newspaper reading is more serious. At any rate, Dostoevski certainly knew the work well in 1847-49, whatever the language through which he came to know it.

13. Helmine Lanzendorf, the mysterious beauty of Berlin society, may have been the daughter of the Napoleonic Marshal Bernadotte, founder of the present royal dynasty of Sweden, and Lucie Hardenberg, daughter of Minister Hardenberg. She was brought up by Lucie Hardenberg together with a daughter of her own first marriage. Her foster-mother was devoted to her, far more than to her own daughter, yet countered inquiries about the girl with the answer that she was the legitimate child of one of her coachmen. It is perhaps significant that the answer did not keep Frederick William III of Prussia from proposing marriage at one point with Helmine.

See Harich: *E. T. A. Hoffmann*, op. cit., Vol. II, pp. 117-118 and p. 224.

14. Walther Harich, who expended much time and effort on the matter of the genealogy of the characters in *Kater Murr*, arrived at the conclusion that Hedwiga was the daughter of Meister Abraham and his lost wife Chiara and that the clairvoyant Chiara substituted her in the palace household. Possibly Dostoevski, who had no more information to guide him than Harich or any other reader, was thinking along similar lines when he so closely associated Alexandra Mikhailovna and the musician "B.", Meister Abraham's counterpart. (See Harich: *E. T. A. Hoffmann*, op. cit., Vol. II, pp. 231-233.)

Hewett-Thayer (*Hoffmann: Author of the Tales*, op. cit., pp. 304-305) admires the ingenuity of Harich's reconstructed genealogical table, but suggests that Harich has relied too heavily on analogies from former works by Hoffmann and not allowed the author, who was at the peak of his powers at the time of writing *Kater Murr*, sufficient leeway for the invention of quite new ideas and combinations.

VII — A LITTLE HERO

1. In other words, *Die Fermate* is a light and humorous variant of the
problem-tales *Der Artushof* and *Die Jesuiterkirche in G.*, which
dealt with the question of whether the artist should or should not
marry his "Ideal." *Die Fermate*, written between January 16 and
February 3, 1815, comes first in chronological order, and its more
gravely pitched concluding passage reads like a prelude to the other
two. Hoffmann read the story to a group of friends, among whom
was Fouqué, who persuaded him to give him the work for his own
publication and to write another for the publisher to whom it had
originally been promised. Hoffmann complied, and composed *Der
Artushof* for the original publisher between February 17 and March
6, 1815. *Die Jesuiterkirche in G.* was composed in the latter months
of 1815 or early in 1816. *Rat Krespel* (September 1816) also deals
with the problem of the conflict between Love and Art, though in
quite a different way.—Dostoevski has now made use of all four of
these "Art-stories."
2. *Die Genesung. Fragment aus einem noch ungedruckten Werke* is a
slight work which was first published in July 1822, a month after
Hoffmann's death.

VIII — EXILE AND RETURN. THE WORKS OF 1861-1862

1. *A Friend of the Family* (Russian title: *The Village of Stepanchikovo
and its Inhabitants*) (Selo Stepanchikovo i ego obitateli) was begun
in 1857, interrupted mid-way for the writing of *Uncle's Dream*, completed 1859, and published in *National Notes* in two installments, November and December 1859.
The story is narrated by the nephew of Yegor Ilich Rostanev, a retired Colonel of Hussars, who has hesitantly called his nephew down
to the provincial estate of Stepanchikovo, where things are not
going well. The Colonel could be very happy in his widower's
state, for he is a kind and modest man, devoted to his fifteen-year-
old daughter Sashenka and his lovable eight-year-old son Ilyusha.
Moreover, he is in love with their governess, the gentle Nastenka,
who is poor but proud. But his boundless good will makes him the
unhappy victim of his tyrannical mother, "Madame la Générale," a
number of parasitical and semi-permanent house-guests, and, worst
of all, the sanctimonious fraud Foma Fomich Opiskin, who, like a
latter-day Tartuffe, dominates the entire household. A sizable
episode is taken up with the intrigues of one of the impoverished
house-guests who tries to enlist the visiting nephew's aid in eloping
with the wealthy and hyper-romantic Tatyana Ivanovna. His
scheme fails, but the rich lady elopes with another fortune hunter
named Obnoskin. After her return, the story rises to its climax
when Foma Fomich finally oversteps his prerogatives and slanders
the character of Nastenka in the Colonel's presence. In a sudden
and never-before-seen fury, the Colonel strikes him and knocks him
through a glass door, down a flight of steps, and into the garden.
But Foma Fomich returns, makes apologies, and is reinstated in
the household. Henceforth he lives, a pampered but much less ob-
noxious guest, in the family. The Colonel and Nastenka marry and
live in genuine content.
Not only does Foma Fomich resemble Molière's Tartuffe, but Colonel
Rostanev roughly parallels Orgon, though far more sympathetic
than the French father of the family; "Madame la Générale" corresponds almost exactly to Mme Pernelle; and the honest neighbor,
Mr. Bakhcheev, is a *raisonneur*, not unlike Orgon's brother-in-law
Cléante. The children are younger than those of Orgon, and the
frustrated romance does not involve them but their father and their
governess.

Uncle's Dream (Dyadyushkin son), composed in 1858-59 between the two parts of the preceding story, is told by a narrator who has no part in the action. The plot revolves about a redoubtable provincial matron named Marya Alexandrovna Moskalov, whose prime concern is to find a wealthy husband for her daughter Zina. Zina is frightfully embarrassed by her mother's intrigues but allows herself to be guided by her against her will. At the opening of the story she is grieving for the young tutor whom she loves but whom her mother drove away more than a year previously. The present suitor sponsored by her mother is Pavel Alexandrovich Mozglyakov, who is at present entertaining a wealthy and senile Prince who he insists is his uncle. Zina's mother sees at once that the Prince must become Zina's husband and promises her daughter that when the Prince dies, as he must soon do, Zina may have her wealth *and* the poor tutor. The Prince is duly entertained and flattered until he does, of his own accord, propose marriage to Zina. At this point, Mozglyakov, the rejected suitor, has the brilliant idea of convincing his senile "uncle" that the whole scene of proposal occurred only in a dream. The poor old Prince is half convinced but more fearful lest, if he insist that the event really did take place, his "nephew" will declare him legally insane and remove him to a lunatic asylum. At the party arranged for the announcement of Zina's engagement he does actually tell the assembled company his "dream" and is bewildered by the stormy scene he thereby creates. Zina's mother is so mortified that she moves away. The Prince dies, and a genuine relative comes to claim his remains. Three years later, Mozglyakov, while on a government mission to a remote province, meets Zina again. She is the wife of the local governor,— and her mother is the queen of local society.

2. The text of *Petersburg Visions in Verse and Prose* (Peterburgskie Snovideniya v stikhakh i proze) is printed in *Sobraniya Sochinenii F. M. Dostoevskogo v 13 tomakh*, Moscow-Leningrad, 1930, Vol. XIII, pp. 154-172.

   A note, ibid., p. 595, states: "Printed without signature in the journal *Time* 1861, January, literary supplement (feuilleton), pp. 1-22." This is followed by the testimony of N. N. Strakhov, taken from *Materialy dlya zhizneopisaniya F. M. Dostoevskogo*, p. 213, and by the statement that Dostoevski's authorship is further attested by evidence from the account book of his journals. The literary supplement was reprinted in its entirety in *Russkaya Mysl'*, 1916, pp. 106-126, with a commentary by V. Komarovich; also in the *Proveshchenie* edition of Dostoevski's works under the heading of *Forgotten and unknown Pages* (Zabytye i neizvestnye stranitsy), 1918, pp. 176-208, with a commentary by L. P. Grossmann. See also: Astrov: *Ne nashli puti*, 1914, pp. 281-291.

3. Ibid., p. 155.

4. Ibid., p. 160.

5. It is not impossible that still other autobiographical details, postdating *White Nights*, enter into the character and life of Vanya.— After Dostoevski's release from the prison at Omsk in February 1854, he had been transferred to the 7th Battalion of Siberian Infantry stationed at Semipalatinsk. In the latter town he fell in love with Marya Isaeva, the wife of a dissipated customs officer. It was, however, not the husband who made the third party of the triangle, but rather a young school teacher named Vergunov. Dostoevski's rôle throughout was rather passive, but fraught with jealousy and torment, for all of that. Oddly enough, after the husband's death the competition of Vergunov was eliminated and Dostoevski actually married the lady. She returned with him to Russia and was living with him at the time of his writing *The Insulted and Injured*. It was she, rather than Dostoevski, who, like Vanya, was soon to die of tuberculosis.

6. The Russian word for "wolf" is *volk*, but in an extended adjectival form in which the accent is transferred to another syllable, the "o" is pronounced like an "a." Thus "Volkóvski" and "Valkóvski" are, to all intents and purposes, homonyms. (The phenomenon is known in Russian as *akan'e*: the pronouncing of an unaccented "o" as if it were "a.")

7. The foreword is reprinted in *Sobraniya Sochinenii F. M. Dostoevskogo v 13 tomakh*, Vol. XIII, pp. 523-524, with the title: *Tri rasskaza Edgarda Poe*. A note, ibid., p. 607, states:

"Printed in the journal *Time*, January, 1861, p. 230, in the capacity of editor's foreword to a translation of E. Poe's *The Black Cat* (Chërny Kot), *The Tell-tale Heart* (Serdtse oblichitel'), and *The Devil in the Belfry* (Chërt v ratushe; literally: "The Devil in the City Hall"). (The translation was done by D. Mikhailovski.) Attributed to F. M. Dostoevski by L. P. Grossmann, who also reprinted this foreword with commentary in Vol. XXII of Dostoevski's works, pp. 232-235."

The full text of the foreword is as follows:

THREE TALES OF EDGAR POE

"Two or three tales of Edgar Poe have already been translated into Russian in our journals. We are presenting our readers with three more tales. Here is a particularly strange writer,—strange, indeed, though with great talent. His works must not be reckoned straight off among the fantastic, for, if he be fantastic, he is so, so to speak, in an external way. For example, he has an Egyptian mummy come to life by means of galvanism after having lain five thousand years in the pyramids. Once again by means of galvanism he has the dead man talk about the state of his soul, etc. etc. But this is still not exactly the fantastic manner. Edgar Poe permits only of the external possibility of a non-natural event (giving proofs, moreover, for its possibility, sometimes unusually cleverly), and once having permitted of this event, is in all other respects wholly true to actuality. Such is not the fantasy, for example, of Hoffmann. The latter personifies the forces of Nature in forms: he introduces into his stories sorceresses, spirits, and sometimes even seeks his ideal beyond the earth, in some extraordinary world, accepting this world as a higher thing, as if he himself believed in the actual existence of this secret, enchanted world. . . . Edgar Poe may be termed a writer, not so much fantastic, as capricious! He almost always takes the most exceptional actuality, places his hero in the most exceptional external or psychological position, and with what power of perspicacity, with what striking verity does he tell the state of that man's soul! Besides this, there is in Edgar Poe one characteristic that decisively separates him from all other writers and establishes his originality: this is the vigor of his imagination. Not that he surpasses other writers in imagination. But in his capacity for imagination there is such a unique quality as may be found only in him. This is the power of specific detail. Try, for instance, to imagine to yourself something not quite ordinary or even unknown in actuality and merely possible; the figure that will form before you will always include several more or less general traits of the whole image or will concentrate on some particularity or part of it. But in Poe's stories you will so clearly see all the details of the form of the existence presented to you, that finally you will be convinced, as it were, of its possibility, its actuality, whereas this existence is either almost wholly impossible or has never occurred on earth. For example, in one of his stories there is a description of a journey to the moon,—a most detailed description which he pursues almost hour by hour, all but persuading you that it may have taken place. Similarly, he described in an American newspaper the flight of a balloon that flew across the ocean

from Europe to America.   This description was done so circumstan-
tially, so exactly, was filled with such unexpected and detailed facts,
had such an air of actuality that everyone believed in this journey, of
course only for a few hours.   Then, upon inquiry, it proved that no
such journey had occurred and that the story of Edgar Poe was a
newspaper canard.   Such power of imagination, or more precisely of
reflection, is shown in the stories about the lost letter, about the
murder committed in Paris by an orang-utang, in the tale of the discovered treasure, etc.
   People call him the equal of Hoffmann.   We have already said that
this is not true.   Moreover, Hoffmann is immeasurably greater than
Poe as a poet.   With Hoffmann there is an ideal, indeed not always
explicit, but in this ideal there is purity, there is real beauty, genuine,
peculiar to the man.   This is most evident in his non-fantastic stories
such as, for example, *Meister Martin*, or that most graceful and most
charming tale *Salvator Rosa* (i.e. *Signor Formica*).   We have not yet
spoken of his best production, *Kater Murr*.   What genuine, mature
humor, what vigor of realism, what malice, what types and portraits,
and with all of these—what thirst for beauty, what bright ideal!   If
there is fantasy in Poe, it is a kind of materialistic fantasy, if one
may speak of such a thing.   It is obvious that he is wholly American
even in his most fantastic tales.   In order to acquaint our readers
with this capricious talent, we present for the moment three of his
short stories.
8.   The group includes *Meister Martin der Küfner und seine Gesellen*,
     the unfinished *Der Feind* (about Albrecht Dürer), and *Meister
     Johannes Wacht*, which, though on a theme closely allied to *Der
     Feind*, is not actually set in Nürnberg.
9.   References to Hoffmann by name in the writings of Dostoevski occur
     as follows:
     1.   letter of August 9, 1838 to Michael Dostoevski, in which he makes
          the claim to have read "the whole of Hoffmann"; quoted on p.
          9 of the present text.
     2.   letter of January 1, 1840 to Michael Dostoevski, in which he em-
          phasizes having spent the past winter reading various authors,
          "particularly Hoffmann"; quoted on p. 9.
     3.   *White Nights* (Second Night), 1848; quoted on p. 76.
     4.   *Petersburg Visions in Verse and Prose*, 1861; quoted on pp.
          80-82.
     5.   *The Insulted and Injured* (Chapter 1), 1861; quoted on p. 120-21.
     6.   Foreword to *Three Tales of Edgar Poe*, 1861; quoted in part on
          p. 133 and in toto in Note 7 above.
     7.   *The Possessed* (Part III, Chapter I, "The Fête—First Part"),
          1870-72; quoted on p. 140.
     8.   *An Anecdote from Children's Lives*, from *The Diary of a Writer*,
          1876; see the following note.
10. *An Anecdote from Children's Lives* (Anekdot iz detskoi zhizni).   See
     The Diary of a Writer translated and annotated by Boris Brasol,
     New York, Charles Scribner's Sons, 1949, 2 volumes; Vol. I, p. 551.
     The Diary of a Writer was originally the title of a monthly feature
     article contributed by Dostoevski to the magazine *The Citizen*
     (Grazhdanin), of which he was editor from January 1873 until
     April 1874, when he quarrelled with Prince Meshcherski, the finan-
     cial backer and political mentor of the magazine.   Under the pres-
     sure of financial need, he revived *The Diary of a Writer* in January
     1876 as an independent monthly publication.   The issues appeared
     very irregularly, however, and the contents were made up of ar-
     ticles of varying length on a very wide range of subjects.   The
     publication amounted to Dostoevski's private editorializing on all
     aspects of current events, with frequent recourse to reporting of
     "human interest stories" which had come to the author's attention.
     The "anecdote" in question is such a "human interest story" about a

little girl who has been persuaded by one of her playmates to run away from home, not for any evil reason, but simply for the fun of it. Within twenty-four hours the girl has had quite enough of freedom and gladly returns to her distracted mother. At this point Dostoevski speculates on truancy in general, particularly as a prelude to juvenile delinquency. Speaking of boys' truancy, he says:

"Generally in days gone by, one or two generations back, dreams and fantasies may have been roaming in the heads of these very youthful folks, just as in the contemporary ones. However, present day youngsters are somehow more resolute and much less inclined towards doubts and reflections. The former ones, having conceived a project (well, for example, to escape to Venice after having read about Venice in the novels of Hoffmann or George Sand—I knew one such fellow), nevertheless did not proceed with the fulfillment of these projects, and at the utmost confided them under oath to some schoolmate, whereas the contemporary ones, having conceived something, put it into effect."

11. Even *Doge und Dogaresse* is told in retrospect by a person *in Berlin*, by way of an explanation of a picture hung at a Berlin art exposition.

A brief flash-back in the story *Rat Krespel* relates the life of Antonie's mother as a temperamental opera singer in Venice.

Hoffmann, who had never set foot on Italian soil, necessarily drew his information about Italy from books and from travellers' accounts. This fact, in addition to his preference for urban locales, limited the possible Italian settings of his stories. The most frequent settings are Rome or Naples and its environs.

X — THE LIFE OF A GREAT SINNER

1. Cited by Simmons: *Dostoevski*, op. cit., p. 241.
2. Mayne: *Letters of Dostoevski*, op. cit., pp. 177-178.
3. Ibid., pp. 180-182.
4. Tikhon Zadonski (1724-1783) Bishop of Voronezh in south-central Russia, noted for his extraordinary piety and goodness and recognized in Dostoevski's time as a saint by the Orthodox Church. His sermons and letters were well known to Dostoevski.
5. Chaadaev—Pyotr Yakovlevich Chaadaev (? 1792-1856), possibly the model for Pushkin's Eugene Onegin, is primarily remembered as a philosopher of history. His *Lettres philosophiques*, composed in French, were circulated in manuscript in the early 1830's, and a few selections from them appeared in print at that time, but it was not until October 1836 that the *Première Lettre*, in Russian translation, was published in full by *The Telescope*. As a result of the publication, the magazine was suppressed and its editor banished to the remote provinces; the hapless censor who had approved the article was expelled from his censorship post and from his university teaching post, while Nicholas I personally cancelled his pension; Chaadaev himself was declared insane, put under house arrest, and obliged to submit to daily (not weekly) examinations by a physician. Though Chaadaev wrote his recantation, again in French, entitled *Apologie d'un fou*, immediately afterward (1837), copies of other *Lettres* were actually smuggled out of Russia and published by the Jesuits in France in 1862. (*Oeuvres choisies de Pierre Tchadaïeff* publiées pour la première fois par le P. Gagarin, Paris-Leipzig, 1862.) The *Lettre* of 1836 was considered as a kind of manifesto by the Westernizers, who, though they might disagree with one or another aspect of the author's thought, such as his pro-Catholic stand, nevertheless agreed with the idea that Russia was a nation without history, confronted with the task of assimilation of European culture of several centuries.

6. Belinski—Vissarion Grigorevich Belinski, the famous critic and political liberal, who "discovered" Dostoevski in 1845 and subsequently rejected him. After Dostoevski's return from exile with ideas reversed from those of his youth, he conceived a particular hatred for the now deceased (1848) Belinski.

7. Granovski—Timofei Nikolaevich Granovski (1813-1855), Professor of history at the University of Moscow and a disciple of Hegel. His glorification of the Catholic Middle Ages in both University and public lectures in 1843-44 made him a controversial figure bitterly attacked by the Slavophiles.

8. Paul the Prussian—Tsar Paul I, 1796-1801.

9. Golubov—? (Possibly Moisei Alexandrovich Golubëv, 1824-1869, Professor of Sacred Scripture at the Petersburg Ecclesiastical Academy, Biblical critic and translator of the Old Testament.)

10. the monk Parfeni (Parthenius)—the name in religion of Pyotr Aggeev (? 1807-1878), who in 1855 wrote a book much admired by Dostoevski: *The Tale of the Wandering and Journeying in Russia, Moldavia, Turkey, and the Holy Land of the tonsured monk of the holy mountain of Athos, the monk Parfeni* (Skazanie o stranstvii i puteshestvii po Rossii, Moldavii, Turtsii i Svyatoi Zemle Postrizhennika svyatyya gory Afoskiya, inoka Parfeniya). Parthenius had in childhood been a schismatic (Old Believer), but subsequently became a devout convert to Orthodoxy and a rigorous ascetic.

11. Kostanzhoglo—the "good" land-owner in Part II of Gogol's *Dead Souls*. Some versions of that novel still print the name as "Skudronzhoglo," as it was in Gogol's earlier manuscripts. Only after 1849 does the form "Kostanzhoglo" occur.

12. Andrei Ivanovich Stolz, the Russo-German friend and good counsellor of the hero in Goncharov's novel *Oblomov* (1859).

13. See *Zapisnye Tetradi F. M. Dostoevskogo,* publikuemye tsentral'nym arkhivnym upravleniem SSSR (Tetradi NoNo 1 i 4) i publichnoi bibliotekoi SSSR imeni Lenina (Tetradi NoNo 2 i 3), edited by E. N. Konshina, Academia Edition, 1935.
For the English version, see *F. M. Dostoevsky: Stavrogin's Confession and the Plan of "The Life of a Great Sinner,"* translated by S. S. Koteliansky and Virginia Woolf, Hogarth Press, Paradise Road, Richmond, 1922. In addition to the translation of the pertinent passages from Dostoevski's notebooks, this extremely useful book also contains two essays on Stavrogin's confession, one by V. Friche and one by V. Komarovich, and an excellent essay on the *Life of a Great Sinner,* entitled *The Unfulfilled Idea,* by N. Brodsky (pp. 147-169). (The same book was republished by Lear Publishers, New York, 1947, augmented by Sigmund Freud's brief psychoanalytical study of Dostoevski.)

14. *Zapisnye Tetradi F. M. Dostoevskogo,* p. 107; (pp. 96-107 deal with the Great Sinner). See also pp. 87-114 of the Koteliansky-Woolf translation for the material on the Great Sinner, and pp. 113-114 for this important passage.

15. Friedrich Joseph Haas(e), 1780-1853, known in Russia as "Fëdor Petrovich Gaaz," was born near Cologne and taught medicine in Vienna. Three times he journeyed to Russia, once in 1803, when he carried on a famous medical practice in Moscow; once in 1809-10, when he made a study of mineral waters in the Caucasus; and a last time in 1813, when he established himself permanently in Moscow. Upon request of Prince Golitsyn he became a member of a committee to attend to all matters pertaining to prisons and deportations. Horrified by the conditions he found, Haas began a life-long and amazingly selfless dedication to convicts of all classes and succceeded in persuading the authorities to abolish some of the cruel practices customarily visited upon prisoners. He interviewed exiles before their departure for Siberia, sometimes accompanied them part way

on their journey, maintained communication with their relatives, sent money and books to the unfortunates in their exile, assumed care of deserted children, and wrote letters of comfort which were in many cases the only contact the deported men had with their homeland. Sometimes scoffed at by the public as a crank, he was known to prisoners as "the holy doctor."

16. Harich: *E. T. A. Hoffmann*, op. cit., Vol. I, pp. 286-287.—The outline of *Die Elixiere des Teufels* in "Acts" is paraphrased from Harich.

XI — THE BROTHERS KARAMAZOV

1. *Die Elixiere des Teufels*, near the beginning of Part I, Section 1.

2. A corresponding dedication of the hero occurs in *A Raw Youth* (Part I, Chapter VI), showing how intimately this idea was linked in Dostoevski's mind with the childhood of the Great Sinner. Dolgoruki is questioning his mother about his earliest recollections of her and discovers that one particular memory is to be associated with either his first, his fourth, or his sixth year,—the choice among the three is not established.

    "I don't know or remember anything," he says, "only something of your face remained in my heart for the rest of my life, and the fact, too, that you were my mother. I recall everything there as though it were a dream. . . . And you, Mother, I remember clearly only at one moment when I was taken to the church there and you held me up to receive the sacrament and to kiss the chalice. It was in summer, and a dove flew through the cupola, in at one window and out at another.
    'Mercy on us, that's just how it was!' cried my mother. . . . 'With the chalice just before you, you started and cried out, 'A dove, a dove!' "

3. *Die Elixiere des Teufels*, very near the end of Part I, Section 1.

4. Ibid., Part II, Section 3, about two-thirds of the way through the section.

5. Book XI, Chapter 2 and Book XII, Chapter 1.—Skotoprigonevsk will be sought in vain on maps of Russia. As to possible candidates for the actual setting of *The Brothers Karamazov*, at least three sites may be mentioned: (1) the actual monastery of Optina Pustyn' at Koselsk, in Kaluga Province south-west of Moscow; (2) two rural villages of the Moscow area, Darovoe and Chermashnaya, associated with Dostoevski's boyhood and revisited by him in 1877, just at the time when his last novel was beginning to take form in his mind; (3) Tobolsk, far to the north-east, in Siberia, native place of the man Ilinski, whose innocence of his father's murder was established only after he had served a considerable portion of his sentence at hard labor in the Omsk prison at the time of Dostoevski's penal servitude there. It may also be mentioned that the activities of Tikhon Zadonski are associated with the province of Voronezh in south-central Russia along the Don River.

6. See Simmons: *Dostoevski*, op cit., 344-345.

7. See Note 22 to the Introduction of the present text.

8. See Hewett-Thayer: *Hoffmann: Author of the Tales*, op. cit., pp. 270-271.

9. *Die Elixiere des Teufels*, Part I, Section 3.

10. *The Brothers Karamazov*, Book XI, Chapter 9.

11. *Die Elixiere des Teufels*, Part I, Section 3.

12. Ibid., Part II, Section I.

TABLE 1

The Works of Ernst Theodor Amadeus Hoffmann
(January 24, 1776–June 25, 1822)

(Dates of publication of individual stories previous to their inclusion in
the collections are given in parentheses; if no date is given, the story first
appeared in the collection where it is listed.)

Novels:
  Die Elixiere des Teufels—1816
  Kater Murr
      Part   I—July 1819
      Part   II—December 1821
      Part III—(scheduled for Easter 1822; unwritten)

Independent Märchen:
  Klein Zaches—January 1819
  Prinzessin Brambilla—November 1820
  Meister Floh—April 1822

The Collections of Tales:
  1. *Fantasiestücke in Callots Manier*
          Volumes I and II—Easter 1814
          Volume III—autumn 1814
          Volume IV—Easter 1815
          (republished in two volumes, 1819)

          Volume I
              Jacques Callot
              Ritter Gluck (1809)
              6 Kreisleriana (1810-1813)
              Don Juan (1813)

          Volume II
              *Nachrichten von den neuesten Schicksalen des Hundes
                  Berganza*
              Der Magnetiseur

          Volume III
              Der goldene Topf

          Volume IV
              Die Abenteuer der Sylvesternacht
              7 Kreisleriana

  2. *Die Nachtstücke*
          Volume I—spring 1817
          Volume II—autumn 1817

          Volume I
              Der Sandmann
              Ignaz Denner
              Die Jesuiterkirche in G.
              Das Sanctus

          Volume II
              Das öde Haus
              Das Majorat
              Das Gelübde
              Das steinerne Herz

  3. *Die Serapionsbrüder*
          Volume I   —spring 1819
          Volume II —autumn 1819
          Volume III—autumn 1820
          Volume IV—spring 1821

Volume I

(frame tale)
Der Graf von P. *(or *Der Einsiedler Serapion**)
Rat Krespel* (1817)
Die Fermate (1815)
Der Dichter und der Komponist (1813)
Fragment aus dem Leben dreier Freunde (1818)
Der Artushof (1816)
Die Bergwerke zu Falun
Nussknacker und Mausekönig (1816)

Volume II

Die Automate (1814)
Alte und neue Kirchenmusik (1814)
Der Kampf der Sänger (1818)
Doge und Dogaresse (1818)
Meister Martin der Küfner und seine Gesellen (1818)
Das fremde Kind (1817)
Eine Spukgeschichte* (or *Der schwebende Teller**)

Volume III

Nachricht aus dem Leben eines unbekannten Mannes (or
    Der Teufel in Berlin*) (1819)
Die Brautwahl (1819)
Der unheimliche Gast (1819)
Das Fräulein von Scudery (1819)
Spielerglück (1819)
Der Baron von B.* (or *Der Schüler Tartinis**) (1819)

Volume IV

Erscheinungen (1817)
Signor Formica (1819) (sometimes referred to as "Salvator
    Rosa")
Der Zusammenhang der Dinge (1820)
Die Königsbraut
Zacharias Werner
Vampirismus* (*Eine Vampyrgeschichte**)

4. *Die Letzten Erzählungen*
    2 volumes—1825
  and miscellaneous
        Datura fastuosa (autumn 1822)
        Der Dey von Elba (May 1815)
        Die Doppeltgänger (1822)
        Der Elementargeist (autumn 1821)
        Der Feind (autumn 1823)
        Die Geheimnisse (autumn 1821)
        Die Genesung (July 1822)
        Haimatochare (June 1819)
        Die Irrungen (autumn 1820)
        Die Marquise de la Pivardière (autumn 1820)
        Die Räuber (autumn 1821)
        Sendschreiben eines Klostergeistlichen (1803)
        Des Vetters Eckfenster (spring 1822)
        Vision auf dem Schlachtfeld bei Dresden (1814)
        Meister Johannes Wacht (1823)

---

* editor's title

TABLE 2

The Works of Fëdor Mikhailovich Dostoesvki
(October 30, 1821-January 28, 1881)

Title	Written	Published	Type
Poor Folk (Bednye Liudi)	(?) 1843 to May 1845	1846 (January 15) *Petersburg Miscellany* (Peterburgski Sbornik)	short novel
The Double (Dvoinik)	1845	1846 (February 1) *National Notes* (Otechestvennye Zapiski)	short story
Mr. Prokharchin (Gospodin Prokharchin)	1846	1846 (October) *National Notes*	short story
A Novel in Nine Letters (Roman v devyati pis'makh)	1845	1847 (January) *The Contemporary* (Sovremennik)	short story
The Landlady (Khozyaika)	1847	1847 (October) *National Notes*	short story
Another Man's Wife and The Husband under the Bed (Chuzhaya zhena i Muzh pod krovat'yu)	1848	1848 (January; December)) *National Notes* (as two separate stories)	short story
Polzunkov (Polzunkov)	1848	1848 the *Illustrated Almanach* (special issue of *The Contemporary*)	short story
A Faint Heart (Slaboe serdtse)	1848	1848 (February) *National Notes*	short story
An Honest Thief (Chestny Vor)	1848	1848 (April) *National Notes*	short story
A Christmas Tree and a Wedding (Elka i svad'ba)	1848	1848 (September) *National Notes*	short story
White Nights (Belye Nochi)	1848	1848 (December) *National Notes*	short story
Netochka Nezvanova (Netochka Nezvanova)	1847; 1849	1849 (January; February; May; fourth installment unwritten) *National Notes*	unfinished novel
A Little Hero (Malen'ki geroi) (signed: "M.——i")	1849 (in prison)	1857 (August) *National Notes*	short story

Title	Written	Published	Type
Uncle's Dream (Dyadyushkin son)	1858-1859	1859 (March) *The Russian Word* (Russkoe Slovo)	short novel
A Friend of the Family (Russian title: The Village of Stepanchikovo and its Inhabitants) (Selo Stepanchikovo i ego obitateli)	1857; 1859	1859 (November, December) *National Notes*	short novel
The Insulted and Injured (Unizhennye i oskorblennye)	1860	1861 (January-July) *Time* (Vremya) (Dostoevski editor)	novel
The House of the Dead (Russian title: Notes from a Dead House) (Zapiski iz mertvogo doma)	?1855 1859-1860	1861 (April; Sept.-Nov.) *Time* 1862 (January-March; May; December) *The Russian World* (Russki Mir)	novel
An Unpleasant Predicament (Russian title: A Vile Tale, *or* A Nasty Anecdote) (Skverny anekdot)	1862	1862 (November) *Time*	short story
Notes from Underground (Zapiski iz podpol'ya)	1863	1864 January-February) *The Epoch* (Epokha) (Dostoevski editor)	short novel
The Crocodile (Krokodil)	1865	1865 (February) *The Epoch*	short story
Crime and Punishment (Prestuplenie i nakazanie)	June 1865 to December 1866	1866 (January, February, April, June, August, November, December) *The Russian Messenger* (Russki vestnik) (in book form, 1867)	novel
The Gambler (Igrok)	October 1866	1867 (in *The Complete Works of F. M. Dostoevski*)	short novel
The Idiot (Idiot)	1867 to January 1869	1868 (January-December) *The Russian Messenger*	novel
The Eternal Husband (Vechny Muzh)	1869	1870 (January-February) *Dawn* (Zarya)	short novel

Title	Written	Published	Type
The Possessed (Russian title: The Devils) (Besy)	first attempts December 1868- August 1870; final form 1870-1872	1871 (January-November) 1872 (November-December The Russian Messenger (in book form, 1873)	novel
Bobok (Bobok)	1873	1873 (February) The Citizen (Grazhdanin) (Dostoevski editor)	short story
A Raw Youth (Podrostok)	1874	1875 (January-December) National Notes (in book form, 1876)	novel
The Peasant Marei (Muzhik Marei)	1876	1876 (February) in The Diary of a Writer (Dnevnik Pisatelya), Dostoevski's newspaper column	short story
The Heavenly Christmas Tree (Russian title: The Boy at Christ's Christmas Tree) (Mal'chik u Khrista na ëlke)	1875	1876 (January) The Diary of a Writer	short story
A Gentle Spirit (Russian title: The Gentle One) (Krotkaya)	1876	1876 (November) The Diary of a Writer	short story
The Dream of a Ridiculous Man (Son smeshnago cheloveka)	1877	1877 (April) The Diary of a Writer	short story
The Brothers Karamazov (Brat'ya Karamazovy)	1878-1880	1879 to November 1880 (at irregular intervals) The Russian Messenger	novel

*   *   *   *   *   *   *   *

Twice in his lifetime Dostoevski issued collected editions of his works, once in 1860 after his return from exile, and again in 1865-66.

1. *The Works of F. M. Dostoevski* (Sochineniya F. M. Dostoevskogo), Moscow, 1860.
   Vol. I—*Poor Folk, Another Man's Wife, An Honest Thief, White Nights, A Christmas Tree and a Wedding*
   Vol. II—*Netochka Nezvanova, A Little Hero, Uncle's Dream, A Friend of the Family*

2. *The Collected Works of F. M. Dostoevski* (Polnoe sobranie sochineni F. M. Dostoevskogo), St. Petersburg, 1865-1866; Stellovski editor; each item was also issued separately at the same time.
   Vol. I—*Mr. Prokharchin, The Landlady, A Faint Heart, An Honest Thief,*
   (1865) *White Nights, The House of the Dead*

Vol. II—*Poor Folk, The Insulted and Injured, An Unpleasant Predica-*
(1865) *ment, Notes from Underground, The Crocodile*
Vol. III—*The Double, Another Man's Wife, Netochka Nezvanova, A Little*
(1866) *Hero, Uncle's Dream, A Friend of the Family, The Gambler*
To this set, *Crime and Punishment* was added as Volume IV in 1870
(*A Novel in Nine Letters* and *Polzunkov* were never reissued during
Dostoevski's lifetime.)

TABLE 3

The Works of Hoffmann
in relation to
The Works of Dostoevski

Novels:
Die Elixiere des Teufels	*The Double*
Part I, end of Section 3 and end of Section 4	the final scene
	general influence
the inset about Franzesko the Painter	*Netochka Nezvanova* Chapters 1, 2 and 3
Medardus-Viktorin-Aurelie	*Crime and Punishment* Raskolnikov-Svidrigailov-Sonya
over-all plan	*The Life of a Great Sinner*
over-all plan	*The Brothers Karamazov* Alyosha Karamazov
Medardus-Viktorin-Belcampo	Ivan Karamazov—Smerdyakov— the Devil
Kater Murr	(praised by Dostoevski in "Three Tales of Edgar Poe")
Part I, Section 2	*The Double*
(8th "Makulaturblatt")	Chapter 5
over-all plan of the Kreisler story	*Netochka Nezvanova* Chapters 4, 5, 6, and 7
Prince Hektor as villain type	*The Insulted and Injured* Prince Valkovski
	Crime and Punishment Svidrigailov
the "unseen maiden"; the talking animals	*The Crocodile*
Independent Märchen	
Klein Zaches	*The Double* (?)
Zaches gets credit for the accomplishments of others	The Double gets credit for Mr. Golyadkin's work
Prinzessin Brambilla	*The Double* (?) (influence claimed by Rodzevich)
Meister Floh	*A Christmas Tree and a Wedding* (?)
the Christmas party for children	the Christmas party for children
the later discovery of the hero's bride in the same household	Yulian Mastakovich's discovery of his future bride
the visionary land of Famagusta	the "Acis and Galatea" vision (?) in *The Possessed* in *A Raw Youth* and in *The Dream of a Ridiculous Man*
The Collections of Tales:	
1. *Fantasiestücke in Callots Manier*	
Ritter Gluck (Volume I)	*A Faint Heart*
the blank pages of music	the blank pages of manuscript

the figure of the urban wanderer

Der Magnetiseur (Volume II)
Alban, the sinister hypnotist

Die Abenteuer der Sylvesternacht (Volume IV)
Chapter I (Die Geliebte)

Chapter II (Die Gesellschaft im Keller)
Chapter III (Erscheinungen)
the motif of the lost mirror-image

2. *Die Nachtstücke*
Der Sandmann (Volume I)
Nathanael's opening letter; the figure of Coppelius
Die Jesuiterkirche in G. (Volume I)
Berthold as "murderer" and artist
Das öde Haus (Volume II)
the opening scene in the confectioner's shop

3. *Die Serapionsbrüder*
Rat Krespel (Volume I)
Krespel as violinist

Die Fermate (Volume II)
the episode of the unruly horse
Theodor (narrator)—Teresina—Lauretta
Fragment aus dem Leben dreier Freunde (Volume I)

the pursuit of the unknown beautiful girl by the sensitive young man

Der Artushof (Volume I)
the over-all plan
Meister Martin der Küfner und seine Gesellen (Volume II)
Die Brautwahl (Volume III)

the inappropriate marriage of the elderly Tusmann and young Albertine

Tusmann's adventures in the streets of Berlin (Chapters 1-3)

An Honest Thief (?)
the figure of Emelyan Ilich
The Landlady
Murin as a sinister hypnotist

The Double
the basic plan
the party; the flight (Chapters 4 and 5)
the encounter with the Double (Chapter 5)
Mr. Golyadkin's dream (Chapter 10)
the motif of the mirror-reflections

The Landlady
Murin as a sinister, half-supernatural character
general atmosphere
Netochka Nezvanova

Chapters 1, 2, and 3; Yefimov as pseudo-artist and murderer
The Insulted and Injured
the opening chapter in the confectioner's shop

Netochka Nezvanova
Chapters 1, 2, and 3; violinist details for Yefimov
A Little Hero
the episode of the runaway horse

the narrator—Madame M.—the teasing lady
(Gogol's *The Nevski Prospekt*)
White Nights
Petersburg Visions: the "Amalie" episode
The Insulted and Injured, Part I, Chapter 8.
The pursuit of the unknown beauty by the sensitive young man

The Landlady
the over-all plan
(praised by Dostoevski in "Three Tales of Edgar Poe")

The Double
incidental details
A Christmas Tree and a Wedding (?)
Yulian Mastakovich and the child bride
An Unpleasant Predicament
Pralinski's adventure in the streets of Petersburg

Der unheimliche Gast (Volume III)	*The Landlady*
Count S——i, the sinister hypnotist	Murin as a sinister hypnotist
Margurite as the accomplice of Count S——i	Katerina as Murin's accomplice
Das Fräulein von Scudery (Volume III)	*Crime and Punishment*
the police officials, La Régnie and Desgrais	Porfiry Petrovich and "the explosive lieutenant" Zametov
Der Baron von B. (Volume III)	*Netochka Nezvanova*
	Chapters 1, 2, and 3; violinist details for Yefimov
Signor Formica (Volume IV)	(praised by Dostoevski in "Three Tales of Edgar Poe")
Der Zusammenhang der Dinge (Volume IV)	*The Eternal Husband*
the final scene	the basic situation; the final scene (Chapter 17)

4. *Die Letzten Erzählungen*; Miscellaneous

Datura fastuosa	*A Christmas Tree and a Wedding*
Fermino Valies and Gretchen in the garden	Yulian Mastakovich and the little girl in the arbor
Die Genesung	*A Little Hero*
Theodor as unintentional observer of the lovers' tryst in the beautiful rural spot	the narrator as unintentional observer of the love tryst of Madame M. and N. in the beautiful garden
Haimatochare	*A Novel in Nine Letters*
the over-all plan	the over-all plan